My first 20 years of Christian service were largely 'not Christ but I'. Thankfully the message of 'Union', of 'Christ in You', got through to me to reverse that – a wonderfully liberating experience. I'm delighted at this skilful compilation by Stewart Dinnen and anticipate with great joy many others being similarly blessed.

Neil Rowe
Former British Director of WEC

Norman Grubb was one of God's giants. His *vision* global, his passionate *love* for Jesus all-pervading, his *faith* creative, he gave himself to reaching the world's unevangelised peoples in order to hasten Christ's return. To experience his dynamic leadership though twenty-nine years (1936-65) whilst a missionary and rsearcher was my unforgettable privilege.

Leslie Brierley
WEC International

Norman Grubb has probably contributed more to my life in both spiritual depth and structures for mission than any other single person.

Patrick Johnstone
Author, Operation World

FAITH ON FIRE

NORMAN GRUBB
AND THE BUILDING OF WEC

Stewart and Marie Dinnen

Christian Focus Publications

Published in 1997
by
Christian Focus Publications,
Geanies House, Fearn, Ross-shire,
IV20 1TW, Great Britain

Contents

FOREWORD

Rubi![1]

What a privilege to be asked by my friends and co-workers, Stewart and Marie Dinnen, to write a few words by way of introduction to this marvellous record of your extraordinary life – and what an even greater privilege to have been your (unofficial) 'adopted daughter' throughout my twenty years in Africa!

Not only did I know you as a strict disciplinarian (as shown by the short story recounted in this book about the stolen tithe that occurred one Sunday when I had put nothing in the offering plate at the morning service): not only did I respect you as a visionary, willing to see beyond the immediate to what God was preparing and planning, (as when the WEC staff would have turned me down for being unable to adapt to team work, yet you persuaded them to give the Holy Spirit a chance to change me): not only do I remember your sense of humour (turned down by two doctors as unfit for work in the tropics, I was asked by you in front of the staff, 'Would you pass *yourself* as fit?'): but, above all, I think of you as a father who cared and loved, and who took time to help and encourage me. (You even managed, when you came over for a hectic tour of Britain, to visit my mother in her loneliness and bring her comfort.)

Always, you listened... you prayed... you saw *through* a problem... and then you encouraged us to do the same until the solution became a reality.

To me personally you became (as to many others) the spiritual father I did not otherwise have. You were always there for me to pour out my happiness (when a dear African co-worker came to know the Lord) or my frustration (when a national seemed so slow to grasp the nettle and get something done).

You always answered my letters – almost at once – be it with appreciation, or humour, caution or rebuke. Your hand-writing sometimes gave me a headache to decipher, but it was always worth the effort!

---

1. The Congolese found the name GRUBB hard to pronounce so settled for 'Rubi'. The WEC family was happy to follow suit, as it avoided using the too formal 'Mr Grubb' and the too familiar 'Norman'.

You kept me on the stretch for Jesus, always striving for higher goals, for more Christ-likeness in daily living and in relationships. You never accepted present achievement as sufficient reason for slackening off. The over-riding emphasis throughout was your deep love for Jesus and therefore for His servants. You were always willing to see 'Jesus in us' and therefore our potential in Him, rather than be side-tracked into unbelief and criticism by an obviously un-Christlike act or thought.

I just pray that many will be blessed and challenged by reading this exciting part of your life, poured out for Jesus in and through our mission, WEC International.

Many of us would not be where we are today if you had not been where you were, yesterday!

Thank you, Rubi!

Thank you, Stewart and Marie!

Helen Roseveare
Belfast
January 1996

PREFACE

'Some of you women in this room will be raped before your missionary careers are over.' Norman Grubb was speaking to a crowded conference of WEC workers on the theme of sacrifice. We bowed our heads in embarrassment as he said this, but he was right. Within a few short years this was the fate of a number of our ladies during the Simba rebellion in Zaire.

With his keen insight and a capacity to understand the swaying battle of faith in the fields of the world, Norman was a prophet, a statesman, a visionary leader. But he was also a man who knew his frailty, and constantly made us gasp at his frankness, honesty, and admissions of weakness. I remember asking him once, 'Rubi, all this talk of victory – is it really like that with you? Are you always up there, in triumph?' He replied, 'Stewart, I just get through by the skin of my teeth.'

What a multi-faceted man he was! How could we do justice to such a life and ministry? We felt we could function as facilitators – those who could identify the crucial episodes in his life, the most insightful of his writings, the most helpful of his letters, and join them up with connector passages, explaining what might be unclear to readers, but largely allowing the man to speak for himself.

We feel our God-given objective has been to help readers gain an understanding of the spiritual principles that made him the mighty man of God that he was.

He was no cloistered saint. He had to hammer out practical, workable, down-to-earth principles that would stand the testings and battles of a worldwide missionary movement. He was a true mission leader, setting the pace by authentic example, by incisive Bible teaching, and by Spirit-led direction in mission strategy.

But he was more than a mission leader. He had a continuous liberating ministry into the lives of myriads of people within and beyond WEC. He knew how to wield the Sword of the Spirit and we have purposely included many testimonies of those whom he touched.

We were commissioned by our mission leaders to produce a record that would give future WECers some appreciation of Norman's place in the development of the work. Hence this book covers the time of his entry into WEC up to his official retirement from it in 1965.

But this was certainly not retirement from active service. Indeed it led to a rapid escalation of an itinerant teaching ministry in the USA, Canada, and to Britain, lasting twenty five years.

Nor did he sever his relationship with the mission. By invitation he remained on the Co-ordinating Council and had a significant input by correspondence. He also attended WEC's international leaders' conferences right up to the mid nineteen eighties.

The man, his ministry, and the mission that he, under God, raised from incredible weakness, will surely inspire the reader with a passion for the will of God, for the life of faith, and for the extension of the Kingdom.

We are tremendously indebted to Miss Diane Griffiths, a former WEC youth worker, for her zealous and accurate work in transforming a hodge podge of Dinnen hieroglyphics to a well laid out computerised manuscript.

Stewart and Marie Dinnen
Launceston, Tasmania.
January, 1996

CHAPTER 1

FOUR ESCAPES FROM DEATH

The year was 1917. Lieutenant Norman Grubb (22), a Christian for three years, was a platoon commander of the Gloucester Regiment in the front line trenches during World War I.

In *Intercession in Action* – a booklet consisting of articles he had written for the *Intercessor* magazine, published by Zerubbabel, Inc. – he describes four remarkable escapes from death 'without which' he says, 'there could not have been the following years of fruitfulness'.

I had taken by faith that word in Psalm 91:7, 'A thousand shall fall at thy side, and ten thousand at thy right hand; but it shall not come nigh thee.' Rather a selfish prayer, but I had said to myself that any others who wanted to could also claim it! Four times over I just escaped death.

The first was when my men occupied a trench about half a mile from the Germans. A narrow connecting trench had been dug leading to a small advanced post, which I occupied with my signallers. Suddenly I clearly felt we should get back from that outpost. So I casually took my men back, meaning to return for our equipment. Within a few minutes the outpost was blown up by a shell. We later found our equipment buried.

Then one night we were digging a trench. A 'crump' – a five inch German shell – fell just to one end of that trench. Curiously, I felt strongly that instead of moving farther away, I should go and stand by that fresh smoking shell hole. As I did so, another crump fell just where I had been standing.

Later we occupied some trenches which we had captured from the Germans. My company captain and I occupied a small inner dugout, with two bunks and just a sheet of three-ply wood between us and the company sergeant and staff of about six in the outer end of the dugout. In the early morning, just when I reached for a tin of bully beef, there was a funny metallic sound and some smoke.

When the smoke cleared. the plywood sheet was leaning crazily over me. On the other side all the men had been killed by a direct hit.

Later I found the finger of one of them blown right into my folded raincoat. God seemed marvellously to have had His purpose in preserving me, when so many of my school contemporaries were killed.

Finally, we went 'over the top' in the Paschendaele battle. As we stood ready at 3am to advance under the enormous barrage of the guns, I gave my last word of witness to my men of how Christ is a Saviour to those who trust Him. Within thirty minutes, after we had advanced about half a mile, half the men were mown down by bullets from a machine gun emplacement. My batman (orderly) beside me turned white. When I looked, I saw a bullet had penetrated his heart.

At the same moment I felt a sharp blow on my leg, and there was blood. Although hit with what we called a 'blighty' (a wound enough to send you home!), I was able to limp back to an advance casualty post. Preserved once again! And by this – much more than a preservation – the final plan of God for my life was to be brought to me. So I was sent home as a casualty.

How our disappointments turn out to be God's perfectly placed appointments! I was annoyed that I was not sent to a London hospital, but instead to a Midlands hospital in Leicester. There the visiting padre was Gilbert Barclay, who I did not know was C.T. Studd's son-in-law. His keenness for Christ, so different from that of the other padres I had met, immediately drew us together.

(reproduced by kind permission of Zerubbabel, Inc.)

One day Barclay dropped a magazine on Grubb's bed. It was all about the mission work in NE Congo founded by Studd and about the wonderful responsiveness of the people there to the gospel.

Again that clear inner voice that had guided him to safety in the trenches, spoke, and he instantly recognised the call of God to join Studd and his little team called *The Heart of Africa Mission.* He wrote to tell Mrs Studd of his call. She was heading up the home end of the mission while her husband remained in Africa. She invited him to come to the Studd home in London for a couple of days and Grubb, still on crutches, went soon afterwards.

On his return from that visit he wrote the following letter (quoted in part):

2 Tichborne St.,
Leicestershire.

Dear Mrs Studd,

I was so sorry not to see you before I left and I hope that staying in bed stopped the cold from getting worse.

I thank God for moving you to ask me for those two days. It has been such a delight to see you personally and arm myself with more tracts about the HAM (Heart of Africa Mission); Mr Barclay, too, is being a tremendous help.

Of course I shall give up the idea of getting ordained and get on with Bible study as far as the army allows me the opportunity, as that is the most important part of training.

Yours very sincerely,
Norman Grubb.
P.S. I should like a supply of more literature.

After being moved to another army hospital in Parkstone, Dorset, he wrote again to Mrs Studd.

I am most deeply interested in the papers of the HAM you have so kindly sent me, especially the magazine, and am praising the Lord for you all.

When I am out of the army my deepest wish, please God, is to offer myself to you as a missionary but that, I'm afraid, is very far in the distance at present.

Till then I shall be most grateful to you if you will keep me in touch with all the news.

I am at present convalescing and have quite three more months in England before they push me out again, and if I could do any work for you, secretarial or otherwise from where I am, I should love to do it. We don't get the chance of doing much in the army except silent witnessing, though we have plenty of time on our hands while in England.

Yours very sincerely,
Norman Grubb.
2nd LT Gloster Regt.

Mrs Studd replied (quoted in part):

Dear Mr Grubb,

How very kind of you to send this generous donation to the funds of the Heart of Africa Mission. I have very much pleasure in enclosing herewith the official receipt with the grateful thanks of my husband

and the committee, and would like to say how much we value your interest in and prayer for this work, and your kind offer to do anything that you can to help us.

I am deeply interested to know that you are looking forward to joining this work when you are free from the army: we shall bear this in mind and pray that you may be kept and brought through this terrible conflict and given the desire of your heart to go forth as a messenger of Christ to the heathen. I do hope that if you are in London before returning to active service I may have the pleasure of seeing you: will you send me a line or ring me up on the phone (Sydenham 220) so that if possible I may make some appointment with you.

The visit to the Studds' Upper Norwood home was fateful for Grubb in more ways than one. It was there that he met the beautiful fourth daughter of C.T. – Pauline. He was instantly smitten and a courtship commenced culminating in their marriage in November 1919.

By January 1920 they were on the ship to Africa.

CHAPTER 2

'WE'RE NOT BIG WHITE CHIEFS'

What kind of missionary did Grubb make? Brought to Christ at 18, having had three years in the army (including one year in trench warfare), he had been married for a month. Here he was, at 24, with no theological or missionary training, in the heart of Africa. With his young wife he was seeking to see strong indigenous churches planted and converts nurtured to a maturity of which he himself knew very little.

He writes of his welcome to Nala and meeting up with C.T. Studd, his wife's father:

> In himself he was all that we expected in his loving welcome, but we found C.T. had no time for special favours to his daughter and new son-in-law. I think we were rather puzzled and hurt that we did not get preferential treatment – we were just some of the new recruits!

Grubb describes his early attempts to persuade the founder to change some of his methods, but to no avail. Instead Studd sent them to an outstation, where again in an attempt to change current practice – particularly regarding clothing – the Grubbs ran foul of the nationals. (He had wanted them to dress in native bark cloth, but they liked to use any bits of Western clothing on which they could lay their hands.)

Attendances slipped from several hundred to about eighty. They soon realised their mistakes and went back to C. T. admitting their pride and self-assertion. He forgave them.

Pauline had her first child a year after they arrived. The little one – Noel – did well for a while but became sick when he began to teethe. Medical help was too far away and he died on his first birthday.

It is clear that this event had a deep impact on Norman – an impact that did not lead, however, to discouragement and depression but in his seeking of the Lord for a fresh anointing. He wrote:

> During a month's quiet last year after Noel's death, my great cry was 'Lord, endue me with power from on high according to thy promise,' and the Lord enabled me to believe He had answered. These last nine months

around Poko have been to me the Lord's marvellous and unexpected answer, exceedingly abundant above all I asked or thought.

While giving some time to pioneer evangelism the Grubbs' main task in these early years seems to have been the encouragement and nurturing of new Christians and the examination of candidates for baptism.

An early brush with the forces of nature must have deepened their trust and commitment to the Lord:

October 28th – November 2nd.
On the road to Ngongo we crossed the worst water yet experienced. We were up to the neck or out of our depth in many places. It was a job to get Pauline over, her hammock on the heads of eleven tall men; she almost went in once. The Lord watched over us; not a thing got wet, yet we might easily have lost a box, not to say a life.

Several incidents highlight their deep desire to identify with the nationals.

We met with a sad reception from the Chief, Ngongo, who, instead of coming to greet us, shouted angrily at the leading Christians wanting to know why we always came out and stayed at his place and why they did not build us a house somewhere else; we felt this was a case of not being received and so we passed on to live with the elder of the Ngongo church, Bangbani (though the Chief cooled down before we left and pressed us to stay).

I believe this step is one of some importance – it has often been in my mind that we ought to live with the leading Christian where there is a group of believers but where the chief himself is opposed or indifferent. Personally I had never taken this step before. One of its chief merits is that it is a step in the descent of a missionary in the natives' eyes from a great white chief to a humble minister of the gospel! Bangbani lives in true native fashion in the depths of the forest, with no other human being nearer than half a mile – just himself, his wife and sister, and the children of a dead brother. We all managed to squeeze into his four little huts. Bangbani and his families in two of them, our boys and evangelists in the other hut, and ourselves in the shelter used as kitchen, dining room and church on Sundays!

It was while living in Bangbani's shed that the Lord met them and led them into a deeper walk with himself through a revelation of Galatians 2:20.

Norman describes how they could not sleep, so, as the moon was full, they took their camp chairs out and sat in the moonlight. They had been receiving a magazine called *The Overcomer* published by Mrs Penn-Lewis, and the teaching in it intrigued them. Her emphasis was not so much that Christ had died for us – that was basic – but that the scriptures clearly taught that we have been crucified with Him. The young Grubbs had never seen this but Norman had been reading Stifler's Commentary on Romans which pointed him in a similar direction. That night they stayed up till 4 am and it was in these night hours that they both entered in by faith to a realisation of this biblical truth. When they arose next morning Norman says he didn't feel any different but he took a postcard and made a drawing of a tombstone. He inscribed it with the words 'Here lies Norman Grubb, buried with Jesus'.

It was two years later, back in England, when he was having a discussion with Mrs Penn-Lewis that the whole concept suddenly came real to him and the Spirit witnessed powerfully to the reality of this crucified-and-risen relationship to Jesus. He later testified that it seemed as if a light had been suddenly switched on in his inner being. This theme of Union with Christ was to dominate his teaching ministry for the rest of his life – a truth that was to bring release and blessing to thousands.

Meanwhile in Congo it is interesting to note their developing strategy of targetting village and area chiefs, knowing that conversions at that level would greatly influence whole tribes.

Monday, May 24th, 1922.
It was a short trek to Gamu's. Gamu is the old great chief of all the Azande land round here, now divided up among his sons – and a true chief he is too: an old, old man with great grandchildren, yet handsome and regal enough to grace any throne, and his face is not marked with sin and cruelty as some, yet it is the face of a man whom it would never pay to disobey – and how his people and his own sons fear and respect him, keeping a respectful distance and approaching him only when called, hatless and on bended knee.

In the evening we sat with the old chief for a personal talk; alas the devil had him hard and fast in his grip and though we spoke to him for an hour and a half, he was not willing to decide. He would not budge from that position, often trying to pin his faith for salvation on the fact that several of his sons have believed. So when we felt we had discharged our full duty towards him and had solemnly warned him of his dreadful position according to John 3:18, we had to leave him, but as we parted we said, 'God is able to get victory in his heart'.

Tuesday, May 25th, 1922.
God indeed did his work in proud old chief Gamu's heart last night. Early this morning while it was still cold, this old man who can hardly walk, came out of his house. He was going to invade our bedroom, had not our boys told him he had better wait. We did not hurry, not having enough faith to believe God had answered our prayer, but when at last we did come to him, he did not give us a chance to speak, but hastened to tell us that he changed his mind and would believe today. How we did praise the Lord! We questioned him closely and he seemed in real earnest so we pointed him to Jesus (of whom he had often heard before). He accepted salvation through Christ by faith there and then. So we had prayer, gave him a few more words and left rejoicing. The reason for this victory was clear. The evangelists and ourselves had, all last night and this morning, prayed especially for him. There are about twelve other believers so they will come each Sunday to pray with the old chief. His son, Mofoi, a strong believer, will also come over and share God's word.

We arrived at chief Gambavudu's village after a heavy trek through much water and swamp. Wonders from the hand of the Lord never cease on this trek! Gambavudu is a changed man. I gave him the Word when passing through some months ago and he definitely refused to give up his witchcraft. This time his whole attitude was different and after a long talk tonight he said that, in the morning, he would break down his shrines for ancestor worship. This is a wonderful miracle that only the Lord could have worked.

Wednesday, 26th May, 1922.
This morning Gambavudu arranged a meeting for us, to which about 40 men came. Before it took place we went out to find that his ancestor shrines were lying on the ground, demolished. Hallelujah! We asked him to speak at the meeting. This he did, nervously at first, but he eventually spoke out clearly. Then he appealed for others to make decisions, and ten responded.

After lunch we finished our talk with the chief. He said that he had fully considered our word to him last night and had definitely decided for God. We feel he gave every indication of being in earnest. One of his soldiers is a splendid Christian so he has asked him to gather the believers every Sunday to teach them and pray with them.

It was inevitable that a work founded by the sacrificial C.T. Studd would take on the same quality. Grubb writes to say how impressed he was by some of the national evangelists and their willingness to pay the price of costly service.

July 31st.

Two of our evangelists and their wives and a little child of two have had the special honour of shedding a little of their blood for Jesus. I have already mentioned the treatment Maduga received at the hands of Chief Kipati who lifted his whip at him twice and blasphemed awfully. He gave the same reception to Mokule who went down there to spend two months preaching in his land, refusing to see him for several days and blaspheming when he did see him

After a week Mokule went to stay three miles away at Makidi's, a Christian who has stood true to the Lord in spite of the hatred and persecution of Kipati, who imprisoned him for no reason except that he believed in God a year or two ago. While Mokule was there, another evangelist Pengeri, passed through on his way to Poko with wife and child and stayed the night.

That evening four men suddenly appeared on the scene with hippo-hide whips in their hands, dashed for Mokule, Pengeri and their wives, seized them and laid about them with all their might, cursing as they did so. They were only stopped from seriously hurting them by the wife of one of the four men who had come up behind and shouted at her husband to stop beating them before they killed them.

When they found that Pengeri was only passing through they left him and fell on Mokule alone, finally making a prisoner of him and his wife, dragging them back to the chief's village and shutting them up in prison for the night.

The next morning they must have taken fright at what they had done for they let Mokule out of prison and even offered him a chicken as a peace offering! Pengeri had already left for Poko and Mokule followed. They arrived with great scars on their bodies, specially Mokule. The wives and little baby had been beaten too.

But Mokule and Pengeri proved themselves to be true soldiers of Jesus Christ: they did not have the scriptures –neither Matthew, nor the Acts nor 1 Peter to be guided by, and so they determined to take their case to the official and get justice, but both Alfred and I felt that the Word clearly shows that to suffer for well-doing is well-pleasing to God. So we called them aside and read these scriptures to them and told of Paul also and other examples. There was obviously a struggle in their hearts but in the end they both got up and said they forgave all for Christ's sake and did not want to make a case of it.

More lessons were in store for the Grubbs. Norman's diary gives an account of two of them, the first about the power of prayer, and the second on the need for a clean heart in the service of the Lord.

Sept. 1st to Oct 10th, spent at Poko Station.
We have spent a busy five weeks here and now at the end have much to praise the Lord for. After our first stay here we felt that we had given too little time to prayer, so this time Kirk (another missionary) and I have had several seasons of prayer together at night. Then we all met together for a day of prayer on the day of the annual meetings at home, spending from ten till two together on our knees and then each alone with the Lord, in the afternoon.

In the morning, the Lord seemed to move Kirk deeply, melting him to tears several times when praying for lost souls and thinking on what it meant for God to give his only Son for our salvation. I can personally testify that the Lord met me mightily when alone with Him in the afternoon. We have also felt the need for teaching the evangelists what it means to lay hold of God in prayer, for I don't think any of them have that thirst to give oneself to prayer which comes when one has learnt the secret of prevailing prayer.

This month has been exceedingly happy. There has been blessed fellowship amongst us five missionaries – real heart unity, joy and love in the Holy Ghost. Especially have we enjoyed reading together each night Paget Wilkes' new book *The Dynamic of Service*. The Lord has greatly blessed it to our souls in a supremely important way, for He has revealed to us what some of us had never even heard of before – the commands and promises in the Word for a full salvation and deliverance from indwelling sin. He has spoken to us all and set us all hungering and seeking and claiming the promises. And again I can personally thank and praise the Lord that He has not only enabled me to stand upon these precious promises of a full and present salvation, but that He has come to indwell me and has already poured in and through me such a river of grace and victory that I believe He has given me a clean heart according to his Word and satisfied a heart that has hungered these long years. I feel as one who has just crossed the Jordan, but 'there remains much land to be possessed' by this child of weak and trembling faith.

Another early lesson was the crucial need for adequate follow-up of new converts, and the need to involve them immediately in witnessing and outreach.

The chiefs we have visited are those in the area where we had such a remarkable welcome in April and May. Many professed to believe, but we have made a big blunder: as an experiment and in the hope that the little groups of believers would be able to stand by themselves, we did not send them an evangelist for six months; no white man had visited them either. The result has been very sad. I think many who believed were in earnest but because they were not immediately discipled the vast majority have fallen away and their last state is worse than their first. Both chiefs and people seem opposed to the gospel, and there are just little groups of believers standing true, often amidst much opposition and temptation.

Well, thank God for them; it has been a testing time and although not all have stood true, we have been greatly cheered nearly everywhere by those who have. We are doing all we can to remedy our mistake by having our Medje evangelist concentrate on them now.

At Mofoi's (the first HAM out-church) December 3rd – 6th and 13th – 17th, 1922.

My last visit here was with Kirk in May 1922 and since then the church has not been visited by missionary or evangelist. Praise God we have at last seen some signs of an independent out-church! After our sad experiences in the newer Medje out-churches which had been left unvisited, we came here fearing we would find the same, but praise the Lord it is very different. We arrived on Sunday morning without warning to find they had just had their meeting. We were greeted by a group of Christians whose shining faces told their own tale. Chief Mofoi is as true and bright as ever, and elder Mombeli and deacon Kelolo the same; both gave such a good account of the members of the church.

What a miracle of grace this is – a little group of believers with their believing chief, surrounded by the opposition – on two sides – of neighbouring chiefs, and indifference from another, without the Word of God (for none so far can read). Yet now for more than five years this little church has been standing and growing, and at every visit I have paid, more have been added to the fellowship.

The chief burden the Lord has given me during my week here is how to help the Christians grow and shine for the Lord. I feel this is the present problem and our most notable failure with the out-churches. The majority of young Christians remain babes, apparently content to believe on the Lord Jesus but not going on to suffer for him – taking in but not giving out – justified but not serving.

What was Grubb's inner heart attitude to the nationals? This entry gives the answer.

Jan 2nd – 10th, 1923 at Tely.
What terrible lives these poor women have. What a wonder of grace and power that God can raise them to live holy lives. Edadra, Mawere's eldest wife, was originally the wife of another man. He committed adultery with one of the wives of a great chief, Boemi, who had a harem of 200. In punishment for this offence, Boemi took Edadra from him. After she had lived with Boemi a little, one of his men danced particularly well one night, so he took Edadra and gave her to him as a present. Finally this new husband, after he had had a child by Edadra, gave her back as a present to Mawere. She has lived with him a number of years and now they are both becoming Christians. But no wonder marriage bonds are loose; they seldom marry for love as we know it.

Another story reveals his sensitive handling of a young evangelist who had gone astray.

October 11th, 1922.
On leaving Poko I had a talk with Mboli, one of the young evangelists. Three days ago he came to the evangelists' class the worse for drink, but I understood he has since made it right with God. He said before conversion he was a slave to drink and spent his days going round to wine feasts in the villages of his friends, but that when he heard the gospel (I think through Alfred Buxton who came out with Studd), he turned to God and was immediately delivered of this craving and it had never returned.

His fall on Saturday was due to suddenly meeting a friend who was selling wine at the edge of the road. He told him it was wine of a special kind he had never tasted, and poor Mboli was tempted to try a little. It turned out to be very strong (probably secretly and illegally distilled) and overcame him. I then asked him, 'Have you made it right with God?' He said, 'In the middle of the night much shame took hold of me, so I woke my wife up and told her we must pray. We both got down on our knees and confessed my sin to God.'

When a native falls into sin, Satan's snare is to keep him from simply believing in 1 John 1:9, and to keep him continually confessing instead of receiving peace by faith in the blood of Christ, so I explained to Mboli that God had forgiven him; he could now praise the Lord and cease confessing. I had a surprisingly blessed answer: 'Yesterday I did that and thanked God He had forgiven me; I have confessed no more'! Finally I said to him, 'I think you ought to go to your friend and tell him you sinned, lest Satan make your fall a stumbling block to him.' Mboli answered, 'Yesterday I thought of that too, and went to tell him.'

Mboli is just a poor dark native not yet able to read properly. I have seen the fruits of his work as an evangelist in the bush – and when God does such a miracle of grace and calls such a person out to preach the gospel, who shall say 'You must spend three years in a theological college first!'

How effective was Grubb in evangelism? Those who knew him in later years would not have said that this was an outstanding aspect of his service. His obvious gifting was in ministering to Christians and seeing them brought into the fulness of union with Christ, but it is obvious from his diary that he had a great delight and considerable effectiveness in both public and personal evangelism. Here are a few pages from his diary.

Nyapate, November 8th – 13th, 1922.
One day during the week I went out preaching and came to the home of a head-man named Tunambu – he seemed interested and so I went next day on my bike, which is the best set of 'church-bells' going, bringing people in crowds who have never seen a bike, nor heard the gospel! Result: a number believed! I went the next day and taught them and then on the Sunday those who really wanted to give themselves to God came to us – a group of about eight. I have left a young evangelist to continue the work there.

At Biendo's the Lord is doing a work in hearts too. Biendo is the brother of Chief Masanga and has a number of men under him – he believed of old, backslid and now has come back to the Lord again – and not only he, but he brings a number of his men with him. I have been to him three times and each time thirty gathered; when I came the third time Biendo told me that after I had left he personally broke down all his ancestor worship shrines in his village and then went into his house and confessed all his sins on his knees before God. He also, I find, has a knowledge of the atoning work of the Lord Jesus and I believe the Lord has heard his cry and saved him.

At the last service I held an after-meeting for those desiring to be saved; nearly all flocked into the room, so, after carefully explaining the way of salvation I told them each to go straight to their homes, throw away any idols, etc. they may have, confess their sins and believe in Jesus. Then when they have done that, go and tell some friend that they have taken the Lord Jesus as their Saviour.

Various stories reveal Grubb's deep commitment to prayer. He had a strong desire both to go deeper himself and to encourage others to do likewise.

At Numangi's we had a meeting each morning for Christians and another for baptism candidates. Each afternoon was spent questioning the latter. In the evening, when it was dark, I said there would be an impromptu prayer meeting, but my faith did not rise to the numbers that came. The first night I slipped down quietly in the dark to the forest and was soon joined by Ongoro and Matabisi, and then, one by one, by about 20-30 black figures! I used not to announce that prayer meeting and told the evangelists not to pressurise people about it, for I wanted only those who had a thirst for prayer to come, but throughout the week the number hardly varied.

I think the evangelists' greatest need is a deepened prayer-life: none of them I think are yet beyond the child stage of ten minutes prayer morning and evening and know nothing of waiting on God in prayer or of having a burden of prayer. I feel the blame lies much with us who do not take them aside and have real prayer fellowship with them. That way, they would learn to pray.

There is no doubt that life in Congo opened Grubb's eyes to spiritual warfare and the intense activities of the powers of darkness as they opposed the spread of the gospel. He wrote:

This month has also been a month of intense opposition from Satan – for he knows the Lord is working amongst us. We came back to find several sad cases of sin. For nearly a week, day after day both Kirk and I heard their stories and tried to lead sinners to confess and the aggrieved ones to forgive for Christ's sake. We lost one lad whom I thought was truly a child of the Lord. He ran away rather than face his sin and we very nearly lost one of our oldest evangelists. There were a number of fierce quarrels and accusations and at times it looked as if Satan would split us up and destroy the work– indeed at one time the evangelists and their wives threatened to cease giving out the Word and settle down again to their old village life but right through all the individual cases and general malaise the Lord had wonderful victory and as far as we know this month ends with perfect love between all, and all seem happy.

In another situation he wrote:

At the evangelists' class this month we spent time considering what fundamental truths should be taught to one who has accepted Christ and been saved and who needs to be prepared for baptism. Almost every day I can testify we felt the presence of the Lord greatly with us and at times very specially. Perhaps Satan's particular temptation to us has been too great a head knowledge without letting the precious truths sink into our hearts.

One message the Lord specially blessed to many was the truth of justification by faith. It is extraordinary how Satan blinds these poor souls in their darkness without the Word, so that very many, even baptised Christians, do not live in the joy of present forgiveness of sins. They believe they are going to heaven, but Satan blinds them to the blessed fact that they are already forgiven and clothed in the perfect righteousness of Christ. You can tell this from their prayers which are almost monotonously 'Lord, I am a bad man' but very seldom 'Lord, I praise you that I am clean by the blood of Jesus'. The Lord gave me a strong message on this and since then several seem to have been led into the light and are constantly praising.

During this time Grubb started to take new steps of faith that gradually increased as he grew in the Lord and came to have greater responsibility in the mission. He trusted God for a definite number to be converted through the evangelists' outreach and then decided on a Matthew 10:9-10 approach on his next trip, taking no food with him. The diary reads:

'According to your faith be it unto you.' In praying the Lord to bless this week to the salvation of souls, I felt I would put my faith to the test and instead of one's usual prayer that the Lord would save many souls, I asked for a definite number, and had faith to ask for ten. When I returned yesterday to Ikibondo's and met the evangelists to hear their reports, exactly ten souls were reported as definitely accepting Christ! Nine were in Meteremembi's sector and one in Masabe's. (Oh Lord, teach me to trust you more practically and largely.) The four evangelists all seem to look bright. I have noticed more than once that after a native has been faithfully preaching for a time he comes back with a new and heavenly light in his face.

Before starting today, quite at the last moment, I felt very strongly that the Lord would have us go trusting him for food along the way, as another missionary, Alfred Ruscoe, did, neither asking for food nor taking money to buy it. This would teach us to lean more heavily on God and to teach the natives that we are not coming to them for or with money like other white men. So I called in the four evangelists and my two boys, Toli and 'Onions', and after prayer explained my feelings. They all unitedly and at once agreed to look to God only, for these four or five days. This is a bigger step of faith for Masabe especially, as for two days he works separately from me, and when a native often naturally gives food to a white man, as a kind of compliment, he would not do so to a black man.

The Lord has more than amply provided. Very soon on the journey a new convert made us a present of a chicken, then another man three eggs; finally the headman, at whose village we are sleeping, gave us two chickens, some cooked potato and two or three eggs! All were of course unsolicited and none taken until the donor had understood the position and was willing to give as a present to God. So praise the Lord for an ample provision for tonight and tomorrow morning.

CHAPTER 3

DARKNESS AND DAWN

Norman Grubb has written that the decade between 1921 and 1931 was the most problem-prone era in the mission's history and that his and Pauline's experiences became 'very chequered'. Not too much information is available on this period, but certain features stand out.

One was the rapid build-up of field personnel on the one hand, and the disturbing rate of resignations on the other. A list is given in an appendix to *Christ in Congo Forests* which is very revealing. It shows that in the decade from 1921 more workers left the mission than stayed in it. 87 new workers had joined the mission, but of that group only 35 were still members.

What were the reasons for this? Because there had been so many instances of converts going back to heathen practices Studd had taken a strong line on the need for practical holiness and the need to persevere to the end as a proof of genuine salvation. But this emphasis was so strong, and so offended these missionaries who believed 'once saved always saved' that they complained to the home committee that a doctrine of 'salvation by works' was emerging. A statement clarifying the mission's balanced position was published but not before a number of missionaries had resigned.

Another issue was Studd's rock-like stand on the faith principle and his absolute refusal to publicise needs. Some felt it would be quite reasonable to trust the Lord but inform His people. The leader wrote to the committee: 'If a man joins our mission he comes out on God. God is his Father, to God he looks for supplies whether in money or kind. If God sends much, he is rather cast down thinking God is afraid to trust him to suffer in patience. If God sends little he thanks Him and takes courage that after all he may be in the apostolic succession. If he has nothing then he shouts hallelujah for he knows he has come to the very entrance of the Kingdom where there is neither eating or drinking...'

There was also a rumble of discontent at the poor quality of housing and general living standards. Studd wrote: 'We are not a bit ashamed if our houses, food or furniture cause Dives (the rich man) to scoff; we are only ashamed that the little sacrifices we have made are so terribly small as to be invisible.'

Another issue arose regarding policy. From the home base came an expression that Studd had become 'bogged down' in Congo and that he ought to visit the home countries to bring the challenge of opening up other fields. C.T. refused to do this in view of the vast opportunities awaiting his team in Congo, but he did write: 'This mission from its very inception has been a worldwide mission and by no means one limited to Africa only. The mandate we received was not Africa, but the world.' He said when it was time for God to call people into WEC for other lands, let them go ahead.

Another damaging controversy swirled around Studd's use of drugs. Finding that great relief from gallbladder pain could be obtained from an injection of morphine, he arranged for others to obtain supplies for him. Some quantities were brought in without being declared at customs. News of this shocked the home committee who failed to realise that Studd's only motive was to remain well enough to continue his work.

One of the 'last straws' was the publication of the DCD leaflet with its clarion call to a 'Don't-Care-a-Damn' attitude to earthly joys and pleasures, so that with total abandon workers could put Jesus and the Kingdom first. The phrase shocked conservative evangelicals. F.B. Meyer, who had accepted an invitation to chair a WEC annual meeting in London, wrote cancelling his commitment. The committee was up in arms feeling that WEC had become the pariah of missions.

This one episode highlights probably the most acute factor in the mission's troubles – the gigantic gulf between two opposite and totally different sides to the founder's character – on the one hand an abso- lutely sacrificial spirit of total commitment to the service of the King- dom, and on the other his irascible dogmatic and condemnatory attitude to those who did not agree with him or whose lives did not reveal the same white-hot intensity of lifestyle that he had. So the mission pro- duced two types of workers – those who looked beyond his human weaknesses and idiosyncracies and committed themselves to an ex- tremist lifestyle, and those who could not stomach his hard-headedness and voted against him with their feet.

Where did the Grubbs stand in all this?

While still in their first four years of service between 1919 and 1923 they flung themselves wholeheartedly into the work, as the previous chapter revealed. But there was an ache in their hearts.

C.T. did not allow a personal father-daughter attachment to influence his handling of them. In fact, instead of accepting his daughter's offer to come and cook for him he packed them off as raw novices to an outlying station.

Home for furlough in 1923 Norman was used by the committee for deputation work over extended periods.

Furlough over, and with Pauline carrying a second child, Norman felt he must return to Africa alone. But Studd never allowed him to remain for any length of time and twice sent him home to sort out differences between himself and the committee. Norman ruefully describes these long wearisome 1600 km journeys up and down the Nile (between Alexandria and Rejaf near Juba in the Sudan) and the slow trip overland from there to Nala in NE Congo.

It was during one of the periods at home that Norman, through force of circumstances, started to develop his literary skills. When Gilbert Barclay was indisposed and unable to edit the HAM magazine the task fell to him. He describes his method as an attempt to avoid cliches and pious platitudes, and to present the missionaries' reports in a pithy, lively and arresting way.

His first book, written in 1925, was on the life and death of Fenton Hall, an ex-heavyweight boxer and officer in the RAF who joined WEC, went through the Missionary Training Colony and then sailed for Amazonia in May 1924. After only seven months on the field he died, alone, on Christmas Day of fever and dysentry in Sapucaia.

The book was published without mention of the author's name (as were many other literary pieces from his pen). It was an immediate success, going on to five editions in two years.

Again while at home in 1928 he was requested by the committee to visit the Heart of Amazonia field. He describes that six-month visit as tougher and more demanding than any other place in the world. When travelling by river canoe he had to live on monkey, piranha fish and manioc. The territory was vast but the team was small and eventually became part of the Unevangelised Fields Mission after it seceded from WEC in 1931.

How did Grubb develop the white-hot faith that was to characterise the life of the mission? Of course he had seen it demonstrated in the life of his father-in-law, but there was another man at whose feet he sat – a man who had a tremendous influence on his spiritual life and ministry – Rees Howells of Wales.

Because of what he had learned about C.T., Howells sought out Grubb during the 1925 Keswick Convention in the North of England and invited him to visit the new Bible College of Wales in Swansea, of which he was founder and principal. That visit, two months later, was as far-reaching in Grubb's life as his contact with Studd.

Mr Howells suggested they take a walk together. Norman testified later that that was the beginning of 'a great light shining in me'. He had a mighty revelation of two things – the principle of faith, and the enabling power of the Spirit to live a life of faith.

A warm intimate bond developed between the two men, and when, later, the major crisis of 1931 developed, it was to Rees Howells that Grubb turned for wisdom and guidance. But more of that later.

Meanwhile, Norman was a man torn in two during these years. His heart lay with C.T. Studd and his burden and sacrifice for the lost, but his gentle spirit cringed from the vitriolic outpourings in Studd's letters to the home committee. He said he agreed with what was written in essence, but not in the manner in which it was expressed.

Returning to Congo he opened up to C.T. about these letters and told him he could not agree with the tone of them. Studd felt that even though Norman was his son-in-law he could not be trusted to take over the leadership of the field, and so he turned to Jack Harrison whom he felt was more capable of running the field and handling the emerging national church.

But once things had simmered down Studd ordered Grubb to return to Britain with a view to taking the reins there eventually. At first he refused, but after a day alone with God he submitted to the founder's direction. He returned to Britain in 1928.

After the death of Mrs Studd in 1929 the committee was somewhat freer to take drastic action. The double impact of the DCD booklet (privately published by C.T.) plus the news that he had been in the habit of taking morphine, brought matters to a head.

The Grubbs were in an invidious position; they were determined to be loyal to C.T. (Norman was actually described by the committee as 'a fox in pants') but on the other hand they had to acknowledge the damage being done to the mission's image at home.

Aware that the committee wished to bring an element of moderation into the mission and to counteract Studd's extreme statements on faith and sacrifice, the Grubbs felt they should make one more visit to Congo to seek a reconciliation. About this crisis Norman wrote:

We had an executive committee in London, good men and women who wanted the best for WEC. But how could they handle the volcanic eruptions of the Spirit of God in a man like C.T.? The Spirit cannot be contained in men's straightjackets, and the committee did like things running to order with its agendas, minute books, firstings and secondings, ayes and noes. The sayings and doings of that God-intoxicated man in Congo were just too much for any respectable board. And so as the news kept coming through of his recurring fever and gradual weakening, plans were carefully laid to build a committee which would eliminate the extremes of WEC as soon as the old man was gone.

However, some of his words and deeds were past endurance and the committee could not wait. What little reputation the ramshackle mission still had was fast going.

So they dismissed him and notified the band of workers then on the field with him, about twenty five of them, that he was no longer president of the mission. Well I remember that evening in Congo when he read the letter to us and then asked what we would like to do. Would we agree with the committee? Then came his characteristic words: 'Of course if you do dismiss me here, I shall just go over there and start again for I am out here to lay down my life for Jesus and these African souls.' Everyone stood with him, and this, in effect, was the rebirth of the mission in 1931 without an outside committee.

It was during that visit that the team unanimously appointed Jack Harrison as field leader and the Grubbs as home leaders. Grubb humbly states, 'They sent us because there was no one else.' But God's hand was in control.

Norman describes their last hours with the founder:

As we were about to go (around 3 am) Studd said, 'Pauline, I would like to give you something.' He looked about his table of gadgets, at the few boxes behind his bed placed on poles to keep them from the termites and then up at the grass roof from which hung various articles not in regular use –banjos, pans, kettles and so on. Then he quietly said, 'But really I have nothing to give you, I gave it all to Jesus long ago.'

Fifty years later, during a video interview on the history of WEC, recorded by CLC, Norman gave this account:

We said goodbye to Studd: we knew we would not see him again. All he had was us. He didn't trust us very much, but we were all he had left. What were we to do? We went home.

Now I'd always had this close friendship with Rees Howells. When I had been in tough times before I'd go down to Swansea and have a time with him. So, when we reached London I said, 'I'll go down and see Rees Howells.' I had with me a copy of our *Principles and Practice*. He was very polite. 'Let me see your *Principles and Practice*.' I went to bed that night and left with him my *P's and P*.

Next morning he said, 'Look here, it says that the founder has the veto over the committee. The whole thing is yours. It isn't theirs. You've got the veto. Go back and take it.' So I went back to headquarters. Col. Monroe, my unsaved brother-in-law was there. He came with me and we crossed over to the offices next door. They had an older man come each day with the keys, to clean upstairs. He had left his keys in the door so David and I opened it. David was an old army man you know, and wasn't saved, so the first thing he did was cut the telephone wires so no one could catch us in the place. We went upstairs and took all the records. We took everything. (I wouldn't have thought of that!)

It is hard to convey to the reader the enormity of the task that faced the Grubbs in that summer of 1931. Norman describes the atmosphere as 'a dense fog of suspicion, condemnation and controversy'. He wrote: 'We were to learn, as an old saint once wrote, that "The way to heaven is through hell".'

The death of C.T. a few weeks after the split deepened the gloom at mission headquarters in London, but of course for those who had stood at C.T's grave the darkness seemed far more intense.

Afterwards Grubb wrote:

For the missionaries it was the moment of greatest weakness in the history of the mission. Their founder and leader had been taken from them. Grave difficulties at home made the prospect of advance look absurd. The number of missionaries had been severely reduced to thirty five. There had been six months of by far the greatest financial shortage in the history of the work – indeed, almost destitution. The outlook was as black as night. And it was then that faith shone out. 'Out of weakness made strong.' The missionaries took up the sword that had been laid down.

In all fairness it is only right to honour the members of the dismissed committee. They were men of God who wanted things to be done 'decently and in order' and in a recent book, *No Fading Vision* by

John and Moyra Prince, the other side of the crisis is given. We are indebted to John and Moyra and the Asia Pacific Christian Mission for permission to quote:

> The Unevangelised Fields Mission had been born in great pain; pain which came first to the missionaries of the Worldwide Evangelisation Crusade (WEC) in the heart of Africa as they saw their once mighty founder age into decline; pain increased to the point of breach when associates at home and on the field, trying to grapple with the situation, were summarily dismissed from their responsibilities. For many in the mission it was now a choice between loyalty to God or loyalty to a once great man. Both together had become impossible. The collapse of their mission and its work stared them in the face.
>
> After much heartsearching, the dismissed English council, with the support of many of the missionaries on furlough, resolved on June 29th, 1931 to set up a new society 'to carry on the work in Amazonia and other occupied areas'. Thus the Unevangelised Fields Mission was born fully grown, with thirty two experienced missionaries, working in three fields, and an experienced council. Under the new name the work of the Heart of Amazonia Mission went on unchecked, all eighteen of its missionaries adhering to the new society. So did the couple working in isolation in Northern India and about half those in the Heart of Africa Mission itself.

The DCD leaflet being of course a public relations disaster, Grubb immediately took steps to counter its negative influence. The home committee minutes record that:

> It was resolved that a leaflet setting out the official position be printed and sent to all those who had objected to DCD as the official and recognised policy of the mission.

Then follows the draft of this letter:

> We have been in correspondence with our co-workers on the field concerning the DCD. We all realise that the phrase for which these initials stand is a stumbling block to many who in everything else are in full agreement with the spirit and message of the booklet.
>
> We therefore wish to make it clear:
>
> 1. That the DCD phrase is not and will not be a slogan of the WEC nor appear in its literature.
>
> 2. That no one joining the Crusade either as a Crusader or a Committee member or missionary will be asked to sign the DCD vow, or to express approval or otherwise of the phrase.
>
> 3. That the policy of the Crusade will be that all who join it in an

active capacity must do so in the spirit of utter abandonment and sacrifice as exemplified in the booklet, namely, that they care for nothing but the glory of Christ and the salvation of souls.

The motto of the Crusade is as it always has been 'If Jesus Christ be God and died for me, then no sacrifice can be too great for me to make for Him', and this is where we stand today.

We ask your prayer that we may be given wisdom and guidance from above as we carry on the work for worldwide evangelisation.

Yours on behalf on the committee,

N.P. GRUBB.

Even by 1931 Grubb's capacity for vision, strategy and faith can be seen in a magnificent article he penned for the magazine soon after the founder's death:

The Future of WEC and HAM

Africa

Through all his years of toil, teaching and example on the field, Mr Studd has founded the work with a tremendously high standard.

In fact there can be no higher standard. I do not think that any of us who have been his fellow-workers realised what a life of uttermost consecration meant until we got on the field and were brought face to face with the claims upon a follower of Christ as shown by him from the Bible and his own life: and for each of us it meant a heart-searching and a struggle, and when followed by a new act of consecration, a new missionary emerged to render an altogether new kind of missionary service: and for some indeed who could not face the price it has meant a turning back.

The standard he set may be boiled down to three principles:

1. A missionary must care for absolutely nothing else but the glory of Jesus and the salvation of souls;

2. His whole faith must be in God alone for the supply of every need;

3. He must not be content with converts one whit below the standard of scripture.

Obvious enough they may sound in reading them, but Mr Studd, by God's grace, lived them out to the very letter, and those who followed him soon found that none could climb those arduous ascents who were not willing to give themselves to the uttermost limit to do it.

We intend to continue the work on the field along these same lines, for we are convinced that God has taught them to us. Our sole objective is to get as many of these natives as possible saved and filled with the Holy Ghost, and on fire for the salvation of their brethren.

Our school work will not be to fill their minds with a lot of knowledge and turn out educated heathen, but to give the gospel plus just enough education to allow them to handle the Word of God for themselves.

Our industrial work will not be to make money or to teach a trade, but to build character by teaching accuracy, industry, etc., as necessary for a Christian.

Our medical work will of course be to do what we can for their bodies, both to relieve pain and to reach their souls.

Other lands

In the course of the last three years, we have had opportunity to go into the question of world-wide evangelisation and find out exactly where the most neglected areas were located. As a consequence, we intend to bring the following six wholly unevangelised areas and peoples before the Christian public:

West Africa:	1. French Senegal.
	2. Portuguese Guinea.
	3. Spanish Guinea.
	4. The Tuareg Tribe of the Sahara.
Asia:	5. An area where 50,000 Afghans cross the frontier yearly.
Islands:	6. The Dutch East Indies (containing numbers of great islands untouched).

In each case there is nothing to prevent a work being started straightaway but the lack of volunteers. In each case hundreds of thousands or millions of people are without a witness to Christ in their midst. We therefore think that the only possible position we can take up before God concerning them is to say that we are willing and ready *NOW* to start evangelisation in all of these places, if the Lord sends us the volunteers.

Funds

If people ask, 'Where could you get the money for all this, not to speak of your existing work in these days of depression, etc.?', our answer is that the *supply of money is nothing to do with us whatsoever.* We neither depend on deputation work, nor on our publication, nor on our Christian brethren, but on *God's Word alone,* which has said, 'Seek ye first the kingdom of God and all these things shall be added unto you'. Which means, without question, that we are *not* to be bothered about ways and means, in order that we *may* be bothered about an infinitely bigger matter – dying souls. That this is the attitude of the missionaries on the field we know, because when Mrs Grubb and I left in March, they definitely told us that they relieved us of any responsibility for keeping them supplied with money; they looked to God alone, and we have come home free to concentrate, putting before God's people the need of the millions going to a Christless eternity.

Crusaders

To be a Crusader means to us and to some of you who are Crusaders at home, a very real thing. In taking the Crusader's vow you drew your sword and started in to fight with us for the salvation of the heathen: you realise that a battle means hardship and toil and sacrifice, and you are fighting by self-denial, by steady praying, and some by going. The death of our founder must be a call to us to face the implications of our vow.

Crusaders ought to have a double ministry: they ought to be so aroused by the conditions of these Christless millions that their lives are counting in some way for world-wide evangelisation; and they ought to be so on fire for Christ and souls where they are, that they are the most vital members of their churches.

CHAPTER 4

THE TUSSLE FOR THE TEN

One early exploit of faith stands out during that first momentous year of Grubb's leadership – the story of 'The Ten'. In reviewing the greatest needs at that moment it was immediately obvious that the priorities were men and money.

Against the economic backdrop of the severest depression ever to strike Great Britain came the vision of ten new recruits, plus all the finance needed. This was to be the first anniversary memorial of C.T. Studd's death, but it was a giant leap for a small mission of some thirty workers. Grubb describes what happened:

At first, with everything so dark around us, the highest point that prayer and faith could reach was that the Lord would fully supply the needs of the field and home; and it seemed marvel enough as the weeks changed into months that the supply still came, although at the end of at least one month there was only one penny over.

But by November another and greater need was pressing upon us. Letters from the field were telling of open doors such as we had never seen before, chiefs and headmen on all sides opening their lands to the gospel, new tribes being reached, new regions entered, and the missionary staff being stretched like a telescope to meet the demand.

The burden came increasingly upon us, 'Had not we been entrusted by the Lord with this field? Did He not hold us responsible to draw from Him the needed supplies of men and money for it? Had He not given us His promises and the weapons of prayer and faith specifically for this purpose, so that we had no excuse if we failed to obtain them?' Then surely now the time had come for our faith to go farther and to ask from Him both new workers and the funds for them, in spite of the apparently hopeless circumstances.

We had by this time two fully trained men candidates with us, Messrs. Coleman and Cripps, and we found that we had just enough money to pay for their passages, plus a small amount for some of their equipment. However, they volunteered to go straight out so as to be able to start on the language, believing that money would come for the remainder of their equipment within a few months, before they would be ready to start work. They sailed in November.

But God was calling us to reach out far beyond this, and a human impossibility began to take shape in our minds and prayers: that we should ask God for TEN NEW WORKERS and the funds for them (about £1500) and that God would send them all before the anniversary of Mr Studd's death, July 16th, 1932. We considered that it might not be convenient to send the whole number out before that date, so decided to ask God to send the full number and the full supply before July 16th and then that we would complete the sending of them out before the end of the summer.

We began praying for this in November at the time when the first two of the ten mentioned above, sailed for Africa. But it was not until January that the full conditions of believing prayer were revealed to us from God's Word, and we were given grace to obey them. We saw that the men of faith in the Bible, for whom God did impossible things, always fulfilled one condition – they demonstrated that they had really believed God by openly stating beforehand what He would do. The Bible abounds with instances of this, two of which are in the records of Joshua and Paul. When God told Joshua to take Israel across Jordan, he demonstrated his faith in God by telling the Israelites three days beforehand that they were going across. When Paul was on board ship in that tremendous storm, and when after waiting on God, God assured him that he and all the crew would be saved, he publicly told them to cheer up and said, 'I believe God, that it shall be even as it was told me'.

First of all we published among our own inner circle that we believed that God was going to send ten missionaries by July; then we wrote to the field telling them to prepare for ten new workers during the summer, and finally we published the fact in the March magazine and the subsequent numbers. How well we remember what fools the devil told us we were, and how we should hide our heads in shame when they failed to materialise.

Easter time came, and by now we had three lady candidates with us ready to go out, Misses Rose, Brown and Peckett – but no money! We faced the situation together, realised that now the time had come to receive a deliverance from the Lord, and believed that He would give it. This is the story.

Two of the ladies went away for the Easter weekend, but before they went they proved that they really believed God by leaving with the third their addresses, so that she could wire them if the Lord sent the money during that time. On Saturday two guests came for the weekend. They lived by faith, and as far as we knew had no money. But as a matter of fact for years they had had a sum in the bank which they had dedicated to the Lord, but He had never revealed to them how to use it. On Saturday night in a prayer meeting before going to bed, the need of the three was mentioned in a sentence of prayer. God had spoken, and next morning they came down to tell us that God had given them the guidance they had been waiting for, for years, and the money was enough for two passages. At dinner time we made the news known and said we must send the wires. But here came the faith of the third, who had not gone away. She said, 'Why not wait half an hour? God may yet send the money for the third passage!' This was said in spite of the fact that there were no mail deliveries or visitors expected, since it was a Sunday. But just about the time she said that, someone had cause to go to the office of the mission, and there found a letter which had been put in on Saturday night. The address was a ladies' club in London, and inside was a cheque for £100! Hallelujah!

Some fifty of us waved farewell to these three at Victoria Station on May 26th – numbers 3, 4 and 5 of the Ten, taking with them also the completed equipment of numbers 1 and 2.

By this time two more young men had offered, fully trained, Messrs Willson and Cottam; and about the same time a sufficient supply of money had come. They sailed very shortly after the ladies, on June 16th, numbers 6 and 7 of the Ten.

During these months we had one missionary home on furlough from Africa, Miss Daisy Kingdom. She was doing a deputation tour in Canada during the winter months, but was now due back in England ready to return to the field. She also wrote to us to say that she was (D.V.) bringing with her another fully trained worker who would be number 8 of the Ten, Miss Irene James. While we rejoiced at the news we wondered what to do about Miss Kingdom. Should we include her in the Ten? But we had been led to trust the Lord for ten NEW workers, so that would not do. Yet when she arrived, Miss Kingdom must obviously be the first to be sent out before any new workers. So we had to increase the number in prayer and faith to eleven. We must confess that even the increase of one staggered our faith, but the Lord gave strength, for had He not said that He gives 'exceeding abundantly above all we ask or think'?

They both arrived from Canada in June, bringing with them a little less than half the sum needed for their outgoing.

And now for the last lap. Six weeks remained, and no applications or money for the remainder. Five weeks, none. Four weeks, no application, but a gift of £100. Three weeks, still none. Two weeks, and a fully trained lady with nursing experience applied: Miss R Sore, number 9.

There were but days left. On the evening of the tenth a fully trained young man applied as number 10, Mr Ivor Davies. It was at a conference at the Bible College of Wales, Swansea. He had spent three days in fasting and prayer to be sure of God's call, and the very next day the Lord set a wonderful seal on his application, and a wonderful completion to the Ten. There was a brother who was a guest at this conference, but who

knew nothing about the offer of Mr Davies. When praying before breakfast next morning the Lord led him to take a blank cheque from his cheque
book, and put it in his pocket, but did not reveal to him what it was for. At
breakfast he heard the news about number 10 and at once knew that the
cheque was for this purpose. After breakfast, when walking toward the
lecture hall, he asked the Lord where he could find the Secretary of the
mission in order to enquire about the amount needed to send Mr Davies
to the field. The Lord told him that the man he wanted was walking on the
path behind him. At the same moment he heard footsteps, and in obedience to the Lord's guidance, without even looking round to verify it, he
asked the one whose footsteps he heard what the cost would be. It was
the man whom he was seeking, and very shortly after, a cheque for £120
changed hands.

Two days later, two of us were in Ireland. We talked together and
came to the conclusion that it would be a complete answer if the Lord
would send £200 more and we agreed to ask Him for this in secret. Two
days later, when we came out of a meeting in which we told the story of
the Ten, our hostess handed us a telegram, and although she had not the
faintest idea about our secret prayer, was moved to say 'Perhaps there
are £200 in it!' When the telegram was opened it read: TWO HUNDRED
POUNDS FOR THE TEN. HALLELUJAH!

And so within six days of the anniversary God had sent the ten, all the
funds and enough, in addition, for Miss Kingdom.

What a wonderful God we have! How literally true that He is just the
same today as in the days of old, and how humbled we feel at the way we
constantly 'limit the Holy One of Israel' by our unbelief. Praise the Lord,
O my soul, and all that is within me, praise his Holy Name!

By the autumn all ten – five men and five women – were en route to
the field.

Of equal significance, though less well known is the fact that during that year ten black missionaries moved out of their home locations
in the WEC areas of Congo to evangelise distant parts of the land
– lame Zamu and his wife to the Balumbi tribe in the south, two
couples from Wamba and another two from Ibambi also to the
southern region.

Another step – momentous in its outworking for the development of an adequate infrastructure at the home end – was the Grubbs'
decision not to accept any share of the general support fund for the
mission fields, but to trust God personally for *all* their needs.

It was a decision not lightly taken and often tested in the early years.
Norman tells of having to go off for a few days of meetings, leaving

his wife Pauline (and others living at HQ) with just four shillings and sixpence in the house. Only two hours after he had gone a large hamper was delivered at the door sent from an address at the other side of London. It was opened before all – and a praise meeting resulted because it was full of 'sensible' items like meat, potatoes, bread and cheese. Later they discovered that the person who sent it had been impressed by the Lord that morning in his prayer time to go immediately and order it.

But often things were 'tight', and for one week the only food available was bread and cheese.

One day a van drove up and delivered half a ton of potatoes. Next day two large sacks of oatmeal arrived, and some days later the same of lentils – all from the same person, who kept up this supply for years.

This decision not to accept a share of the mission income released Grubb to bring the need of home staff to the Christian public with the knowledge that any additional personnel coming in on the same 'personal faith' basis would not diminish the flow of finance to the fields. It also meant that sending bases run on the same basis could be established in other countries.

During 1933 applications were received for four new fields – Colombia, Arabia, Central Asia and Spanish Guinea. They were part of the new faith target of fifteen workers for that year.

Again it was a swaying battle of faith against unbelief. Grubb recounts how he was preparing a magazine article announcing the faith target of fifteen, but was unwilling to send it to the printer without a final seal of £100 towards it. He set a deadline of 11 am. The time came, but no £100. As he was about to scrap the article Colonel Munro came over to his office waving a cheque for £100! The fifteen (ten men and five women) came forward, and were equipped to go by the anniversary date, 16th July.

Right from the early days of the Grubbs' commission to take up the leadership role at the home end, Norman's keen mind was researching and exploring the then unevangelised areas of the world. WEC's first move to another country (after he became leader) is described by him as follows:

The first [advance] was in the Republic of Colombia in South America. What a mountain it seemed to us then – to start a new field in our weak-

ness. We would never have done it had not Principal Drysdale of Emmanuel Bible College said, 'Why don't you go to Colombia?' God spoke
to Pat Symes in Australia and to us, 12,000 miles away in England, by the
same printed survey on Latin America which pointed out Colombia as
the least evangelised and most fanatically Catholic of the South American republics. To both of us came the challenge 'Go in' and both of us
were reluctant to accept it. Pat's arrival in England en route to another
field brought about a meeting, and the surprise discovery of our mutual
calling. We could resist God no more.

Pat continues:

The call to Colombia in 1932 was clear and plain and it led me to leave
Brazil and the untouched Indians I had hoped to reach. This call put me
into circumstances in England that called for much prayer and waiting
upon God, and at last when I had given away my last penny [to a tramp on
the London Embankment] God gave me the promised £100 with which
to commence work in Colombia.

Writing a ten year review in 1941 Grubb wrote:

When Pat joined us he told us that the Lord had assured him of fifty
workers in ten years. Great though this seemed, larger than the whole
personnel of the Crusade at the time, we joined in faith with him. The
fifty were completed last year, 1940, eight years from the date of the
Lord's promise to him, although the number has now been reduced by
six, four by illness, one by entering business, and one by marrying into a
brother mission.

Today there are some twenty congregations, varying in number from
fifty or sixty downwards, each gradually appointing their own elders and
leaders and beginning to function as a living witness in their district.
Amongst them are men and women from the depths of sin – drunkards,
adulterers, wife-beaters. Some use their own home for meetings. One
has even built on an extra room for the purpose. Another starts his evangelistic activities as early as 5am on Sunday to hold meetings in remoter
parts. The missionary staff occupy twelve centres. A Bible Institute has
been opened to train Colombian evangelists. Four are already on active
service, financed by believers. Another three are in training. The objective is to send forth fifty evangelists and fifty Bible women.

The opposition to the simple gospel was appalling. Only those with
total commitment and sacrificial determination could have stayed on

and reaped an abundant harvest. Twenty five years on, Grubb looked back on all that happened then and described the persecution:

From the beginning there was persecution. Eight years ago fierce persecution swept over all the Colombian church. Church buildings were burned, two schools closed. The missionaries working among the Indians have been forced out by the Roman Catholics and the government. Bill Easton and three men believers were attacked in their chapel, beaten, jailed and tortured all night. Ralph Hines and a Colombian helper were beaten and driven into the flooded Magdelena River at rifle point. A Colombian girl of eighteen was imprisoned all one night. One congregation was driven out, three homes burned and the chapel thrown down; another group had to flee, leaving their homes to the enemy. A group at another place was expelled and homes burned. A missionary and believers were attacked in a meeting, and the same evening all expelled from the town. Another missionary, Julius de Gruyter, was attacked, along with three Colombians, all badly wounded. Bert Snider, a missionary, was jailed for 33 hours. Others have suffered in different ways, but all rejoicing that they have been counted worthy to suffer for Christ's name, and in doing so will fill up the sufferings of Christ for his body's sake. Prayer has been answered and when the enemy's hands were extended to kill and burn, God's hand was extended to restrain and force back.

CHAPTER 5

VISION, VENTURE AND VINDICATION

As the early thirties wore on the blessing on Norman Grubb's leadership was abundantly evident. The crucial areas were recruitment and the finance needed to support an enlarging band of workers. The first two recruiting exploits – 'the Ten' and 'the Fifteen' (among whom was Pat Symes for Colombia), were followed by the 'Twenty-five'. Grubb wrote in the magazine:

> Readers will remember that in the last magazine Pat Symes wrote from Colombia, 'God has given me five of the next twenty-five for Colombia'. It is most remarkable that five of the nineteen applicants so far are for Colombia.

Some of that twenty-five were for new fields, including Ivory Coast, and in the next year (1934-1935) the Lord moved Grubb to believe for fifty. But the big 'mountain' was finance. £5000 would be needed to send that number out. However a virtual stranger who had stayed at headquarters for ten days and had attended the prayer times became aware of the ongoing battle of faith and when he returned home was led to send a cheque for the total amount needed.

New fields entered by these recruits were NE India and Portuguese Guinea in W. Africa. The next year's faith target of seventy-five (for the 5th anniversary of C.T's death) was achieved, so the number of workers in the mission at the time of Studd's death, about 40, had grown to 175 – a 437% increase. And finance? A magazine article written in 1935 tells the story:

> We are full of praise to God for His abundant mercies to us this past financial year. He has sent the largest sum we have ever received in the history of WEC. The greatness of it will best be seen if we compare the totals of the past four years:
>
> | 1931-32 | £ 5866 |
> | 1932-33 | £ 6639 |
> | 1933-34 | £11312 |
> | 1934-35 | £15384 |

The deputation expenses were only £186, an increase of £34 on last year. On the other hand, the expenses for the Mission House have gone down from £180 to £0! Not that an average of fifteen to twenty five folk live on air, but because the Lord blessed us so much in the life of faith in the previous year, that we were led to take on the whole expenses ourselves this year. Once again we have proved overwhelmingly that it is good to trust the Lord, for the more we step out on His promises, the more abundantly He pours His good things upon us. The previous year, although we had £180 less to pray in, we were tested by ten days on bread and cheese! But this year, every meal has been provided for amply; very often twenty-five have sat down to a meal. Whole sacks of potatoes, oatmeal, lentils, rice, peas, legs of mutton and lamb, very many gifts of money, one of which was used to buy 3000 eggs. Gifts both from near and from many thousands of miles off, have just arrived at the right moment. But in addition to this regular supply, there has been the 'exceeding abundant' – first an electric washer which is always on the go and serves the household; then a beautiful cooker of such an economical kind that it only used £4 of fuel a year, where we were previously using £36 worth; finally a friend made a present to us of her own new Ford car! So what are we to say to all this, except to us it is yet one more testimony to the blessedness of trusting the Lord?

Just one more thing ought to be added. All of us in joining WEC have joined for WAR, not ease and comfort; and we expect to have hard times and testings. Thus although we give abundant thanks for all blessings and provision, by God's grace we are not dependent on the supply but on the PROMISES, and will go on and go through, in the dark days as well as in the bright.

During the early thirties basic changes came about in the government of the mission, largely stemming, in a negative sense, from the harsh confrontation between Studd and the executive committee in London, and partly from Grubb's own personality and convictions.

On the one hand he viewed with distaste the heavy handed legalistic methods of the committee and the tug of war between its authority and the autocratic stance of Studd on the field.

On the other hand his own impatient temperament and almost socialist leanings to champion the underdog – quite apart from scriptural principles of equality and unity – pushed him to dismantle an authoritarian structure in favour of each field being self-governing within the over-all framework of the mission's *Principles and Practice*.

A high-powered executive and the use of an 'outside' council of reference (of well-known Christian leaders) were anathema to him, and at home a new simple formula for government developed. The workers themselves would meet quarterly to make executive decisions regarding on-going strategy and policy.

This principle of 'internal responsibility' also produced a second: equality in fellowship. Norman wrote:

> A functioning fellowship should manage its own affairs without outside control; this is the only basis of total fellowship when all ... have the same rights of exploring, discussing and deciding courses of action. The division between managers and managed is deadly to heart fellowship and freedom, unless the managers are merely members of the managed, chosen for management by the team.

There were some very practical implications arising from this concept. It meant that a key factor in the consideration of new applicants was their spiritual maturity and capacity for discerning God's purposes both at a personal and group level. So the merely formal interview was abandoned, and a requirement adopted that those who wished to join would be invited to take up residence (of indefinite length) at the headquarters. During this time they would receive teaching on the mission principles and practice, be involved in the work of maintaining the headquarters, and participate in the prayer-and-faith fellowship times. Eventually applicants would be accepted on the basis of their attitude and spiritual maturity as evidenced by their participation in headquarters life.

One more significant achievement during these early years must be mentioned – the writing of C.T. Studd's biography. The research was completed in one month. Grubb exiled himself to a lonely village in Scotland and collated all the material ready to dictate it back at headquarters.

It was an instant success and the first edition of 3,250 copies was sold out within a few weeks. The Marechal (daughter of the founder of the Salvation Army) wrote: 'No record of a life has so moved me. C.T. is a flame of fire. You bring out with such disarming simplicity the amazing steps of faith he took in the face of opposition from doctors, committee, family and friends. This book is after my own heart. Put me down for 300!'

The Crusaders Union which had hundreds of Bible classes for schoolboys sent a recommendation to every leader to read the book.

It has gone through twenty one impressions in English and has been translated into twelve languages. A report printed in the mission's magazine in 1936 said:

> *The Life of C.T. Studd.* This book continues to carry a stream of blessing everywhere. Times without number people have told us that they have never read a story like it. One authority on missionary literature said that in all his reading along this line he had come across nothing like it, since reading the life of John G. Paton, in his boyhood. A Methodist minister, who is superintendent of a circuit told us that he had given sixteen lectures on it. Another, the minister of a Central Hall, came to say, with considerable emotion, that his spiritual life had been different since reading it, and that he had just completed his fourth time through. The publishers even said that for many young people of today, it may take the place of *Pilgrim's Progress,* for the simple reason that it is present-day and grips them.
>
> But best of all has been the publication, now taking place, of the first USA edition. Mrs Henry Woods, of the Worldwide Revival Prayer Movement, wrote and told us that she published a gift edition of the life of Hudson Taylor years ago, and for some time now has been asking the Lord to guide her to another biography which could bring the challenge of Christ to the students of this generation. She picked up a copy of C.T. Studd somewhere and immediately felt this was the book she was looking for. Further readings of it and the opinion of friends, has only confirmed her impression. 'I am entirely convinced that the book will prove of inestimable spiritual value to students throughout the world.... The book is a message for the church in general.... My husband was so much impressed with it that he could hardly lay it down after beginning it' she writes. The result is that she is bringing out a gift edition of 5,000.
>
> Owing to the fact that our Canadian and USA Crusade Leader, Alfred Ruscoe, will also need many copies, perhaps a larger edition will be printed. But it anyhow means that the total number of copies is now at least 40,000, in three years, far beyond 'our asking or thinking'.

Ideally, it was Norman's intention to have experienced missionaries open new fields. Sometimes it happened that way, sometimes not. The stories of the opening of the Spanish Guinea and Ivory Coast reveal his confidence in two experienced couples – Alex and Dora Thorne, and Sam and Lilian Staniford.

For two years God had given us our marching orders to occupy every remaining unoccupied region of West Africa not in the programme of our brother missionary societies. A map of Africa was hung on the walls of our London prayer room with arrows directing attention to these lands, and daily we brought before Him the names of the seven lands of West Africa, which, so far as we could ascertain, were wholly or partially unoccupied. Daily we used to thank Him in faith and enjoy looking forward to the coming days when He would send us as a preliminary, two pioneers for each. Amongst these lands, the smallest, yet always with an especial attraction to us, was Spanish Guinea.

The Lord worked for us at the Emmanuel Conference in Birkenhead where we gave a survey of West Africa. It has never been our policy to urge people to become missionaries, but rather the opposite, to make people see the full cost entailed and leave the Holy Spirit to do the thrusting out. This was particularly so in the case of West Africa, because we had asked the Lord not for a tenderfoot, but a man of experience to pioneer the work. In Mr and Mrs Thorne, God gave this first full answer – not one but two! They had considerable Christian experience having had a taste of the mission field, and they were filled with the Holy Ghost. Out of the seven lands their knowledge of Spanish made the little land of Spanish Guinea the obvious choice. Even in natural qualifications, although *they* stressed their lack, *we* saw a very different side of things, Mrs Thorne being a fully trained nurse, and Mr Thorne both a trained male nurse, and very practical in the handling of cars, carpentry, etc.

If they felt their weakness and let us know it, we also made sure that they should know our human weakness as a crusade, and have no temptation to trust in the WEC rather than God. 'If God is leading you to go to West Africa and in fellowship with the WEC,' we wrote, 'we are ready to go along with you. If God is in it – and it certainly looks as if He is – then He will also supply the necessary funds. I say this from the deepest poverty, for we are even being tested in the Congo field at this moment by shortage, and in addition we have Arabia, and now Central Asia, and another with us to open work in South America. Not a penny for all these projects, but all the same God will do the lot and more, if we will steadfastly look to Him alone and not to man.' To which their answer was, 'We believe God is calling us to Spanish Guinea, and if God calls us, there will be the necessary supplies. We are prepared to go where the Holy Ghost leads and leave the consequences to Him.'

There was one more test, short and fierce. A few weeks before the date of sailing, we received information from a reliable source that it was useless to send missionaries to a Spanish colony, as their recent laws (this was some three years before the Revolution) forbad the entry of missionaries unless of Spanish nationality. It was a heavy blow, and we have to confess that the faith of the WEC staggered. Other lands were open in West Africa; why should they not go to one of them? We put it to the Thornes. They prayed but returned to say that God had again spoken

clearly and asked them what they were doing considering another country when He had said Spanish Guinea. It took us a weekend to agree to
going forward against the laws of a government – a weekend of darkness
which only lifted when we heard God saying the same thing to us, recognised His voice and yielded. *He* had said Spanish Guinea; very well, if a
government said no, it was a chance for a trial of strength between a
temporal power and God.

The Thornes arrived on December 14th, 1933. They were the first
British missionaries ever to go there, although the American Presbyteri-
ans had opened work years ago in the northern part, abandoned it, but
recently re-opened with a couple of workers, just in time before the new
Spanish ban came into force. We had obtained the names of these missionaries and sent them a letter. We also made our four definite requests
to the Lord for the Thorne's arrival: that at the port of arrival someone
would be raised up to befriend them: that some native should come along
who could speak English: that the American missionaries would help
them: and above all that in spite of all we had heard, the Lord would make
the Spanish authorities not only willing for them to stay, but even be
favourable to them.

Their own diaries tell the romance of their landing:

December 15th, 1933 [Mr Thorne continues]. Arrived, and our feet
planted on the shore at Benito, praise God. A German is standing there
talking to the ship's officer. Coming forward he is introduced – Mr Heid
– and he said at once, 'Well you must come with me to my house; the
lady can stay there, and we will see about Customs later.' So we turned
and accompanied him, in some bewilderment. Well, this trader and his
wife made us as welcome as if we were their own people. He would not
hear of payment, either for bed or food! Now is it not just like the Lord
to raise up someone like this?

Our next discovery was that the American missionaries had their station at Bolondo, just across the river, and although temporarily out of the
country themselves, left the house at our disposal. So the next morning
two boys came over from the house and we duly all crossed the river to
our new temporary abode.

December 28th. A car is going to Bata, and the Governor returned yesterday. Off I go to see him. Well, now. What would you expect the governor to do or say? I went up to his house and had to wait in his secretary's
office for half an hour. The secretary can do a great deal of wire-pulling,
and so I believe the Lord arranged every detail. I told him quite frankly of
our hopes and aspirations, then followed splendid opportunities of testi-

fying to what great things the Lord has done for us. Then the bell rang announcing the presence of the Governor in the next room, so in went the secretary, and after a few moments I was sent in. The governor greeted me in a friendly but not enthusiastic style, gave the merest glance at my passport and said, 'Oh, you are a missionary.' Then I again started explaining our object for being in the land. He did not say anything at all to oppose our going; in fact, when I told him we did not know where we should settle down, he said that was all right, and that when I let him know, he would do what he could for us. But still so far he had not given the help I was expecting in answer to prayer, so I said, 'May I ask, could you give me any idea as to where would be the most likely parts for me to find the people we want?' And then he told me the best ways to investigate the land. The Governor himself has given the idea of looking at the land, north, south, east and west. Hallelujah, I just felt 'The land is before you, go up and possess it.'

Thus all stages of their arrival became a string of answered prayers, culminating in the Governor himself acting contrary to what he should legally have done (as was officially admitted a year later, namely, to refuse permission to work), to being a friend and first adviser of the Thornes. The weak are God's strong ones!

Grubb also describes the commencement in Ivory Coast:

The entry of Ivory Coast was accomplished the following year (1934) by the Stanifords from the Congo who had been compelled to return to England for medical reasons. Permission was not easily obtained from the French administration to open work amongst an inland tribe called the Gouros; they had an evil reputation for poisoning. Work was only allowed amongst the northernmost 10,000 of a tribe of 120,000.

The sufferings of Christ were shared by the leader who lost his beloved wife, Lilian, after three days of yellow fever. Also, he lost the sight of one eye and the hearing of one ear through a motor accident, all within a few months. He was invited to return home, although we knew that to leave the infant work might mean that the permit would be withdrawn for the future. John 12:24 was the answer received – the corn of wheat had fallen into the ground and died, now the harvest was awaited, and no return home was going to interfere with the reaping of it.

Many villages were visited; reinforcements arrived. But very little in conversions was apparent; and still the door was shut to the majority of the tribe. Then, shortly before the war, clear guidance came to re-apply for permission. The local official, who had become a good friend, said that he would pass the application on to the Governor-General at the coast, but that there was little hope of a favourable reply. As the letter was on its journey, an official document crossed it on the way up to this local administrator, informing him that administrative boundaries were being changed; in future the Gouro tribe would be under one official, and that he was the man appointed. His first act was to open the whole tribe to the gospel! The one station amongst the Gouros was extended to three, north, centre and south. The endurance of faith had inherited the promise.

The testimonies of Dr Wilf and Mrs Nancy Morris pull the curtain back and give us an intimate picture of the Grubbs during this period. Nancy gives her impressions:

It is well nigh impossible for me to write of Norman without including his wife Pauline. From the summer of 1934 till I sailed to India in 1937 they were both an unfailing source of challenge, inspiration and spiritual help. Their Christianity was so delightfully practical as they lived out their faith and set an example of willing sacrifice for the sake of releasing the gospel into the world. As a young teacher my weekends, frequently spent at 17 Highland Road, left me in no doubt as to the kind of mission I was hoping to join.

Those were the good old enamel plate days with Rubi at one end of the table, Ma Rubi at the other, and Daniel in his high chair at her side. It didn't seem to matter what was on the plates because conversation was so absorbing. I would always ask how I could help, whatever the task, and however mundane it seemed to be. I knew it counted toward worldwide evangelisation. One day Ma Rubi took me to the basement and showed me an empty, very dirty room. She said, 'Nancy, coal was stored in this room but now we have a better use for it. Could you do something about it?' As I wielded a scrubbing brush and used endless buckets of water my heart was singing: 'I had rather be a doorkeeper in the house of my God than dwell in the tents of wickedness'. Headquarters was in such a real way 'the House of God'.

Wilf gives his story:

My first meeting with Norman was when, as a medical student, I became interested in WEC through its magazine. On visiting the headquarters, I was much impressed with him. Here was a mission secretary who really lived by faith in daily life and who was consumed by a burning desire for God and for world evangelisation! From the first, he inspired me to go all out for God.

In 1932, after I'd qualified, I went to live at headquarters. There was

no formal candidate course. I did some practical jobs there with Fred
Chapman and Olive Moore. The Grubbs were at the table at meal times. It
was very much a family affair.

Norman was very much one with us. He made no difference between
himself and the candidates. You would never have thought that he was the
chief. Really he was the first person who taught me how to stand against
one's feelings and the 'visible' and go by God's Word and what God says.
It was the school of faith, and I needed it very much because I had determined to put that faith to the test in England before I went to India.

Norman Grubb was the same off the platform as on it – more uni-
formly Christian in his daily walk than any I have known. By steadfast
faith he bore great burdens and overcame in many crises. At times these
took their toll, but the Lord always carried him through to victory. His
impulsive, outgoing nature was under the Holy Spirit's discipline.

While a candidate at headquarters it was his messages applying the
Word to many issues that prepared me and many others for the setbacks
and triumphs, wounds and victories which lay ahead.

On the India field from 1934 it was letters from Rubi which helped
sustain me in the early years. He always held me to the highest, encouraging me to walk by faith – not by feelings or the visible. He always saw
the best in people and counted on that.

With Wilf on the field and Nancy still at home Norman was sensitive
about their separation. Nancy continues:

Mr Grubb spoke to me: 'Well, Wilf's on the field and I don't want you to
wait for ever to join him.' He was impressed, I think, that we had put God
first and were willing for the separation. So he said, 'I want you to go
down to the Bible College of Wales at Swansea for a few months: I don't
want you to go for years, just a few months to get a taste and the challenge of it.' I'd only been teaching two terms so had to give my notice.
This caused great distress to my parents and I found it hard to bear. The
headmistress was unhappy too. All I could say was 'I believe God is telling me to do this.'

I always remember Mrs Grubb saying to me, 'Nancy, do you realise
that when you join WEC you're going to live with people who are trusting God even for postage stamps?' I knew they were trusting God for
food at headquarters and sometimes I made a little contribution, but postage stamps!

I went off down to Swansea and my father who had always been very
generous and looked after us very well, said, 'What are you going to do
about money while you're at this Bible College of yours?' I said, 'It's all
right dad; while I've been teaching I've earned enough for the six months

Mr Grubb wants me at college.' So off I went, paid the first term's fees and put the rest in a savings account at the post office, keeping a bit of loose change.

After about three weeks the Lord started to speak to me: 'Here's your opportunity.' I'd read *Hudson Taylor* and He kept bringing back to me how Hudson Taylor was put in the position where his parents thought the mission was looking after him, and the mission thought his parents were taking responsibility for him. The Lord said this was my opportunity. I remember spending the afternoon praying, and then that night I couldn't sleep. Round and round in my head went the thought 'Can God supply a table in the wilderness?' In the morning I got on my knees and said, 'Yes, God You can, and I'm going to trust You to do it.' So on the Saturday I went to the post office, took out the savings and gave it away, except for a very small amount of loose change for stamps.

Later, when I had two important letters to write I took my last six-pence to buy stamps. As I reached the door of the post office the Lord said, 'Go back and give that sixpence to Bessie Fricker' (later Bessie Brierley). So I walked back to the college and though it was embarrass-ing, I found Bessie and very hesitatingly said, 'Bessie, I feel the Lord wants me to give you this sixpence.' She said, 'Hallelujah, I've got to go to a meeting in town tonight and I didn't have my bus fare.' So, I thought 'Well, praise God. So far so good. Now what do I do?' I thought, 'Well, all my life I'd been trusting my father and he's always given me stamps when I needed them. Now I'm trusting my heavenly Father. Is he less kind, less generous? No.' So I wrote the two letters, put them on the dressing table and said, 'Heavenly Father, I need stamps for these letters by next Monday morning.'

Monday came; I went down to breakfast and one of the girls came in waving an envelope. She said, 'Someone has sent me so many stamps, I'll never use them. Here girls, help yourselves.' 'Thank you,' I responded. (But in my heart I was saying, 'Thank You, Heavenly Father.')

1935 was a crucial year in Norman Grubb's life. He passed through a spiritual crisis that could well be described as 'the dark night of the soul'. Very little is recorded covering this year. We do know that Rubi's reading of James' *Varieties of Religious Experience* seemed to under-mine his spiritual convictions. Jock Purves, a Scottish WECer who had worked for a time in Kashmir and who was then on the home staff, realised something of the inner spiritual struggle that was going on. He became Rubi's deputy for that year. A gentle, insightful, wise brother, he carried this task responsibly in Norman's absence.

Norman and Pauline spent the year in various locations which included a time in Swansea with Rees Howells. His son Samuel remembers:

> He had that breakdown in 1935. It was a difficult time because he seemed
> to have lost his faith and stability for a while. He and Mrs Grubb came
> down here to Swansea for a time. Father was very gentle and dealt with
> him in great sympathy because he knew that it was a real breakdown and
> if the Spirit didn't touch him it would be difficult for him to assume
> responsibility again. Father carried a very great prayer burden for him.
> He felt responsible for him.

Norman started to find answers in the writings of William Law and Jacob Boehme, largely centring on the truth of our realised union with a Christ who died, a Christ who rose again, and a Christ who ascended. This was to become the major, indeed the only, continuous theme of his subsequent books. He would often say in later days, 'The self was never meant to be anything other than a container of the divine.'

The mists cleared by the end of the year. Later he tells of having a fixed consciousness of Christ within, as his all-in-all. He felt it was a step further on from his Galatians 2:20 experience in Congo when he saw his dying and rising with Christ as a key to his own personal release and empowering.

So he was back in business, not constantly bridging a gap between himself and Christ but living in a settled awareness of Christ in him as his all-in-all.

CHAPTER 6

PROGRESS AT A PRICE

The second half of the thirties brought continuing expansion, but such were the logistical problems of seeing so many recruits settled into new fields that the strategy was altered. Reviewing the situation a few years later, Norman wrote:

> During the earlier years, 1931–1935, when the ten, fifteen, twenty-five and fifty came in, it was made clear that although we asked God to send them in by a certain date, it might take longer for them to go to the fields, as a certain testing was necessary to ensure that their calling was truly from God, and their spiritual and physical fitness manifest; also in opening new fields there were sometimes European languages to learn and delicate negotiations to make with reluctant governments. This proved to be so to such an extent that although these four batches were all in to date by 1935, they had not all finally sailed until 1937.
>
> As a consequence, from 1938 onwards we slightly changed our method, asking God for the new seventy-five, but spread over three years, at a rate of twenty-five a year, with the intention of getting each twenty-five out to the field within each year. The first of these 25s sailed according to plan in 1938. The war intervened when less than half of the second twenty-five had sailed in 1939, but we were led to go straight on with our programme in faith. All but one of that twenty-five sailed (the 25th remaining in USA to take an extra course), although the last few were several weeks late leaving England. In the yet tighter conditions of 1940 all the twenty-five and their money came in; twenty-one sailed, but four still awaited boats or permits from England. But meanwhile in early 1941 eleven had sailed from Canada and USA, thus by that means completing the total of seventy five, although a few months behind schedule.

One of the most significant happenings of these five years was the re-acceptance of Alfred Ruscoe ('Rusiko') into WEC. He had been a missionary with Studd but had disagreed with his policies and left the mission. His return to the work, and his commissioning to establish a sending base for WEC in North America was something of a miracle because Norman Grubb had very little confidence in him initially. It was only when they realised God was clearly drawing them together that both men dropped their differences with each other and committed themselves to the work of the mission.

It is even more significant to realise the total freedom that Grubb gave Ruscoe. He simply acknowledged that God was in this, that He would provide, and that He would show Ruscoe how he was to develop WEC in N. America. This was always, in his view, God's way – the independence of faith – and often the expression was used, 'If you have the vision, go for it!' Ruscoe had a vision of four headquarters in four years, and sure enough they came into being in Toronto, Charlotte, Seattle and Pittsburgh.

On the value of this 'independence of faith' Grubb wrote in an unpublished article:

Another valuable product of the faith life in a community is a basic independence of man as the reverse side of a total dependence upon God. Each person remains inviolably an individual before God. Team work demands loyalty, team discipline, team leadership, but that is only a relative horizontal relationship, never to rival the absolute vertical relationship between the individual and God and in this the life of faith maintains the subtle difference.

Money is power. He who controls finances, controls lives. If, down underneath, the heart reliance of a servant of God is on his board or denomination for his livelihood and daily bread, then there is bound to creep in a human subservience. If down at the grass roots God alone is the provider, ultimate allegiance is rendered only to Him. It puts a freshness into mission relationships – not the dullness of compulsory duty, but the spontaneity of freely rendered service. It is a preservative against the danger of mission magnification. If the society is our life-centre and life-security, we shall magnify the organisation and seek its prosperity. If God is our life-centre, we shall not make too much of any human organisation, ours or others, for we shall only boast of one real membership – in the universal church of Christ.

Healthy, humbling, liberating – like breathing pure mountain air or surveying the scenery from the summit – is this community faith relationship. Yet in this also the same law operates – to find your soul you lose it: and a society which lays no claim to human loyalty and allegiance actually has a binding affect on it members; they are the individual strands which, twisted together in one cable, carry every kind of weight without breaking.

If the way of faith is, as we believe, the only safeguard in a Christian organisation against worldly security, prosperity, complacency, against

man pleasing and its reverse, man-domination, if it is the only preservative against creeping corruptions of secularity, debasing an agent of the
Spirit from a living organism to a mechanical organisation, then the way
of faith is also the only unfettered, unconquerable principle of advance.
The man of faith breathes the fresh air of eternity away up above the fogs
and mists of time. He moves in the freedom of the heavenlies out beyond the limiting pressures of earth's atmosphere.

In the area of strategies for advance Norman was quite flex-
ible. In two cases he 'picked up' works started by non-WEC personnel. The first of these related to the handing over of Dr
Katherine Harbord's ministry on the Nepal Border. He describes
the circumstances:

Among those who believed that God was going to open the closed land
of Nepal was a woman missionary doctor, Katherine Harbord. So moved
was she by the spiritual and physical needs of these little people, quite
different from the Indians, who sometimes mingled with the sufferers at
her hospital in North India that, with no mission willing to back her, she
went alone to the western half of the rugged 500 mile frontier, along
which there was not one missionary witness. She rented a house at
Nautanwa, and for eight years ministered to the souls and bodies of the
Nepalese who came down through the passes. The fame of her medical
ministry was carried back into the closed land, and she even made a few
secret journeys to attend the women folk in the households of some of
the ruling classes; a few hidden disciples of the Saviour were left behind.
    After eight years a grave medical condition necessitated her return
to England for an operation. But God's strength was made perfect in her
weakness. In her hour of need God brought us of the Worldwide Evangelisation Crusade into touch with her through reading a magazine article
on her work; our Doctor Wilfred Morris had just arrived in India, and the
guidance was clear that he was God's choice to take her place. This was
the beginning of the WEC work in India.

Another instance came in 1938. A small mission based in Canada
had commenced a work in Liberia, W. Africa in 1928, but decided to
disband. However, a number of its missionaries were determined to
carry on. About the same time our N. American base started to have
something of a vision for commencing in that land. When those on
furlough from the original mission heard of WEC's interest they applied
to join. Result – an instant field with eight workers.
But fast expansion brought its problems. The increasing stream of

recruits brought considerable strain to the crowded London headquarters. To 17 Highland Road was added number 19 and in 1932 number 34, opposite, through the loving provision of a Miss Gristwood who herself joined the mission. A further enlargement was desperately needed. It then came to light that, through a quirk in the borough by-laws, a larger building could be erected on the ground of No.19. Rubi wrote the following while the building was still in progress.

The modern Goliath stood in our path – finance! Needless to say we had no intention of erecting a hostel in the homeland with money given for the field. Then in one stroke God thrust us into building. We received information that a sum of money in the region of £1,800 was coming to us, specially to be used for a missionary hostel. And yet the amazing thing was that the donor had not known what was in our minds about extension.

Now we began to turn our attention to the practical details of building. First this thought came to us. Why should we not ask the Lord for a volunteer building team of recruits, including sufficient experts in the various departments of house-building? God had previously given us individual electricians, plumbers, etc. to make large structural alterations in the 'stables', so why not now a whole team? We began to pray and expect. We realised that if we had a voluntary building team who worked for the Lord then all the money could be put into the best possible material, so as to put up a hostel worthy of the Lord. No effort was made to search about and invite this one or that to come and help, but we merely asked the Lord to send along candidates or volunteers fitted for the job, just when we wanted to begin to build. It would seem like a fairy story if it were not a fact that at this very moment we have here now a team of fourteen crusaders, climbing like cats over the steel structure that they have themselves erected, and they include three experienced builders: Wilfred Watt (who acts as a foreman), John Byers and Frank Miller; three trained carpenters: David Davis, Martin Davies and Phil Dyer; one who is skilled in erecting girders: Kenneth Cairns; one plumber: David Barron (at present in France, but returning when plumbing is needed); four Jack of all trades: Norman Kennedy, Jack Lenny, Will Purves and Max Jahn, with Fred Lyons of the home staff helping and Leslie Sutton in general control! And the Lord will send the plasterer and electrician when needed!

Yet even now by far the best wine has been left to the last. One further matter confronted us, of such importance that we reckoned that God's provision in this respect would be the crowning seal. In our ignorance of building and our desire for the very best job to be done for the Lord's glory, would He guide us to a Christian contractor for the drawing up of the plans, provision of best materials, and responsibility for putting up the building with our team of volunteers, when obviously an ordinary contractor would not do it? Also one who would provide scaffolding, concrete mixer, etc. One of our number knew such a one, both a contractor in a large way and a true brother in Christ. He came over to see us, expecting to find a very small job in prospect. When he came and saw for himself the crowd of folks here and the greatness of the vision, he caught fire. Then he fell ill. But the sick-bed, instead of cooling him off, made him ten times hotter. For he later came to tell us that, as he lay there, God spoke and said that He had laid him aside in order to give him a definite commission to put the building of this hostel FIRST before all other jobs. And first he put it. His architect, another dear brother in Christ, put aside other work to draw up plans.

The name of this contractor was Will Hopkins ('Uncle Hoppy' as he was called by the WEC team).

Searching among the archives, we came across this notice written in Uncle Hoppy's own handwriting:

June 1930
This is written for one purpose – to glorify God.

Will Hopkins turned down a £25,000 contract because it would have interfered with the desire to assist in building the Hostel which Praise God we now see by sight.

His debts are £21,000 or a little more and by putting God first he believes that He is able abundantly to clear all these.

He is very happy in his fellowship with The Father, The Son, & the Holy Spirit. Amen
Will Hopkins

And, yes, indeed, God honoured Will Hopkins. His business was greatly enlarged and blessed by God.

After the hostel was commenced Rubi went to North America. For some time he had realised the potential for missions there. Indeed that was really why he had sent Ruscoe over. At the end of his first tour he wrote:

My ten months tour of the USA terminated on November 25th. It has been one further illustration of this wonderful life in which we do nothing of ourselves, but what we see the Father do, that we do also. In co-operation with Alfred Ruscoe we long had had the desire to see the Crusade in action in USA, but we knew that, combined with the desire, we must also know God's time; for with the few links we had in the country, humanly speaking, our going could only mean a lot of hard struggling and a few small meetings, but when God's hour struck, it would be a triumphal march. And so it has proved beyond description.

Dr. and Mrs Henry M. Woods of the Worldwide Revival Prayer Movement, who, as already mentioned, had published the gift edition of *C.T. Studd* for students in USA a year earlier, invited me over. This opened unnumbered doors through their nationwide links with Christian workers. Ten years ago they had been led to publish a gift edition of the life of Hudson Taylor which was largely instrumental in the calling out of the 200 who at that time went to China; they had now been led to publish *C.T. Studd* with the same object in view – of rousing young men and women to evangelise the world; yet when they asked me to come over, I had no idea that they had had this vision, and they had no idea that I had been praying for two years for an opening in USA for the very same purpose! Such are God's perfect ways. Not only that, but the door was thus opened to me just at the time when we had completed the sending out of the first hundred by faith, the opening of nine new fields, and the establishment of the faith headquarters in London with the erection of the new hostel, thus enabling me to go with a concrete all-round testimony of what God had done.

The result has been overwhelming. How well Fred Anthony and I remember arriving at Dr. and Mrs Woods' home near New York on January 26th, feeling strangers in the land and knowing only a handful of folks. How wonderful to start with that 'home from home', which has been open to us during all our stay. And since that date we have never ceased to be busy.

Meetings must have averaged at least two a day, and numbered some 600; some 14,000 miles have been covered; congregations have been from nearly 4,000 at Moody's, 3,000 at the Church of the Open Door, Los Angeles, many others of 1,000, down to house meetings of 20 and 30; in universities, Bible Schools, and I should think, every denomination there is. There were many unusual gatherings such as when one couple turned their silver wedding anniversary party into a buffet supper and revival challenge to the seventy leaders and their wives of a big Methodist Church. The chief results have been the transformation in the lives and outlook of numbers of Christians concerning victorious living and service. Testimonies have come by the hundred to this effect. Wherever a series of meetings in one centre has been possible, the numbers have increased till the place was full at the end, such as our last four-day rally of this kind, accompanied by Alfred Ruscoe, where the numbers rose from 500 to 1,000. I have learned from this that God has given the Crusade a message for this hour, in bringing God's people to see the life of victory and authority in darkening days.

Mr Vernon Patterson of CBMC in Charlotte, N.C. invited Rubi to speak to his group. Other Christians were stirred and a gift was pledged that would cover the rent of a ten-room property suitable for a WEC headquarters. The first USA HQ was in business and within a year there was a staff of three, plus two candidates preparing for the fields.

Back in Britain, 1937 was the year that the WEC Youth Department was founded. It was to have a significant impact on British WEC as young people were challenged about true discipleship and missions.

Ena Pethybridge who, with her husband Bill, were the pioneers, tells her story:

In 1936 John Lewis, who was one of our local young people in Southend was getting interested in WEC and so persuaded some of us to go up to HQ in Upper Norwood for a weekend. That just revolutionised my life because I really had no missionary vision until then.

I learned that they were having a meeting in September for people who wanted to form prayer groups or help WEC in some way, so I decided to go.

Norman Grubb was the chairman. I think that was my first close contact with him. The drawing room at No. 17 Highland Rd. was full. There was a young lady there who brought five of her Bible class children aged 10 – 12, so of course Norman and some of the others were very interested to find who these children were. The leader, Miss Leitch, explained that as far as she knew they were the only children's group officially linked to WEC; they were wearing WEC badges. Norman, with his usual charm, drew them out and asked all about it. A middle aged gentleman suddenly spoke up and said, 'You know Mr Grubb, it's about time you had a properly organised youth section of WEC.' Norman Grubb, with his lovely smile turned to him and said, 'Oh yes, brother, perhaps you're the one to do it.' And this man said, 'Well, of course I'm a middle aged man with a home and children and I couldn't possibly go round the country founding a youth work.' Meanwhile I felt as though a spiritual bomb had hit me and I prayed, 'Oh Lord, don't let that man do it because I think you've told me to do it.' Of course I was scared stiff. I never said anything to anybody. I felt the Lord just had to work it out.

We finished the meeting and the more I prayed the more I felt it was right to join WEC. So I sent for application papers. I didn't wait for any acceptance at all, I just went straight ahead and gave in my notice at the bank where I was working. Then I wrote WEC and told them I was coming up. I learned afterwards that Norman Grubb heard about this and said, 'Oh, what is she? An office worker? We don't need another office worker.

But anyhow she seems determined to come so we had better find her a bed.'

The morning after my arrival Norman Grubb took morning prayers. I was fresh and nervous but I was astounded to hear him bring up this proposed youth department. When he asked for prayer I just opened my mouth and prayed about it and asked God to guide. When the meeting finished I was told that he wanted me in his study. I was very nervous as I went in. He said, 'Look here, I sensed something in your prayer. Have you come here with a burden to form this youth department?' Very tremblingly I said, 'Yes.' He slapped his knee and in his usual enthusiastic manner said, 'I believe it's of the Lord; I believe it's of the Lord. Go right ahead and I'll back you up all I can. Do you have contacts around the city with other youth departments of other missions?' I said, 'One or two.' 'Go ahead, don't wait to be accepted on the staff or anything. That'll be all right!' So he just pushed me on. I did get quite a few contacts and he gave me more. Then we discussed the theme of this youth work. I have much to thank the Japan Evangelistic Band for, because I got the idea from them that it should be for saved children who would be led on to a missionary vision. He was 100% for that. We decided to call it 'Young Warriors'.

I asked the Lord for a monetary seal if it was His will and the Lord sent in some money for the new work. It was launched during the summer conference at the Bible College of Wales in the summer of 1937.

I had the privilege of going round the country with a missionary team headed by Norman Grubb so I was getting more and more of his lovely teaching all the time. At the end of 1938 I became engaged to Bill Pethybridge who was interested in WEC and now wanted to come in as a candidate. He joined during March of 1939 as a candidate for the home end. We were supposed to wait two years before being married but the Lord told us He would bring it to pass in September. We did not tell anybody. So in the summer holidays we were allowed to go down and stay with my parents. The war clouds were gathering as we went back to WEC. The very next morning after our return to headquarters war was declared. Well, now we saw Norman Grubb at his best. He called us all together – missionaries, candidates, home staff, and said, 'First of all we're going to have a praise meeting and praise the Lord that the devil is on the run and God's going to turn this to further blessing.' After we'd had some prayer he said in the light of possible bombing there were too many of us at headquarters. He told us to seek the Lord and find out what he wanted us to do. Some could stay but some should scatter. Well, we didn't need to pray because we knew what the Lord wanted. We felt we should be married on September 14th and this was September 2nd.

We went to see him and told him how the Lord had led us and we felt the Lord wanted us to go to Scotland and open the first headquarters there and of course carry on the Warrior work at the same time. He looked at us and said, 'If you'd told me that yesterday I would have squashed it flat. Bill's supposed to do two years here and he's only done six months, but I'm sure it's of the Lord, (slapping his knee again with great enthusiasm). Go ahead. Make all the plans for the wedding and we'll back you up.'

We had about eighty people at the reception, and the WEC staff said it was the first cheerful thing that had happened since war was declared. They made all the jellies, blancmanges and sandwiches! We left for Scotland the next day.

We forgot all about a honeymoon. We wanted to get on with the job. We did open the very first Scottish HQ and later on we went down to Wales and opened the first Welsh HQ. All the time it was Norman's teaching on faith that was inspiring us to launch out. And of course he was really in the work with us. Eventually we were freed to concentrate fully on the youth work and later, after seeing a number of groups formed, we launched into the summer camps which brought much blessing. We thank God for Norman Grubb and the wonderful foundation that he gave us.

In the thirties there were virtually no set structures or procedures for applying to and joining the mission. Everything was totally informal. Eric Smith, now a very senior WECer remembers meeting Norman Grubb.

I had an interview with Rubi about joining WEC. He struck me as a very educated man, interesting to talk to. When I said that I wanted to join, he simply put two questions to me: 'Are you ready to die for Jesus?' and, 'Have you led souls to Christ?' That was all. I was able to say 'yes' to both so was accepted on the spot!

It was subsequent to that that I went to Bible School and when I returned I simply lived at the headquarters for a year. There was no structured candidate course. I spent most of my practical time whitewashing the ceilings of No. 17 Highland Road!

Rubi was pre-eminently a man of vision. He carried tremendous burdens – you could tell when he was weighed down. We just sensed it. He would share quite a lot in morning prayers. He knew where he was going and he got us involved with him.

What was life at mission headquarters like? There is no doubt that the outstanding feature was morning prayers. Norman led these in his own inimitable way.

Leona Bartlett (née Passmore), a Canadian worker for Spanish
Guinea remembers:

He always started off with a good rousing hymn. One thing I was pleased
about – he didn't let the singing drag. Other mornings when he wasn't
there the singing was a real drag, but when he was there he had us really
singing from our hearts. And the thing that I most enjoyed at morning
prayers when Rubi took them was he was always teaching; he could get
out of a verse something that I had never seen and it wasn't just the teaching but the application he made. He wanted each of us personally to dwell
and think on the portion he had explained to us and to apply it to our own
daily lives. It made a real impression on me that here was a man of God
who lived what he taught and he wanted the rest of us to do the same.

Leslie Brierley, retired International Research Secretary, recalls:

He used to come in with scripture, generally the Old Testament patri-
archs; then he would bring one or two letters just received from the fields,
sharing a problem or a blessing and then he would explain it and try to
link the scripture with the situation on the field and draw his lesson from
that. This led to faith and prayer, and sometimes a challenge for a particular thing that had to be obtained – a visa for an outgoing missionary,
or a new country to be opened, or a people to be prayed about and so on.
Then we would get down to prayer, and pray through. Sometimes we would
sense there was a rise in faith and we had obtained that for which we were
asking God.

John Whittle of England, who later moved to USA with WEC, recollects:

In morning prayers he sat there, and very hesitantly and leisurely – not
trying to be an orator or Bible teacher – tried to extract some of the
deeper aspects of scripture and apply them to the operation of our work.
There was never anything very ordered about what he said, it was often
meandering, but it was a meandering in the realm of the Spirit, into the
deeper things of God. Most of us took hold of the principles that he
brought out, and learned to apply them to the actual job we had to do.
    My strong feeling about him was that he always set people free to be
themselves; he gave them any pointers, suggestions and nudges that he
thought could help them. Of course if anybody came for a definite project
he would help shape it up, but he was not dictatorial – he was largely
advisory. He based his actions on the things he was learning in the Spirit.
The only time I saw him 'off key' (I don't know what other word to use)

was when anybody opposed him with a totally different idea; then he would veer away somewhat or make it very clear that he was following another path.

He was the most generous and thoughtful person imaginable. He was easy to travel with, easy to live with and although some may have found that disagreeing with him brought out a disagreeable retort (that was possible), I suppose I never disagreed with him because I was so profoundly moved and blessed by what he had to give.

His consuming passion was the investigation of unreached areas of the world where he felt WEC should enter as soon as faith could take hold of the necessary personnel and means to do so. But he had a double life – a glorious double ministry, his obvious mission leadership role plus a personal learning and sharing with those who would follow him in the deeper things of the Spirit.

Marjorie Cheverton, retired English WECer, describes life as a candidate at WEC HQ.

Morning prayers were really wonderful times. Rubi would come down and lead them. There was no time limit. He always brought letters from the fields and various bit of mission information and these were read out. He always expounded the word and was very keen on Joshua. Then we really spent hours in prayer in the mornings. That meant we had a long afternoon at work because we'd spent all morning praying!

He was great fun really. People would send in gifts of potatoes and lentils and things like that. So at dinner time Rubi used to sit at the top of the table and we all sat around. You daren't ask for a small helping because he'd say 'Who's grumbling about the food?' You had a big ladleful of lentil and potato, and he had it too, and we girls used to sit at the other end and pray 'Lord let's have a small helping' because you daren't leave any. His own children were sometimes at the table at lunch time, and he handled them firmly. Priscilla wouldn't eat her cabbage so had to sit there (I can see her now) with her dad until she finished, while we all cleared up after the meal.

He was a very kind-hearted man and extremely thoughtful to all of us. We were tickled over his attire. He always wore those flannel shirts. He would say he was a fool for Christ's sake and would go out amongst all his society friends wearing them!

As the decade drew to a close two more countries were entered – Senegal (in 1936) and Upper Volta (Burkina Faso) in 1939, plus, of course, Liberia, already mentioned.

In strategies for advance is it wise to open a new field with totally inexperienced workers? Rubi often took huge risks as far as giving responsibility to the untried, and Senegal was no exception. When Ted Gibbons and Leslie Brierley went to Senegal they were alone. Rubi drew attention to the fact that North of them there were no missionaries for 1,200 miles. To the East, none within 1,000 miles, and to the South, the next country was totally unreached.

Was it all success, achievement and glory over those years? By no means. New fields were not without their casualties. At one stage in 1938, three young men and a young lady from Canada sailed from Britain to Colombia. One of the men had an understanding with Anne Robinson of Liverpool, but a shipboard romance commenced between him and the Canadian girl who had a similar attachment. Anne was heart-broken to receive the news, and since Norman Grubb had come to know her through her visits to HQ he made a point of visiting her home to express both his sympathy for her and his disapproval of what had transpired. (In fact mission policy was changed as a result of this event and mixed groups of single workers were not allowed to go to the field unchaperoned.)

He maintained a long and lasting link with Anne for many years, and although she never joined WEC officially, she has given a vast amount of time to working with the WEC team in London as a voluntary helper. She has some vivid recollections of Rubi:

When I visited WEC headquarters I always found him to be very kind, courteous, gracious. understanding and sympathetic. Sometimes I found him very strong-willed, even intolerant to a point, and yet it was not a nasty intolerance. He would be gracious and listen to you but you never felt you got anywhere! We would have heated discussions on his favourite theme 'Christ in you'.

In another situation – Arabia – Norman admits that our efforts did not meet with success.

Our attempts to enter one field have failed – Arabia. Four approaches have been made, but it has now been proved that to go to the Arabs merely as a preacher of the gospel is not acceptable to them.

CHAPTER 7

APPLES OF GOLD IN SETTINGS OF SILVER

It was in the late thirties that Norman's ability to crystallise spiritual principles started to emerge. This was evidenced in the leading articles of the magazine *World Conquest* around this time, in which we see, not only his in-depth understanding of Biblical truth, but his ability to express it succinctly and apply it incisively. These were the early forerunners of full length books dealing with similar themes. Here are some articles, slightly abridged.

HOW TO OBTAIN GUIDANCE

There is hardly any question that is more frequently asked than this. The reason is obvious. Until we know God's voice and how to hear Him speaking, we are conscious of instability in our Christian service. In multitudes of cases our difficulty is not unwillingness to go here, do this, or say that, but uncertainty as to whether God is telling us to act. The lack in our prayer life is not so much lack of zeal, or failure to ask, but lack of faith and assurance in asking, derived from uncertainty as to God's will. 'We know not what to pray for as we ought.'

Now the opposite is manifest in the scriptures. The keynote to every great life there described is that they merely did what God told them to do. 'The Lord said unto Moses.' Paul 'heard a voice saying unto him'. And supremely, Christ said, 'The words that I speak, I speak not of myself, but the Father that dwelleth in me, He does the works'.

Christ here says that He was guided by an indwelling voice, not an external appearance. And I discovered that in the great majority of instances in Bible history the same is true, for we have no right to imagine an audible voice or visible appearance, unless it is distinctly stated to be such.

This important fact brings guidance within my reach and that of all believers. Visions and voices are extremely rare, indeed unknown in the experience of the writer, though we have no right to limit God in His manner of revelation, but communion with an indwelling Person is the privilege of all, and the unceasing experience of some.

The best method of obtaining guidance known to the writer and practised continually in our daily headquarters meetings when dealing with our Crusade problems is as follows: First, we make as sure as possible that we approach the subject upon which we are seeking light as God's servants seeking the fulfilment of His will in His way; this of course, should not and does not take long, for it is the normal attitude of Christ-indwelt lives.

Then we recognise and utilise the mind on its right position. The mind is a useful servant, but not the final arbiter of truth. The exaltation of human reason to the throne of authority is the sin of 'the wise of this world'. Moses made this very clear concerning guidance in Numbers 16:38.

Thus we examine thoughtfully our situation, know all that we can about it, let the scriptures throw any light upon it, but then we refuse to make the decision. That must come from the Inner Witness. Now, in order to know His voice, we change our tactics. When God speaks, He always speaks in stillness. While our hearts are disturbed and our minds busy on a situation, His voice cannot be heard. Our inner attitude must be like a pool of water. If disturbed no reflection can be seen in it. When still, the features can be seen. So the best thing we can do, having stored our mind with the facts, is to leave them with God. It is not a state of forgetfulness, but a redirection of our attention. We were concentrated on the problem; now we concentrate on Him, the Solver. When our eye is single, our whole body is full of light.

Often circumstances arrange themselves so as to make a certain course obvious – this is a very usual method. Sometimes a verse of scripture or a strong inner assurance is the way. But the point is that whatever means the Spirit uses, He communicates, through a mind stored with the facts, a solid certainty that thus and thus is God's way. That is the peace of God sitting as a referee (Col. 3:15).

World Conquest, Nov/Dec 1938

THE ADVENTURE OF ADVERSITY

Amongst the great principles of victorious Christian service which God has been teaching us in our morning headquarters meetings has been the true method of facing, handling and using for good all forms of adversity, all experiences of what we call evil – shocks, suffering, difficulty, disasters, unjust treatment.

The first key, put in a sentence, has been this: that our 'evils' are never the happenings in themselves, but the effect we allow them to have upon us. No matter whether objectively an experience is apparently good or evil, subjectively, to the one who fears and doubts, all is evil; to the one who trusts, all is good.

To all appearances Calvary was totally evil, and the scriptures themselves say that Calvary was Satan-engineered ('Satan entered into Judas'); but Peter later confirmed his Master's attitude by the inspiration of the Holy Ghost, when he declared, 'Him being delivered by the determinate counsel and foreknowledge of God'.

But the adventure of adversity goes even far deeper than this. When seen in its true perspective, it is found to be the doorway into God's most transcendent secret – that adversities and sufferings, which in their origin are the effects of sin and instruments of the devil, in the grasp of faith become *redemptive*. They are transfigured from the realm of merely something to be endured as an opposition of Satan, to something to be used to conquer their author and redeem his victims. Faith in time of adversity makes the serpent swallow itself! Once again the supreme proof of this is that when Satan made his fiercest attack in history on the person of Christ, God used that attack through the faith and endurance of the Sufferer, to bring about the world's salvation. God uses evil to bring about good – not causing it, but using it.

If God's gifts are our blessings, and the devil's assaults are also our blessings, what remains to harm or depress us? If good is good, and evil is equally good to the enlightened, then a realm of life is entered where we rejoice always, in everything give thanks, and in all things are more than conquerors.

World Conquest, Mar/Apr 1938

THE LAW OF SPIRITUAL HARVEST

There are three ways in which we must understand and enter into the underlying principle of life in the Spirit – the way of the Cross. The first we all know. As sinners, we see and receive Christ crucified as our substitute.

The second aspect of the Cross, clearly expounded in scripture, and realised in the experience of all who go on with God, is identification with the Cross of Christ. The believer comes to see that he has not only come to the Cross, but is himself on it. For if Christ died for me, then in the sight of God it was I that died. 'I am crucified with Christ' sums up in a sentence the teaching of Romans 6, 2 Corinthians 5, Colossians 2 and 3, etc. And as the believer yields to and lays hold of this more profound aspect of the Cross, the dying of the old man and rising of the new man in Christ becomes a permanent inward experience in the personality, bringing with it the corresponding outward transformation of look and lip and life.

But the third meaning of the Cross for the believer is much less realised and practised, and it is concerning that aspect that this article is written. It is the way of the Cross embraced and lived out as the law by which the spiritual harvest in a fallen world is reaped. The two former aspects of the Cross are for my benefit: this third aspect is for others through me. It is seen supremely in Christ. He went forth from His baptism and anointing with the Spirit to walk the way of the Cross for others.

He did this to fulfil this law of the spiritual harvest. It was a necessity. With this 'joy set before him' the joy of the harvest, the joy of the mother who travails to give birth, 'he endured the Cross, despising the shame' (Heb.12:2).

From Christ we follow on to the first members of his church. Here we see the same principle recognised and accepted by those who see the full stature of Christian living to consist, not merely in the enjoyment of the fruits of Christ's passion, but in the sharing of the passion itself for the saving of others. Thus Paul says, 'So death worketh in us, but life in others'.

We see then a fact of vast practical importance and a door of unending opportunity. If I am Christ's, the 'deaths' to personal advantages in the flesh, such as comforts, loved ones, material advancement, enlarged income, pleasures, leisure, give me the right to claim and receive the harvest in the Spirit. Instead of regarding such as losses and deprivations to be endured if necessary but avoided if possible, we come to see and deliberately embrace them and glory in them as the way of the harvest. Equally we turn all life's unsought trials to our use for the bringing forth of the harvest: tragedies, injustices, slights, insults, losses. Each gives us our chance of reckoning the injured self dead with Christ and in its place finding the risen power of Christ to triumph in trial and thus minister joy to the tried, to love the injurer or insulter and thus win him.

I know no man who understood this better than C.T. Studd. In the evening of their lives, the call came to Mr Studd to go out to Africa, while Mrs Studd, at that time an invalid, could not accompany him.

They both realised that the call could only be fulfilled by a broken home and maybe years of separation, and both were able to accept – only because they understood the law of the harvest, 'death in us... life in others'. And from that attitude, accepted in 1913, and endured un-flinchingly till their long separation ended in their glorification in 1931 and 1928 respectively, has sprung this Crusade with its harvest of souls in Congo, and the first blades of a fresh harvest showing above ground in a dozen other lands.

World Conquest, Jan/Feb 1939

LIGHT ON THE SPIRIT-FILLED LIFE

The original nature of man – the human nature as we call it – the nature with which both Adam and Christ were endowed, is inbreathed from God and consists of His own attributes, for man is made in His image. Such are the endowments of mind, imagination, intuition, which can be put to the service of self or God: the emotional life which can alternate between love and hate, joy and sorrow, compassion and jealousy; the powers of will which can choose good or evil. And of this divine-human nature it is said, 'And God saw everything that he had made, and behold it was very good'.

When stated thus by itself, this is a commonplace truth. But we Christians have put such a necessary emphasis on the truth which follows this in point of time – the fall – that many fail to differentiate between the original God-given nature and 'the flesh' – that same nature under the dominion of sin. They mistakenly regard some of the very attributes of our nature as being the result of the fall, and wrong in their origin instead of merely wrong in their use. For Satan, the author of the fall, originated nothing, but was merely the mis-director, misuser, usurper of a nature whose endowments and capacities were originally created to manifest the glory of God.

Now the importance of all this is seen when we come to examine the ground-work of a Spirit-filled life. Exactly where does the truth lie in questions concerning the flesh and the Spirit which have exercised, and often divided, earnest men and women? What is the flesh? What does the Spirit do when He sanctifies us?

An insight into the workings of the two spirits spoken of in scripture – the satanic spirit and the Holy Spirit – has answered these questions for us. Of the one Paul has told us that in our fallen condition 'in time past ye walked according to the spirit that now worketh in the children of disobedience'. Of the other he has also told us that in our redeemed condition we are born of the Holy Spirit, filled with the Spirit, led by the Spirit, used by the Spirit. Now here we can see the executive heads of the two invisible kingdoms of darkness and light, which are in utmost and eternal opposition to each other, yet alike in their method of operation in and through those who own allegiance to them, for both indwell, control and unite with human nature, using it to express the characteristics of their respective realms.

In other words, our God-given human nature, is a dynamic potential which can be directed, according to the aims of its chosen overlord, to good or evil. In the fall it has been 'sold under sin', but now in the redemption that is in Christ Jesus, 'we' (our original selves) are brought back from the usurper, and bidden to reckon ourselves 'alive unto God' and to 'yield ourselves unto God as those that are alive from the dead'.

The root of this release is found in the substitutionary death of Christ and our realisation of our identification with him in the cross: 'Likewise reckon ye also yourselves to be dead indeed unto sin'. But this does not mean that some part of us is to die, but that we are to see ourselves in Christ as those who have passed through an experience of death so far as any further acknowledgement of the lordship of Satan and union with sin are concerned. From this particular aspect of truth, nothing in us ourselves has died. There is no such thing as the death of self or death to self. Rather 'self' is our glorious God-created personality which God now reunites to Himself for the purpose of expressing His own glory through our 'selves'. We have passed on beyond the cross, out of the tomb, into the resurrection, and are now fully alive unto God, every inch of our original natures; the emotions now express love for God and man, pity, hatred of evil, jealousy for God's glory, pride (glory) in the cross; the imagination and intuition are vibrant with a constant sight and sense of Him whom having not seen we love, and with a vision of His love for the world; the will makes choices and declarations of faith; the body uses its capacities both in sounding forth His praise and sharing in the preaching of the gospel to every creature. The same self, the same'I', but now the willing servant and son of the Spirit.

Thus, in a word, we have seen the way of the Spirit to be transmutation, the losing of nothing with which God has endowed us, but the transmuting of the whole self from a fleshly to a spiritual kingdom. And this fact has meant to us a new and exhilarating freedom, a knowledge that in Christ we have come to full manhood and womanhood, with every endowment of the human nature 'holy unto the Lord'.

World Conquest, May/June, 1938

PERSONAL POSSESSIONS

There were two distinct stages in the life of the Lord Jesus on earth, between which a great contrast is to be seen in His manner of living. During His early years He was the equivalent of a present-day wage earner, living a normal home life under His parents' roof. When the time for His public ministry came, He left all, parents, wages, home, and occupied Himself with His work of teaching and healing, leaving His temporal needs to the care of His Heavenly Father.

When He called special disciples to follow Him, He required of them the same standards of consecration. 'Lo, we have left all,' said Peter. 'If thou wilt be perfect,' He said to the young ruler, 'go sell all that thou hast, and come follow me.' Even to the 'great multitiudes' He plainly stated, 'Whosoever he be that forsaketh not all that he hath, cannot be my disciple.' Yet at the same time He had other devoted followers, who remained in their normal occupations, such as in the home at Bethany.

At Pentecost, when the church was founded, all believers accepted Christ's standards of discipleship. 'As many as were possessors of land or houses sold them.' They had all things common. As the gospel spread to the Gentiles, its chief exponent lived in the same way, 'having nothing', at times working with his own hands for his daily supply, at times ministered to by the gifts of the churches, and sometimes 'hungry, thirsty and naked'.

On the other hand, as the church took root in the cities of the Gentiles, it is plain that the large majority of its members continued their normal way of life and maintained their personal possessions; and that this was approved by the Holy Ghost through Paul by such instances as his exhortation to wage-earners (1 Cor. 16), to the rich (1 Tim. 6:17), and to individuals such as Philemon.

What conclusions, then, are we to draw from a balancing of these various scriptures? We would say first that community sharing as against personal possession is the ultimate standard of life in Christ. Me, my, mine came in with the fall and disappear in full and final redemption. All through history, since the first example of communal living at Pentecost, there have been both individuals and communities of God's people who have seen this to be the highest way of life and endeavoured to carry it out.

On the other hand, in present world conditions, the adoption of such standards seem left to individual choice.

But God seeks and finds those ardent souls who say with Paul, 'I have suffered the loss of all things and count them but refuse that I may win Christ'.

C.T. Studd joined this pioneer band, when as a young man he literally sold all and followed. To the Crusade which he founded in later years, he bequeathed those same convictions. No law was laid down, but all fulltime members, and many who are equally its members though called to remain in their home towns and occupations, have joyfully followed. Crazy? Yes. Hazardous? Yes. But apostolic.

To such come also the apostolic fruits ('these that have turned the world upside down'), and the apostolic fellowship ('the fellowship of his sufferings'). Precious fruit, precious fellowship. Not loss, but infinite, eternal gain. And of such the world is not worthy.

World Conquest, July/August, 1939

ALMIGHTY MEEKNESS

Two rival principles of action, an old and a new, joined battle at Calvary, and call the world's attention to their relative claims – force versus meekness.

The way of force the world has known and practised from its infancy.

But in the fulness of time the true light shone forth. A new revelation, God's final word, fulness of wisdom and brightness of His glory, illuminated the world in the person of His Son; and He brought to light by word and action a new way of conquest, a new method of government, a new dynamic power which is to swallow up the old way of force, unconquerable, eternal, irresistible, for it is the very nature of the Creator – Redeemer God in action – the way of meekness.

Contrast the use of force and meekness, and what do we find? Force is power on the circumference, meekness power at the centre. Force, power on the outward, meekness, power on the inward. Force, power visible, meekness power invisible. Force is man's unregenerate spirit putting forth its energies, mental, verbal, physical, to attain its end. Meekness is God's Spirit, reigning in a man who first dies to all self-attitudes and activities, and working through that man by his ways

of love, faith, lowliness and long-suffering, the almighty works of God
in the particular situation.

Who won at Calvary, and is still winning and will win? The outward
might of deep-laid scheme, mob violence, and Roman law, or the inward, hidden might of the Lamb who opened not His mouth? Which
have been more powerful, the legions of Caesar or the gospel of Jesus?

The meek inherit the earth.

World Conquest, Mar/Apr 1939

CHAPTER 8

WARFARE IN WARTIME

Norman's outlook on the war was interesting. Some might justifiably accuse him of being a pacifist. His convictions about God's supreme purpose for the church and the Kingdom were so profound that he virtually said that involvement in a worldly war was a dereliction of duty in a spiritual one.

While he intended to leave each one to come to his own individual viewpoint he clearly expounded his own personal convictions.

God's servants in an organisation such as WEC are set aside for a single task, to present to the world by lip and life the whole gospel of the Lord Jesus Christ. They proclaim a 'newness of life', which begins by salvation from wrath and introduction into God's family through the atoning death of Christ, and goes on to holiness and harmlessness, meekness and loving service. Its precious possessions are an inward liberty untouchable by outward conditions, an invisible and eternal inheritance which makes the owner despise claims to earthly possessions, and membership in a family circle which has lost all sight of differences in colour and language.

This new life in Christ they are themselves endeavouring to exemplify by leaving all to follow Him; by overleaping national barriers to become all things to all men that by any means they might save some; by going defenceless amongst savage and fanatical people, clad in the armour of love, the one irresistible weapon of offence and defence; having, as their sole objective, the winning over to Christ, the Truth, of multitudes enslaved to the false principles and programmes of the fallen world.

If then a conflagration breaks out which would compel us, should we be involved in it, to raise up again those carnal barriers between the nations; if we should have to take up again those futile and devilish weapons of carnal warfare which we have foresworn and replaced by the eternal weapons of love; if we should have to fight for rights of outward liberty or the restitution and defence of outward lands and property, when we now know and preach that the only true liberty and true possessions are in the inward ownership of the unsearchable riches of Christ; then, should the summons to do this come to us who have seen the vision and received the high and holy calling, we could only answer, humbly yet sincerely, as did Nehemiah, 'I am doing a great work, so that I cannot come down'.

Some may say that this is correct if the liberties affected or the properties seized were our own, but are we not bound to stand for the rights of others, even to the use of the sword? Not if one has discovered that man's only eternal right and unalterable happiness through grace is not to claim this or own that, but to fulfil the commandment to love God with all his heart and his neighbour as himself. This he can do, whether in the concentration camp or as a member of a subjugated race, or as a so-called free man.

God's servants in such movements as this Crusade are called to a higher form of ministry and warfare, a higher method of relieving distress than the use of gun and bomb, that of giving our all, our loved ones, possessions, life itself to bring the eternal light, liberty and riches of Christ to the world.

God's way of handling evil was the cross. His revelation of almighty power was the cross, and this same way of the cross the Lord Jesus passed on to His disciples as their way of life. He defended neither Himself nor His disciples, although He could have done.

War conditions meant that the magazine had to have a change of format; Norman explained:

THE MAGAZINE IN WAR DRESS

For the period of the war we are producing *World Conquest* in this new form. The advantages are many. It enables us to help towards the national need of economy in paper. It reduces our own publishing expenses by over half. Yet it actually allows as much reading matter as before. It will enable us to present in shorter form and with headings which will more easily catch the eye the various aspects of the testimony God has given us; and we shall endeavour to make every piece of news vital to our readers for inspiration, teaching, challenge and testimony to the victories of living faith.

A welcome effect to our readers will also be the halving of the price in these days of rising prices, from 2d. to 1d.

Readers wrote in after the first edition was published:

From MANCHESTER, 'I enclose the price of the five dozen received and shall be glad to receive a further five dozen. I believe it is in the plan of God for *World Conquest* to be put in its new order, for the circulation is bound to be much greater and bring much blessing.'

From NEWCASTLE, Staffs., 'The new war edition meets a great need for propagation of the truth in these dark last days of misinformation. We feel that we here could dispose of at least three dozen copies. We are greatly encouraged by the inspiration received. It comes as a real tonic for the perplexed.'

A new reader from LANCASTER, 'Throughout my whole life (and I have been amongst missionary influence since babyhood) I have never come across such faith, daring and victory. I am amazed at the content of every paragraph... I feel I must empty my purse and trust for next week's supply – so am sending £2, the widow's mite, and the 2s.6d. my daughter sends for one dozen of the magazines to distribute.'

A SOUTH AFRICAN writer says, 'I have no hesitation in saying *World Conquest* is the most inspiring paper I receive.'

Finally, a London minister writes: 'This is a note of real appreciation for your splendid paper. I am delighted to find that spirit of holy aggression in spite of so much to depress the Christian testimony. Go ahead with your paper!'

What impact did World War II have on the life and work of WEC? We quote below an article that Norman wrote at the onset of war in November 1939:

THE CHALLENGE OF CALAMITY
The War and the Crusade

In times of great emergency, we find that all men of God through history took one essential first step. They found out what God had to say to them. They took care to guard against the swaying of their minds through mass suggestion, the calls to action or responses to fears inspired by sudden crises. Thus Moses met the sudden revolt by falling on his face before the Lord; David the tears and threats of his despairing followers by encouraging himself in the Lord his God; Joshua the challenge of those grim walls by an interview with the captain of the Lord's host. Then from the hidden place they came forth as giants refreshed to handle situations with ease and triumph which baffled their contemporaries who were 'careful about many things', but neglecting the 'one thing needful' – to sit at His feet, to do the chief of all works, 'this is the work of God that ye *believe* on Him'.

First Act in Crisis

So in this tremendous world crisis, we understood that our first work was, not to do things, but to hear Him. We have already described in our emergency letter how we gathered in the new hostel in London immediately war had been declared. In such tremendous moments, with the air raid sirens still sounding in our ears, the mind is too numb to see the details of future action. But we had already learned by many past experiences that the foremost act of a believer under all circumstances is to honour God by *praise*. This at once turns the thoughts from selfish fears to the worship of Him who says that 'all things work together for good'. It delivers the mind from despairing distraction to hear the 'Thus saith the Lord'. So we started right away 'to sing and to praise' (2 Chron. 20:22).

The Holy Spirit has been speaking to us over a long period concerning our attitude in the event of war. We are to concentrate, unmoved by any outward circumstances, upon the greatest of all wars, the deliverance of the devil's captives by the preaching of the gospel to every creature. How would the war affect the Crusade? We had always made our boast in the Lord that faith in Him lifts men above the effects of all world conditions; that the devil's mountains are changed by faith into God's highways (Is. 49:11). Now, was this world crisis to be regarded by us as a disaster or an opportunity for proving God and furthering world-wide evangelisation? If the latter, what great things could we expect of God in this situation to manifest to the world that He is the God of the impossible? The answer to this question became clear.

We would obviously expect smaller sums for the upkeep of the existing work, but we believe the Lord will do the opposite for us. We believe that by the end of the war we shall be able to point to the fact that we have received a larger regular supply than previous to the war. In order to help our readers watch the Lord's faithfulness, we shall comment in each issue on the monthly supply that God sends.

The commencement of World War II inhibited many from thinking of mission, of the opening of new fields, and of home base development. But not so for Norman Grubb. Here is the testimony of Ray Oram of Bristol (later a worker with WEC and CLC).

I recall vividly the time when World War II broke out. Many were in panic. Store windows were being boarded up, air raid shelters were being built or dug in the ground and we were learning how to wear gas masks and how to distinguish gas bombs. Churches were cancelling evening meetings; much Christian activity had been reduced and the outlook was generally fearful.

It was at this time, with all the backdrop of fear and concern, that a letter arrived from Norman Grubb. It was sent to all the friends and supporters of WEC in Britain. What a contrast to the prevailing spirit. What a boost to faith; what a message from God! 'This is not a time of retreat,' he wrote, 'but of advance; God is Sovereign. Hitler can only go so far. We may have setbacks, we may have to suffer, we may be faced with dire hardships but God is still on the throne. He is still in control. He will work out His purposes and the earth shall be filled with the glory of God as the waters cover the sea.'

Then, as I recollect, he went on to spell out the advances for which WEC was trusting God during the war years – increased ministry to the Lord's people, multiplied home bases about Britain, foundations laid for a great missionary push after the war. What a shot in the arm this was for me. How faith rose! My mouth and my heart were filled with praise. Who did Hitler think he was? Did he not know that there was a God in heaven who ruled over the affairs of men? One who causes the wrath of men to praise Him. God used that letter to set me and others going. Home bases were opened in wartime in Britain. The Lord's people were blessed and strengthened through the message of faith in the living God. The missionary challenge did go forth and many went into missionary training when the war ended.

It was, I suppose, the Spring of 1940 and John Whittle from WEC headquarters and I were travelling on a bus in Bristol. We had a conference arranged that was soon to take place, but I looked out of the window and saw something up in the sky. I said to John, 'Let's get out of here, quick!' 100 – 200 German planes were coming over, with a few of our Spitfires buzzing around the side of them like gnats. They were heading for the Bristol airplane works. They missed them but hit houses, and within a matter of minutes the hospitals began to be filled up with the dead and wounded. It was just after that, that this conference started in Bristol. Norman Grubb stood up and preached a message of faith. People gathered, day-time and night, a time when many people were afraid to go out. That was such a blessing. It put iron into our spirits and greatly blessed many.

In 1940 Rubi wrote to the WEC home-end 'constituency':

TRIALS MAKE, NOT BREAK
It seems a long time since we heard Mr Chamberlain use those dread words on the radio, 'England is at war with Germany', on the morning of September 3rd, followed in a few minutes by the fear-inspiring wails of the air raid sirens. Things looked black as night. Our world seemed falling in ruin around us. The nation would take all the men. Bible Schools were closing. Christian agencies were evacuating their headquarters from London. It was inevitable that finances must dwindle.

Down to Root Principles

At such moments only principles which have been examined to their roots and embraced with the whole heart can stand the strain. All mere theory, truth toyed with but never digested is swept aside. If ever we thanked God that the WEC vessel had journeyed through many a stormy sea in its history, it was then. For through the years we had learned by God's patience and grace something of the principles of gale-navigation. With growing conviction we had come to see and teach that the whole essence of victorious living is that difficulties are the life-blood of faith. They are the 'bread'of the believer (Num. 14:9). No storms, no opportunity for the word of faith, 'Peace be still'. No Red Sea, no stretching forth of the rod to divide it.

Since it was obviously impossible to proceed with a programme of recruitment for overseas fields, how could advance in the work be achieved? Pat Symes, writing from the Colombian field gave the answer:

To us here in Colombia the war brings a challenge from the Lord. We are living today in adverse circumstances. If we do not look out, Satan will try to make us panicky: but we must refuse him, take hold of the adverse circumstances and use them for God's glory.

He is the same God who sent us out to Colombia and provided so liberally for so many years. So let us make this a time of advance: when we definitely set out to make an offensive. We must not retrench, nor only hold our own – we must advance. This can be done best by trusting the believers more and putting responsibility upon them. I believe they will rise to the occasion and surprise us.

Writing in the Jan-Feb '42 issue of *World Conquest* Norman outlined how the sending base of WEC could be expanded and strengthened.

THE FULL PROGRAMME OF WEC

At the start of a new year it is helpful to review the ways of advance and expansion into which we believe the Lord is leading us. We have for years been conscious that God had a home-front programme for us to fulfil. We must be God's messengers to the church of Christ at home, if the mission field is to be occupied. New converts must be added to the home ranks, if new pioneers are to arise. For this reason deputation teams, headquarters conferences, etc., all have had as their main objective, not the enlistment of interest in the WEC, but the surrender of lives to the full will of God.

Not until war was declared in 1939, however, had God's time come for the revelation of the full home-front programme. Then God spoke. We were now for the next few years to throw ourselves as completely into home developments, as we had previously into field advances. We were to seek and find exactly what God's plan was to be, by what means we were to be His messengers at home as abroad.

Hours, days were spent seeking God's mind and consulting together. The lesson we learned again was, 'As thou goest step by step, the way shall open up before thee'. Take the first step, and the next would come to light. Launch, and there would be the multitude of fishes. Many indications had shown us that the first advance was to be the opening of a headquarters at Scotland; volunteers had come forward the week war was declared. So the plunge was taken, and the Glasgow HQ came into being.

The Twelve Headquarters

But what next? The new headquarters was seen to be an evident blessing. Young people were getting called to the mission field (some ten are now in training), Christians quickened, souls saved, good fellowship established with all branches of Christ's church. The same must be repeated in other parts of the country. It took a year for the next move to be seen in clear outline, until it gained final shape in an advance conference held in January, 1941. It was then decided that Britain was to have twelve WEC headquarters – two in Ireland, two in Scotland, one in Wales, two in Northern England, three in the Midland belt, one in the South. Of these, eight (including Glasgow), were to be functioning by January 1942. It would be by far the largest annual advance in our home history, and that in war time. It could only be contemplated by once again receiving and decreeing God's promises, based on the assurance that the programme was His will. The step of faith was unitedly taken at that conference.

Soon the answer began to appear. Four homes were offered by friends of the Crusade in four different parts of England, in which branch headquarters could be started – first in Bristol, then Colchester, then Cardiff, then Macclesfield. Workers came forward for each, full-time Crusaders on the faith lines of all home workers, some quite new to the work and only one with any length of experience in connection with WEC; indeed the raising up and growth of the workers, as the openings came and as each has boldly gone forward with their new responsiblities, is one of the wonders of this year. Three more open doors have followed, to complete (with Glasgow) the eight for the year – Belfast, Nottingham and Bournemouth.

Meanwhile a further question was greatly concerning us. Exactly what

was to be the work of these new headquarters? By what methods were
they to minister to the church of Christ? What share were they to have in
the church's ministry as Christ's beacon of light in a chaotic world? Many
hours were again spent on this. Gradually a five-point programme became clear. They were given the alternative name of:

CENTRES OF ACTION

Centres of:
1. Revival in the church.
2. Missionary challenge.
3. Christian instruction.
4. Home evangelism.
5. Unity.

Bookshops in Every Town

Altogether new light on the development of the third point (Christian
instruction) came in the middle of the year by the unexpected formation
of the Evangelical Publishing House as an associate branch of the Crusade.

The start had been the bookshop at Colchester; but we soon found
demands coming from all parts of the country where a need had long
been felt for centres for the purchase of Christian literature. Here then
we soon saw a call to something much more extensive than the twelve
headquarters. There would be the necessity for bookshops in pretty well
every decent sized town in Britain.

Was WEC to become a denomination? Rubi continues in the same
article:

Full Home Front Programme

The full home front programme is now taking clearer shape. What had
started by being just a London WEC headquarters for the British Isles,
was extending to twelve sub-headquarters; then to a further unlimited
number of bookshop-headquarters, called Centres of Action, with a five-
point programme, probably every town in Britain of over 30,000 having
one of them. They are to have no membership, hold no Sunday services,
do nothing which would possibly constitute them as churches; but they
are to be the humble servants of and co-operators with all Christ's servants and all churches in their towns; they are to help forward or initiate
all kinds of co-operative evangelism: help all missionary societies.

As the war came to an end, Grubb wrote:

The day war broke out, as we gathered for prayer in London, in spite of
the restrictions we would naturally expect in manpower and money, we
definitely asked God to give us advances in both these respects so that
the war would actually mean a strengthening and increase of the work
rather than decrease. As we prayed and considered, one special objective
was impressed upon us for the war years, and that was home advance. We
had given the past ten years to a rapid field expansion, from one country
to thirteen. We had long felt that home extensions were not keeping pace
with this, and that something must be done to reach out over Britain with
the challenge of world evangelisation. So we followed up that first meeting at the declaration of war with a conference of home leaders, who
gathered round the map of Britain and took it by faith from God that He
would enable us to occupy with Regional Headquarters the twelve areas
into which we divided the British Isles.

Of course, the main headquarters in Highland Road continued to be the
focal point of sending base activities. The building actually withstood
the countless bombing raids on London.

A close friend of WEC, Peter Guest, now a resident of Vancouver, B.C., describes a visit there with his father in the early forties:

My wife, Anne, and I came to know Norman Grubb through my father,
Edward, who acted as a local representative for WEC in the Birmingham
area. At one stage he decided we would move to London in order to be
nearer the headquarters.

He used to go over there quite often and I remember accompanying
him one day to share in the normal fellowship-and-prayer time that took
place each morning.

One of the faith-requests came from a staff member in charge of the
catering who mentioned that there were no potatoes for the evening meal,
so this was brought before the Lord in the ensuing prayer time by the
thirty or so people present.

Sometime during the late afternoon a truck turned up and dropped off
about a dozen sacks of potatoes!

Nearing war's end, Norman wrote the following for the magazine:

Five years of war have now gone by, and we would look back briefly and
pass in review what God has done, as a testimony to His grace and faithfulness in the midst of the strains, dangers, and sometimes setbacks that
all have experienced.

1. FIELDS. Two new fields, the Northern Territories of the Gold Coast, and the Island of Dominica, West Indies, have been occupied. Of the other eleven fields, the work in eight has gone steadily forward, though in all cases with only a dribble of reinforcements, and with the existing staff holding on to their posts in spite of much weariness. In the other three fields, there have been setbacks, but in two the ground is now being regained: in Senegal, the missionaries had to leave for a period, but are now back; on the Tibetan border, the station has been left empty owing to the pioneer being in the army, but preparations are now in hand for reoccupation and new recruits are arriving on the field; only in Portuguese Guinea is there a definite hold-up at the moment, the visa not yet being granted for the Brierleys' re-entry, but we are standing in faith for this.

In all 76 new recruits have sailed for the fields during these five years; 46 missionaries have come on furlough; and 22 missionaries have returned from furlough to their fields. In all these crossings and re-crossings of the ocean, we thank God that no lives have been lost. Five of the new workers have been captured by the enemy, three in the Atlantic, two in the Pacific; two of these have been released. One other was on a boat which was sunk, but she was rescued. This is indeed a record of God's mercy.

2. FINANCES. We have recorded annually the steady increases in the Lord's supplies, from £12,500 in 1939 to £33,214 in 1944.

The figures for the financial year which ended March 31st, 1945, should be ready by next issue. We would judge that they show another slight increase. In company with so many other societies that have received financial increases, we thank our faithful God.

3. HOME BASES. As remarked above, our special prayer objective these war years has been home advance, and in this God has greatly prospered.

We began by praying for twelve Regional Headquarters. The number was later enlarged to fourteen. Of these, thirteen have been occupied.

As a result of investigations that went on during the war the leader was able to announce a list of faith targets for the post-war era:

With the post-war era now opening before us the call is plain to us to re-dedicate ourselves to the calling of God given to Mr Studd at the foundation of the Crusade, 'to evangelise the remaining unevangelised parts of the world in the shortest possible time'. This means that we stand ready to enter any area for which God sends volunteers and which is not being occupied by another mission. But recent investigations seem to crystallize our attention upon certain main areas and to these we call the attention of Christ's people, and appeal forthwith for God-sent recruits for them:

1. AFRICA. 36 areas, mainly on the west coast. Population 12,000,000. We are asking God for 150 pioneers in ten years.

2. INDIA. 100,000,000 in the eight provinces of Sind, Punjab, Kashmir, Rajputana, U.P., Bihar, Orissa, Bengal.

3. S E ASIA. 20,000,000 in Indo-China and Siam.

4. NETHERLANDS EAST INDIES. 12,000,000 in unevangelised areas of Borneo, Sumatra, Java, Celebes, New Guinea and smaller islands.

5. MANCHURIA. 20,000,000 in the northern province of Heilungkiang.

6. WEST INDIES. 500,000 in the islands of Guadaloupe and Martinique.

7. NEAR EAST. Parts of Iraq.

8. EUROPE. Parts of the Balkans.

9. ESTABLISHED FIELDS. The completion of the task in areas and tribes already occupied, especially Belgian Congo and Colombia, South America, and the introduction of the young indigenous churches to their responsibilities.

10. CHRISTIAN LITERATURE. Centres for distribution at key places throughout the world.

We recognise with thankfulness that other agencies also have these various unevangelised millions on their heart and are making preparations to enter, and with them we co-operate in calling on the church of Christ forthwith to complete this task of world evangelisation; we ourselves stand ready by God's grace to pay our share of the price in faith, labour and sacrifice.

CHAPTER 9

LENGTHEN THE CORDS, STRENGTHEN THE STAKES

If the dominant note in the thirties was the expansion of WEC into new mission fields, the dominant note of the forties was the enlarging and strengthening of WEC's infrastructure. Certainly several new fields were opened such as Portuguese Guinea, West Indies, Canary Islands, Pakistan, Thailand, Uruguay, Indonesia, but WEC's potential for attracting and processing personnel was vastly improved by the enlargement of the British Base, additional headquarters in USA and Canada, and the establishment of bases in Holland, Switzerland, Germany, Australia and New Zealand.

Norman was always alive to the fresh strategies of the Holy Spirit and very open to unorthodox methods of expansion.

'We ought to have Christian bookstores scattered all over the place – sort of spiritual Woolworths, up and down the country.'

Was this a carefully considered official minute from a responsible board? No, it was an off-the-cuff comment by the leader of WEC in war-time Britain; the year, 1941. But it was a flash of divine inspiration given to a man sensitive to the Spirit.

The background: Ken and Bessie Adams of Colchester knew the life of faith. They had worked for the Friends Evangelical Band evangelising in country areas of Britain without a salary. They realised the need for Christian literature for new converts and started a bookstore in their home. But now they were under the urge of the Spirit to join a larger mission which would give scope for their vision.

Norman Grubb was invited to Colchester to meet them and immediately realised the strategic value of WEC having a literature arm.

On his return journey to London he spoke at a meeting in Chelmsford. Over tea he met a more senior couple called the Whybrows and immediately started to share his encounter with the Adams. God had been preparing the 'Whys' for a move into Christian work and they sensed God leading them to join with the Adams. The Christian Literature Crusade was born and raised within WEC, then a few years later became an independent mission in its own right.

Grubb wrote:

It really is something to see and laugh at the rickety starts of these various launches of faith, and then see emerging a properly run literature
organisation which can meet the commercial world on its own level –
yet the end and aim of it is the bringing of Christ-centred literature to
millions of people in many countries. The primary activity and interest
is not sales but souls, not a business but a ministry.

Another example of unorthodox strategy concerned the development of the work in Australia and New Zealand, for which Norman had both the vision and faith.

An early visit of Mrs Studd in 1925 had sparked off deep interest in WEC in these countries and local councils had been formed,
but it needed the continuing presence of full-time WECers to cause
deep and lasting interest to develop.

Arthur Davidson from New Zealand went to London as a candidate in 1936, then became a missionary in Colombia. Within a
year he had strange guidance that he should terminate his missionary career, and asked to be transferred back to New Zealand
or Australia for home end representation ministry. He writes in his
biography:

I plucked up sufficient courage to write a confidential letter to Norman
Grubb who was visiting the Canadian base at the time.
    I felt it was wise to prepare myself for an unfavourable reply. In a
surprisingly short time Mr Grubb's answer came. He wrote:

Your surprising letter reached me today. Your thought of starting a
WEC headquarters in Australia is certainly a revolutionary one especially as you have had only one year on the field. Under the circumstances it is most unlikely, humanly speaking, that God would lead
you and Lilian to leave Colombia so soon. Yet I feel I should add that
it may be the Lord's plan, for only yesterday I received a letter from
the New Zealand Council urging me to send a worker to start a headquarters there. Alfred Ruscoe and I immediately placed the matter
before the Lord and took by faith God's man for Australia and New
Zealand. Now, the next day your letter has come...'

Further confirmation came when Arthur suffered toxic goitre –
common in the high Andes – and was advised to leave Colombia.

Lilian, his fiancée, had physical problems too. Both needed to go to USA for treatment.

Arthur expected they would both return down-under after that but Norman, who was then visiting USA, had other ideas. Arthur wrote:

> We found that he had an unshakable conviction that, after medical attention in the USA, we should spend a year in North America to gain experience with Alfred Ruscoe in the rapidly expanding home base work. He clarified his view by stating that he was never deeply impressed with outward signs, except as a confirmation of guidance. He felt that an important scriptural principle must take priority – namely that workers set apart for a responsible ministry needed adequate preparation for their task. The work in North America, under Alfred Ruscoe, provided a rare opportunity, he felt, for us to get such training.

Arthur and Lilian submitted to his direction. They were married in Toronto and went on to spend a valuable period in USA.

In 1940 the Davidsons went to New Zealand and had their first tour. The story is full of miracles. Safe travel from Vancouver to Auckland – (the ship was mined on its return voyage and sank) – the provision of accommodation – a godly Presbyterian minister, Rev. George Yule who chaired the Council and who liked WEC's faith principle – the provision of a car – and a projector – the installation of a telephone within two days (while the waiting time was generally one or two years) – the provision of petrol coupons by interested friends – and gifts that covered tour expenses.

Davidson wrote afterwards:

> When sending an account of our New Zealand tour to Mr Grubb, I reminded him that my main commission was to Australia; would it not be timely for me to share our vision with the Australian Councils? He wrote back quite thrilled about the blessing and developments in New Zealand, but he strongly urged me not to breathe a word to any of the Australian Councils concerning our call. If, later, we were to transfer there, the initiative must come from them. This, he said, would be the final seal that our going was of God.
>
> Because of Mr Grubb's strong insistence on this point we realised we were shut in to prayer and faith regarding our vision and its fulfilment. (Years later Mr Grubb told me that he never felt we would 'take on' with the tough Aussies, although he was prepared to see God work for us and reveal His will.)

A few months after this correspondence I received a letter from Conrad
Lieber, WEC Literature Secretary in New South Wales, stating that he
had read the account of our New Zealand tour in the British edition of
World Conquest. He enquired if there was any possibility of our coming
to Australia for a nationwide tour. WEC in Australia, he said, was greatly
in need of deputation assistance. If we could come for a period in 1941
he would be glad to place the matter before the Melbourne and Sydney
Councils.

In a short time warm invitations came from both Melbourne and Sydney, suggesting that we should try and arrive in time for the main summer
Keswick Conventions in Victoria and New South Wales. The New Zealand Council agreed to our going for a deputation tour of six months.

As we prepared for this period in Australia the Lord gave us a deep
assurance that although we were going ostensibly to take meetings, the
main purpose of our visit would be to see a headquarters commenced
before the end of 1941. Furthermore, we became deeply convinced that
it would be located in Sydney, despite the fact that the majority of missions had established their headquarters in Melbourne.

And so it transpired, with a headquarters being established in Sydney in
December 1941.

In Britain, one significant development of the early forties was
God's wonderful provision of a home for missionaries' children in
Arbroath, Scotland. The Lord had been preparing Charlie and Lily
Searle for this task. They both had gone from humble circumstances to
Congo where they had a great ministry for eight years. But their health
deteriorated and they returned home. Charlie accepted a pastoral ministry with the Calvary Holiness Church in Bradford. But the stress was
too great and he had a heart attack. Lily, whose health was returning,
was asked to take over. She felt she couldn't, but in prayer God mightily rejuvenated her and she carried the task as well as home-nursing
Charlie and caring for four children.

Eventually the Lord spoke to them separately about terminating their
ministry and about Charlie having an itinerant ministry publicising the
need of Congo, all this with a view to returning to the field. Lily had a
marvellous testimony of proving God's sufficiency over this time.

But now Norman Grubb stepped into the picture. Having returned
from his 1939 USA trip he came to see them and asked, 'What are you
doing out of WEC?' They explained their health condition. Grubb said,
'I can't give you any hope of getting out unless your health continues
good for a couple of years; but anyway you ought to be back in the WEC.'

They rejoined, but were firmly and finally turned down for the field. That was when the Lord called them to care for other missionaries' children as well as their own. The miracle story of the Lord's provision of property, finance and staff can be read in *Going Through With God.*

Lily later wrote:

From the beginning Mr Grubb gave us wonderful encouragement, praying with us, and in every way seeking to advise and reassure us.

Norman wrote in the foreword of Lily's story:

It had always been our aim in the WEC to watch for really only one essential characteristic in a candidate: 'Those with a perfect heart who came to make Jesus King.' Not the intellectual first, not the physical, but the heart firmly set on God, and with a go-through spirit. Mother Studd was adept in spotting God's anointed among the unlikely, and Lily Searle was one of her 'bull's eyes'.

Lily Searle only scraped through on the health level, and after eight wonderful years in the Congo, left the field with many more tears than when she left her homeland. But her field experience, then the inability to return, and finally those years of desperate testing when Charlie and she seemed to be on the scrap heap, were exactly God's ways to their true life calling.

This is Lily's life story, her side of a married partnership in which in an amazing way they have been father and mother not only to their own six children but to so many others entrusted to them. A commission as delicate, self-sacrifical and exacting as any could be.

Another episode in which the deft hands of Norman Grubb had a part was the solving of a crisis in Spanish Guinea. Leona Bartlett (née Passmore) was trained at Prairie Bible Institute and after a couple of years in country evangelism came to the Toronto headquarters of WEC in 1943 as a candidate for Liberia. She recalls:

At our morning prayers in Toronto headquarters a letter was read from Mr Grubb in London. He said that they had heard that in our headquarters there were several girls heading for Africa and would they pray because a great need had come up in Spanish Guinea. Emma Munn, from Ireland, was alone there. The Thornes were back in London where Mrs Thorne was sick. So Emma needed help. Norman asked if we candidates would pray that the Lord would show if one of us should go and join her. As I prayed that night the Lord made it clear to me that I was to go.

They sent word that they wanted me in London as soon as possible. It would be a good idea for me to become acquainted with the British side of the work since I would be with Emma, who was from N. Ireland.

The first time I remember meeting Mr Grubb was when he had returned from a two-month trip overseas and was leading morning prayers. After that session he made a point of greeting me and talking with me.

He called me one day and asked me whether I was positive I was to go to Spanish Guinea. I said 'Yes, I am sure.' And he said, 'Do you realise there are three of you here willing to go to Spanish Guinea but the government will only let one in. I'm going to call in each of the other girls and talk to them. What I want you to do is to pray tonight earnestly that the Lord will show which one is to go. I, as head of the mission, am making no choice in this whatsoever.' So the three of us prayed and the next morning when we met in the dining room the other two girls shook their heads and I nodded yes. So I knew I was going to Guinea.

Two other Canadians who had close links with the Grubbs were Frank and Winnie Chapman of British Columbia; they became field leaders in Spanish Guinea. Frank writes:

My first contact with Norman Grubb was during World War II in 1944. When I was in the Canadian Army I went to 19 Highland Road, Upper Norwood and met him there. I went several times actually. (No. 19 was the office and hostel, as distinct from the Grubbs' home, No. 17.)

His life has been a constant challenge to Winnie and me. He was a man of God, a man of faith who knew how to plough through in the Spirit. After the war I joined WEC and have appreciated the times of fellowship we've had with him down many years. Our contact with Norman has always been very positive. There was one occasion while we were in Spanish Guinea when we had a disagreement but that was settled. We were reconciled 100% as soon as I came home on furlough. Some time after that he called me in and said, 'You're going back to Spanish Guinea. Could you not make a stop-over in Liberia? They have a problem out there and you have some experience. Would you not go and help them? They really need a neutral person to come in.' I said, 'Well, we told the Lord we would do anything He wanted us to do.' Norman said, 'I believe that's what God wants you to do.'

The particular issue in Liberia was the matter of missionaries adopting African children and because we had had some experience regarding this on our field, Rubi felt that we could give some good advice.

When I met the field leader he said, 'It's over to you,' so I stepped right in. The fellowship was divided – 50% one way and 50% the other.

The problem was this. The adopted girls had fallen into sin and were bringing disrepute to the name of Jesus. Half the fellowship said, 'Deal with that; we're up against it. It's a bad testimony.' The other half said, 'If you throw them out then we'll resign.' We knew the thing was to go to prayer. We arrived there on the Monday and went to prayer Monday night. We were supposed to have business discussions but we never got down to these. All day Tuesday it was nothing but prayer and waiting on God. On the Wednesday there was still no business session. This thing was so monstrous that we kept praying all day Wednesday. About 10pm I dismissed the group. Some went home; others stayed to pray and Winnie and I stayed with them.

We urged: 'You've all got your treasures, your convictions; are you not willing to put them on the altar? Don't worry about a thing. If they're not good the Lord will throw them away, but if they're all right He'll keep them.' So, one by one they started coming forward and putting their conviction on the altar. 'I've been strong-headed on this but now I'm giving it to the Lord.' As it started to break someone went and woke the others. 'Hey, come back, the Lord's breaking through.' And He broke through that night – it was a tremendous experience. The Lord spoke to the missionaries who had adopted the girls and told them they had to ask for leave of absence in order to get their house in order. They weren't being thrown out so nobody had anything to grumble about! God broke through in a marvellous way.

We continued to correspond with Norman and when I next saw him and described in detail how God had worked, he was so happy; we just hugged each other.

When we were ready to return to the field I went to see him again. I'd just had news that my son-in-law's brother was killed in a truck collision in Saskatchewan, so when Rubi heard that he said, 'Wouldn't it be good for you to go to the funeral? You've got time.' I told him we were praying about it. So he pulled out a cheque book and wrote a cheque for $US200. He said, 'Maybe this will help you decide.' I thanked him and that gift covered my flight. He was generous. He was always willing to help others.

He was a great encourager through letters. He was a well educated man and yet was so very humble. He never wanted his picture to accompany any magazine articles. He had a very meek and humble spirit.

He was very approachable and never lacked interest in what workers would bring to him. He took time with people. He was so available. It has been a great blessing to have a mentor who would feel the heartbeat of a field leader.

One of the most significant events of Rubi's USA tours in the early forties took place during his visit to Minneapolis. Harold Brokke, past president of Bethany Fellowship, recounts how Ted Hegre, founder of the Fellowship, passed through some early experiences.

He was at an evening service in Minneapolis when the congregation sang, 'Every day with Jesus is sweeter than the day before' and 'I am satisfied with Jesus, but the question comes to me: is the Saviour satisfied with me?' Ted, a young grocery store manager at that time, tried to sing these songs but he felt they were not real in his life. After the service he sought out the most spiritual man he knew and told him he was not satisfied with his Christian experience. The man answered, 'Ted, I'm not satisfied either.'

Ted went home concerned about the way he felt and why there seemed to be no answer. Being an avid reader he knew something about the writings of Andrew Murray. He took down one of his books called *Absolute Surrender.* He read these words, 'Get down on your knees and give yourself completely to Jesus Christ'. Inwardly he argued with Andrew Murray even though the author had been dead for many years. He had tried to surrender many times before but he never found the release he sought. Then he read the next line, 'Get up from your knees and believe that the Lord has received your surrender'. The Spirit's light turned on in his mind and he saw for the first time God's part in this spiritual transaction. The Holy Spirit alone could make this entire surrender a reality. Ted walked in a new sense of blessing, power and victory over sin.

Shortly after this, he heard that a local pastor had invited Norman Grubb to speak in his church. At that time Mr Grubb was the Director of the Worldwide Evangelization Crusade. At these sessions he pointed out the importance of Romans, the sixth chapter. He spoke about the message of the cross. He shared the truth of being identified with Christ in His death and resurrection. He declared he died WITH Christ and that Christ is IN us, the hope of glory, (Col. 1:27).

This message served as a catalyst for a new spiritual adventure. Ted found the secret of union with Christ – the true Treasure of the redeemed heart. This message became a vital part of his life and ministry. He loved to teach it. Others began to see the truth that God's grace included victory over sin and a life of fruitful service. As he preached it and wrote about it, other Christian families came together to share the possibilities of grace and to express it in their daily lives.

On Palm Sunday in 1943 several couples with their families (about sixteen members) formed a church called Bethany Chapel in South Minneapolis. They called Ted Hegre to be their pastor.

By 1948 I was a member of Bethany and we were led to start a Missionary Training College. Ted asked Norman (again in USA) to meet with him. I was included in this meeting. Norman knew that we wanted it to be a place to train missionaries. He challenged us with the thought that Bible Schools may not be the best way to do that. He thought that a reckless abandonment to Jesus plus a zeal to know Christ and to teach and preach His word were the main issues.

With that he shared that if we are to have a training centre let it be a place where we present the claims of Christ and His cross. Also a place where young men and women are called to true discipleship, holiness and obedience to the great commission by the Spirit's power. We started our training school in 1948. That was the kind of school we wanted too.

Cath Brokke remembers Norman's visits.

We appreciated Norman Grubb's ministry so much in those early days because he gave us the message for which we were so hungry. In my church, I had received strong teaching on the two natures and that our spiritual life was a constant struggle. To know that we could be unified within and that Christ is our life is the message that I remember.

There is something else that I recall. He emphasised such a close intimate walk with God – such an awareness of our union with Christ and His presence with us, that even having a lengthy quiet time didn't seem so important to him. He shocked us by the things he said because to him it was the moment by moment fellowship with the Lord that counted.

He was a tall man and spoke with a delightful English accent but when he got excited the words came so fast that it was sometimes hard to catch what he said. Then he'd get this typical little smile on his face and duck his head and then you'd lose what he was saying. But those were things that endeared him to us. It was both the message and the man that had such an impact on us. It reinforced the things that we were being taught by Ted.

Harvard Strand, one of the founding members of the Fellowship, remembers:

Norman Grubb lit a fire, as it were, under Ted, showing him possibilities of the Christian life that he had not perhaps thought of. Ted had already tasted the deeper life of the Lord but these meetings with Norman Grubb brought that thing into flame and really inspired him.

Grubb's message enabled Ted to step out in faith. If I remember correctly it seems to me that he instilled into him the magnitude of the faith that God had available for him. It must have made Ted realise that there was much more in following the Lord than he had seen in his own life. It perhaps gave him more of a determination to test God.

Norman seemed to be so full of life. He would say 'Hear, hear' when anyone would say anything worthwhile. He was so full of life and enthusiasm that it was catching.

Norm Carlsen, staff member of Bethany Fellowship reminisces:

He was best when he talked to a small group of fifteen to twenty people. That's when he really shone. He was always radiating the possibility of the impossible. He was so positive!

I don't remember a lot of what he said; it was more what he radiated. He was a man that laughed at impossibilities and cried 'It shall be done'.

I have a few chosen books that I live with. One of these is *Touching the Invisible*. I've quoted from it and talked about it in meetings. I quote Grubb every chance I can without being offensive, because of what he says, especially in the first two or three chapters. You find the Lord's mind and once you find it you go for it. Then comes the laugh of faith in having the assurance of the answer before it comes. What happened here at the Fellowship was a result of what Norman Grubb preached and taught about sacrifice, about finding out what God's will is, and then going for it.

His impact on Ted Hegre was profound. The Fellowship got these principles through Ted. Grubb came for a summer conference when we had just built the temporary chapel in thirty days. It wasn't finished but we had the conference in it. Frankly we were so tired from building (we worked forty hours straight to get it done) that when he spoke we were in a daze, and I had a hard time understanding him! But that isn't what struck me – it was the man, the quality of the man; that's what stays with me.

Elaine Linder, another Bethany Fellowship staff member recollects:

We were intrigued with Norman Grubb's messages and with his free personality and his wit; you sensed a depth in him that made you want to go deeper yourself. I know he was very straight-forward, he didn't beat around the bush at all. I'll give you my example. We were standing by a big fireplace after a meeting. Al, my husband, was telling him that we were here in training to go to the mission field. Mr Grubb listened for a little while and then he said, looking right at him, 'I don't see how you'd fit in on any mission field.' About three years later Norman was back here again. By this time Al was in a state of mind to understand what Grubb was talking about. The Lord had shown him many things in his attitude and life that needed to change so he went up to him and said, 'I understand now what you talked about three years ago when you said you didn't think I'd fit in on any mission field.' It was such a good thing that Norman had been honest with him and told him of his limitations.

CHAPTER 10

THE EASTENDER AND THE RESEARCHER

No entry to a new field was more daring, sacrificial and exciting than WEC's commencement in Guinea Bissau (then Portuguese Guinea).

It revolved round two people who were deeply influenced by Norman Grubb – Bessie Fricker, a raw recruit from a back street mission hall in one of the poorest parts of London, and Leslie Brierley, who was to become WEC's international researcher and whose findings profoundly affected the future development of WEC.

Rubi recounts the first years of Bessie's early life and call to the mission field:

I first met Bessie Brierley (née Fricker) in a little slum meeting place called Arthur's Mission, in the East End of London. I was speaking on the missionary challenge for several nights, and noticed an eager-faced girl who listened attentively. She came to me at the end of the meetings and in her bold cockney way said, 'Mr Grubb, is there any chance that a girl like me could become a missionary?'

'Yes,' I replied, 'it is the Holy Spirit Who makes missionaries; if you give Him your life He can make you one.'

I found that her background was not the most favourable. She came from a poor home and was employed as a waitress. However, with the help of church friends at Arthur's Mission, she enrolled in the Bible College of Wales. There, under the ministry of Rees Howells, the Holy Spirit did take hold of her; she learned the walk of faith and even prospered in Greek and Hebrew studies.

God's call to Bessie was to the then unentered land of Portuguese Guinea in West Africa. After her testing period in London headquarters she encountered a formidable snag. The other volunteers for that field were single men. Obviously she could not accompany them. We found a solution by sending her to Angola for language study and then to the Cape Verde Islands which are three days' journey by boat from the Guinea mainland.

While there she came to the crisis moment of her life. World War II had broken out and the three young men left Guinea for home. I cabled Bessie to say there were funds available for her passage and said that she, likewise, should return.

'Thank you for your consideration,' she replied, 'but it was not you who sent me out. It was God, and I must wait to hear what He says.' The Word of the Lord to her was 'Am I limited to men? And is not my word "The Lord can save by many or by few?"' I was not surprised.

Many were her personal battles with discouragement and loneliness during this time, the hardest blow being the breaking of a relationship with one of the male missionaries. Norman wrote to her:

My dear Bessie,
Your sad but grand letter stirred us again. What a path you have had to walk and what a resurrection is coming. God has allowed Satan to search you to the bottom, and all he has found has been the pure gold of steadfast faith and devotion. We honour you to the hilt, but much more, God honours and will honour you. You have stood steadfast in a great storm and you have put God before all human affections.

I can only say that I am thankful that you did not link your life to one who would have taken you from your objective. God will surely give you a resurrection from this. He must be a good man who is to be worthy of you.

A month later he wrote again.

How I wish I could help you in the way of fellowship; but I can only say, Bessie, stick it in Christ's name, and He will open a large door before you in His own time. Learn even in the depths of your loneliness and weakness to turn it into a honeymoon with Jesus. Recognise unceasingly that your fellowship is to be found within yourself, where Christ ever is in fulness. Your fellowship is with Him and the Father, and they dwell in you. Claim that this period of longing for human fellowship may be turned into a marvellous revelation of the Son of Righteousness shining in all His glory within you, so that, instead of hungering for fellowship, you will be able to say, 'To be alone with Him here is heaven below, and I don't want a human companion until God gives me one'. Turn it like that into a victory.

Don't mind what folk around you say. If they talk about you at the cocktail parties, you are indeed in high company, for your Jesus was 'the song of the drunkards'. Let them talk. We are DCDs. All that matters is, what does God say to you? You said you were going into Guinea alone. I still believe you ought to stand for that, unless God Himself, not men, tells you not to.

In spite of criticism from Christian workers on the Cape Verde Islands she sailed to Guinea, overcoming the fear she felt about going alone, and about meeting the authorities. The latter was completely dispelled when the Administrator welcomed her into his office and arranged all formalities for her stay. She was accompanied by a Capeverdian Christian seamstress, Dona Libania, who had volunteered to go with her.

Her labours were rewarded; within a year thirty were meeting on Thursdays and Sundays, and several men were converted.

Now we pick up Leslie's story. He and one other British WECer sailed for the southern (Casamance) area of Senegal in 1936 as part of the new WEC advance into seven W. African countries. Two and a half years later, Leslie, with his predilection for exploration and survey, took a short trip to Portuguese Guinea, just a few hours away by road. Two new British WECers had arrived there, but shortly after, when war was declared, they felt they should return home. Meanwhile one of them accompanied Leslie as he made a survey of all the unreached tribes in the colony.

Some time later the Vichy government was installed by the Germans in France, and an expulsion order came to the British missionaries in Senegal, then a French colony. Leslie, now joined by David and Margaret Barron, moved to Portuguese Guinea as refugees. By this time Bessie had arrived in Bissau and the four made a happy team for a short while.

However Lisbon was not happy with three British refugees on its hands. Leslie was given 24 hours to leave the country, so the pleasant interlude of fellowship came to an abrupt end just as romance was about to flower between Leslie and Bessie.

Leslie takes up the story:

God worked a miracle for me. It so happened that a British frigate was in the harbour (it had been searching for German submarines amongst the Bijagos Islands) and was under orders from the Portuguese authorities to leave that very day. I asked permission to go on board and this was given.

So I went wherever they went, and they took me to Freetown in Sierra Leone. There was one particular man on board who wasn't a naval person. He got hold of me and made friends with me. Unbeknown to me he was in the diplomatic service, seeking touchy information – intelligence. I had no idea of intelligence or clandestine warfare in those days. I told him that I was a Britisher, that I spoke French, Portuguese and the Fula native language. He realised that I would be very useful to him on the linguistic level in his work, and after arrival in Freetown he offered me a job, which I accepted. I became a member of the intelligence service and worked as a liaison officer with the free French in Freetown.

Meanwhile a sad and lonely Bessie was left in Bissau. She wrote to her sister in Britain:

I don't know what I shall do alone. It is almost too much for me. (My friend) Dona Libania leaves on the 25th... I had hoped that at least Leslie would have been able to stay but all had to go. My nerves are upset and I don't sleep at nights...

She became weak with fever and the local doctor ordered that she should have a break.

She wondered where she could go and thought of Sierra Leone where the climate was more temperate. Leslie sent her a cable and it contained the first hint of his affection; she went. The friendship flowered and they were married there on 2nd February, 1942.

Leslie wrote to Rubi:

We are at last united – and it feels as though we have known each other for years. We have gone through similar testings – and she, the woman, came out top! Thank you for the telegram of congratulations. We are not yet sure of any future moves – we are just waiting for any door to open, always with our eyes Portuguese Guinea-wards.

Rubi replied:

16th April, 1942.

My dear Leslie and Bessie,
It was a delight to get your letters of Feb 4 and 24 (Leslie), and Feb 8 (Bessie), and to hear all the news.
Feb 4 was the wedding letter, and I am so glad you sent us all the details. What a happy time, and how really splendidly the missionaries especially have gathered round you and made everything like home for you. You've certainly seen God's hand upon you. How good the bishop and his wife have been, even providing you with a honeymoon! We are now praying continually that God will give you both a new release of life, spiritual and physical, after the storms and trials of these years.
I am so glad for the way the Lord has brought you both together and

that you feel as if you have known each other for life. You will have your
married problems and battles. WECers are strong willed or they wouldn't
be WECers, and strong wills clash and need adjustment. But go steadily
on. Mutual trust is the secret. Trust Christ in each other even where opinion and outlooks differ. The beauty of human love in marriage can only
last fresh and true if it has another love at its foundation, the divine love
of Christ in one for Christ in the other. These two loves combined give
marriage its true beauty and meaning. There will be hills to climb where
you seem to be going up on different sides, and it may take time before
you both reach the top and your viewpoints fuse into one. But it will
come, and marriage based on true and deep mutual understanding in the
flesh and in the Lord is a most wonderful thing. I wish I could have a talk
with you. Married folk have problems, as do single ones; but that must
wait. I count it a great honour that you mention, Leslie, that Bessie looks
upon me as a father. No greater thing could be said, although I think it's
more like an older brother! But I certainly will count it a privilege if you
make me a confidant, and allow me to share in life's inner battles with
you.

Leslie continues his story:

I worked on research intelligence in Sierra Leone. This included the gathering of information with regard to a possible invasion by German Forces
into West Africa. An aspect of this work was to visit the chiefs up country, encouraging them by propaganda and social chat to stay loyal to the
British Empire. Although such work and the social and spiritual ministry
in my spare time were never allowed to mix, Bessie and I managed to
minister to two African churches, and to organise social and spiritual
activities with some of the Armed Forces.

The year there enabled me to understand the spiritual needs of the
country and towards the end of my stay I was able to write a fifty-page
survey about many matters missiological. This was sent to Norman Grubb
who saw the value of this research regarding the needs of unreached peoples. He immediately recognised God's answer to his prayers for he had
longed to have someone feeding such information into WEC.

When I got home, after a full term of service, I had to report to the
PERO (Political and Economic Research Office) HQ in London with
the hope of going back again. I went to them first and then to WEC, and
Norman said, 'I'd like you to do a survey – a world survey of remaining
unevangelised peoples'. That was a staggering thing to ask of me, but
from then on I tackled it. There was always a tension during that time; we
had married during that twelve months in Sierra Leone on the condition
that as soon as the door opened I would go back with Bessie to Portu-

guese Guinea. From the time we got home she was hankering to get back there! We applied to different embassies and consulates for visas, and to Lisbon itself, and never had replies, so I went ahead and commenced this survey. The Lord did not allow us to leave for Africa until all the information needed was in hand.

The war was drawing to an end, but with the door to Portuguese Guinea still firmly closed it was agreed that they go to Senegal where Leslie continued to put his material together for what became known as the *Black Spot Survey*.

On its arrival in London Rubi wrote:

The whole bundle of survey stuff has just arrived with the map, all complete. I think you have done magnificently. I wonder how it managed to get through the mail, but it has done. I can't speak too highly of the job you have done, nor say how thankful I am that you have completed it. I believe you would always have regretted it, if you had not put in the extra time to finish off surveys three and four. This fully rounds off one of the finest bits of work God has given to WEC, and really sets us going for the post-war programme.

The impact of this survey was significant, with recruits coming forward for these areas, and senior workers from existing fields being willing to move into positions of leadership in the new places.

It was while they and their little son, Norman, were stationed at Kounkanne in Southern Senegal, only a few dozen kilometres from the border of Portuguese Guinea, that Bessie faced the biggest challenge of her life.

With all avenues of obtaining a visa exhausted, there remained one possible route. Norman Grubb wrote suggesting that Bessie cross the Guinea border without a visa and trust God to enable her to reach Bissau where she could make a personal appeal to the Governor. The Lord confirmed this to her spirit – Leslie did not have enough Portuguese to handle such a tricky situation. Little Norman was placed in the care of Margaret Barron, and off she went.

The Administrator at Bafata, near to the border, gave her permission to proceed to the capital, Bissau. She was there for forty days (the Biblical period of testing) before her resident permit was granted. Then she hired a truck, went back to Senegal to pick up her husband, son and furniture, and returned in triumph to Guinea, where God used them in a wonderful way to raise up a vibrant national church.

On hearing the news of this breakthrough Rubi wrote to them:

6th July, 1945

My dear Leslie and Bessie,

You have been giving us some thrillers. First, comes your venture of faith in Bessie going to Bissau. Once again she has stepped out on God, and it was grand that you both confirmed it by asking for future money to go to Portuguese Guinea.

And now here's a thriller for you. A gift of £500 to build your first station! The donor gave it for that purpose.

Brierley's response to this was:

25th August, 1945

My dear Rubi,

Just received your letter giving news of £500. I'm afraid we didn't shout hallelujah, we were too full for that!. We shan't be able to stand much more – visa, ideal house, growing church and now sufficient (we trust!) for the first station! We do indeed praise the Lord.

The cut and dried plans I had before coming to the colony have already undergone some changes in view of the new situation here. You see, we already have a church here which is shouldering some financial responsibility – they pay tithes monthly, and fast weekly giving the money for the building of a church. The fasting money comes to 13 or 14 shillings ($3) weekly. And the tithe will be quite a good sum. But costs are SO HIGH. It will probably cost over £1000 to build even a smallish church! And as regards the colony, the tract distribution has been done so well and been blessed by God that already in the majority of centres where literate folk live, there are small groups of those who are either believers or are interested in the gospel. Bissau becomes the centre of all this work, for all these up-country folk look upon Bissau as their centre for social life, business, etc. Most of them visit us when in the city. So Bissau will continue to be the headquarters of the work in spite of the heavier cost of living, etc.

And now I leave the rest of the space for Bessie. She fairly goes at the folk in preaching and gets on well – even with the Governor, chatting to him about her crocodile skin handbag yesterday!

Later there came a classic letter from Norman Grubb encouraging them to maintain a positive spirit in spite of setbacks and to give the Africans the freedom to move as they are led by the Holy Spirit, yet always upholding Biblical standards of holiness:

24th October, 1945

My dear Leslie and Bessie,

Your various letters are thrilling, and are eaten up by us, including the long and full description by you, Leslie, of the move into Portuguese Guinea. It certainly is marvellous to see what God has done, and another glorious victory of the obedience of faith. Now perhaps the slogging times will come, and you have already met with weaknesses in the church. But you are no longer missionary chickens, and so know how not to be soured and set-back by these things, but to have the patience and love, and yet faithfulness and firmness necessary in dealing with sin amongst believers. We must fight to the last ditch for an utterly holy church; rather a handful such, than dozens of the other sort; yet at the same time there is a way in which we can fight with a hard spirit, and do more harm than good. I believe you are entirely right in trusting the Holy Spirit in the Africans, and in taking risks. You will have your crashes; but never mind, get up again and go ahead. It is thrilling to watch your method of throwing responsibility on the believers. They will have to learn right from the beginning that not even their precious Señora Bessie is their 'pastor' but the Holy Spirit working through their own native leaders, and would it not be good from earliest days to give the leadership of meetings to the nationals and you yourselves take the position of helpers and teachers?

Rubi's loyalty to and enthusiasm for the fledgling Portuguese Guinea field knew no bounds. He continually referred to it in his public meetings – with good results.

He writes at the end of a tour in USA:

8th August, 1946

My dear Leslie and Bessie,

Returned to England now. Portuguese Guinea has been in the front rank of my speaking and praying in USA, and I have been specially set on seeing God raise up co-workers. God did set indeed a final seal on my tour, because the very day before I left USA, without my thinking of it or speaking of it, the two whom the staff considers the finest and most spiritual and solid women that they have amongst the USA candidates, have volunteered for Portuguese Guinea! Perhaps you will have heard from them by now. I don't even know their names, beyond 'Marie' and 'Val'! They are from a deeply spiritual group, called Bethany Fellowship in Minneapolis. This group is something of an offshoot of the Lord's working through WEC in that city, Ted Hegre being their leader. There is a whole bunch of them, families and all, who have given up everything and live together in this big home, carrying on in business. They have quite a church membership of 150 I suppose, and are extending. These two will be their first missionaries and I think they will be responsible for their support. So thank God for this.

Leslie, writing in 1996 and looking back on these early days, notes:

The ladies mentioned by Rubi, together with a third – Ruth Bergh – were the Lord's provision in more ways than one! They were our first reinforcements, arriving in 1947, seven years after the initial opening of the field. Bessie and I had had time to find our feet, establishing the first rudimentary beginnings of four centres. They were mature ladies, able to adapt to local conditions. All proved to be gifted pioneers, Marie Bakken among the very primitive but intelligent Bijagos tribe, Valborg Esping with the rebellious Papel tribe which had harassed the Portuguese Colonials, and Ruth, working among the largest tribe in Guinea, the Balanta. They, along with their African brethren evangelised these peoples, saw the first ones enter the Kingdom of God, and trained them in witnessing effectively for Jesus. There are now long-standing and flourishing churches among all of these peoples.

Eventually the Brierleys returned to Britain for family reasons in 1959 where Leslie continued his research ministry. Ten years later Bessie was killed in a car accident.

CHAPTER 11

POST-WAR PROGRESS

As the war ended the home base in Britain saw some remarkable developments. One of these was the Scottish summer holiday conferences run by Elsie and Fran Rowbotham. Many young people (including the writers) were greatly challenged and blessed by WEC speakers at these times.

Florence Smith, a retired Scottish worker, remembers:

My first meeting with Norman was at the Aberfoyle camp in the summer of 1945. It was also more or less my first contact with WEC. I was very new to the whole set up and the leader's ministry was an absolute revelation to me. The thing that stands out is the way he handled his Bible. He chased backwards and forwards through it and it was obvious he accepted the Bible as a whole and was extremely familiar with it from cover to cover. I think that was the thing which gripped me, rather than what he said. It gave me a different angle on Bible study and even on my own quiet time. I saw then I had to become familiar with the whole Bible and not just the allotted daily portions.

The following year we went to the Middleton camp and the memory there is of a group of missionaries standing around talking, out in the grounds. Suddenly Norman appeared; they laughed, ran up to him and started chatting. I thought this was wonderful. This was the 'great leader' yet his team was like sons and daughters around a father. I could see he was very approachable just from noticing how the missionaries reacted as soon as he appeared.

Charlton, my husband, told me that he had written on one occasion commiserating with Rubi because he was away from home so much. His reply was 'Home for me is the will of God.' When I joined WEC and moved around so much from pillar to post, that was the thing I hung on to – 'Home for me is the will of God.'

Jack and Peggy Aitken of Britain and Canada also remember the first Scottish camp organised by the Rowbothams.

Norman came to the first Scottish WEC camp in Aberfoyle in 1945. His messages were dynamic. He was full of enthusiasm. He was very approachable and ready to talk with any young person. Norman joined in the long walks, taking the opportunity to get alongside to discuss aspects of our Christian experience. We have memories of stopping at the village store to buy icecream with Norman along with the rest sitting on the low stone wall all licking our vanilla cones.

Later, as missionary candidates in the London headquarters, we did not see much of Norman because of his extensive travels in UK and abroad. But we treasure the memory of his talks in morning prayers on Moses, Elijah, and other Bible characters. As he flipped the pages of his Bible a wealth of teaching flowed from him.

In those postwar days, after morning prayers, candidates worked on the mission houses. We stoked boilers, cleaned rooms, moved furniture – usually from the top of one house to the basement of the house across the road! Weekends were spent in evangelism and helping in churches and Sunday Schools. When the staff felt that candidates were ready for overseas, they would be invited to one of the weekly meetings to be informed of their acceptance.

Time was passing and Jack had not been asked to attend a staff meeting. In the dining room one mealtime Norman was pouring himself a cup of tea at the counter and Jack came up to do the same. Norman looked at him and said, almost casually, 'We were discussing you last night. We think you should prepare to leave for India.' So Jack was in WEC!

The ending of the war also removed the prohibition on travel, but it was still very difficult to obtain bookings. Retiree Wilf Overgaard of USA remembers this 'cliffhanger'.

'GRUBB WIDEVANCRU LONDON STOP READ THRONE LIFE STOP EXPECTING YOU FEBRUARY 10TH EARLE'
The cablegram originated from Toronto headquarters of WEC. The year was 1945, in the month of December. The war had ended only a few months earlier and Norman Grubb was scheduled to visit the USA for an extensive tour of ministry, beginning at Barracha Church, Philadelphia. It was to be a full week of teaching.

Earle Frid, Canadian Secretary, had just been informed by Rubi that in view of limitations and restriction on travel between Britain and the US, the earliest possible passage available to him would land him in Philadelphia on February 20th, too late for the first ten days of the tour.

Convinced that the Lord had guided in the scheduling, and was still in charge, Earle, who was responsible for the Philadelphia portion of Rubi's tour, together with the Toronto staff, expressed their stand of faith by means of the above cablegram. *Throne Life* was the title of a leaflet, written by Rubi, setting forth a basic principle which had become the hallmark of WEC. We are seated in the heavenlies with our Lord and from that position have authority to command situations here on earth. He was thus exhorted to stand with us for travel reservations which would bring him to Philadelphia by February 10th. The problem can only be appreciated when one recalls that commercial traffic across the Atlantic, after the war, was almost non-existent, except for persons with a priority rating.

The weeks slipped by. Rubi did not respond to our cablegram. January passed. Then came the early days of February. The latest word from Rubi was still that he would arrive in Philadelphia. by boat, on the 22nd. Earle was, nevertheless, obliged to go to Philadelphia to finalise details of the meetings scheduled to begin on the 10th.

Saturday morning, the 9th, Earle was in the office of the pastor of Barracha church. Having covered the essential issues to be discussed with the pastor, and assured that all was in readiness, Earle rose to leave, but paused to remark, 'There is another matter which I suppose I ought to mention. The last word received from Mr Grubb was that he would arrive in Philadelphia on the 22nd! However, you need not be concerned. The Lord has told us that he will be here tomorrow morning!'

A few suspenseful hours followed. Where was Norman Grubb? Who would preach the sermon at 11 am the next day?

WEC headquarters, Toronto, 3pm. I was in the office when the telephone rang. The caller was Norman Grubb. He had just landed in Montreal! Knowing that an overnight train would get him to Philadelphia by the morning, I gave him that information and called Earle. I do not remember Earle's reaction. Perhaps he simply said that he had been expecting this all along!

But faith would confront another seemingly impossible hurdle. The noticeboard at the railway station indicated that Grubb's train was running very much behind schedule, a common occurrence after the war. For Grubb to keep his speaking appointment now seemed to be humanly impossible. The pastor, when informed by telephone, stated that Grubb's coming would be awaited by many and to bring him as soon as possible. Then the unusual happened. The stationmaster stepped up to the noticeboard to change the arrival time. The train would arrive much earlier than posted!

Rubi was rushed to a car and Earle declared that all traffic signals were green as they hurried to their appointment. The congregation was singing the first hymn as he was escorted to the platform!

Earle had been led to write to Canadian Airways who had a very limited schedule to London. He explained the problem. The London office of Canadian Airways discovered an extra seat at the last minute and informed Rubi that he might travel with them.

Another fascinating aspect of Norman's leadership was his uncanny ability to discern where workers would find and develop their ministry. He never directed anyone – he was supremely conscious that this was the Holy Spirit's task – but time after time (as can be seen with the Searles in the previous chapter) he was God's instrument in helping workers move into a fruitful sphere of service.

So it was for Jack and Dina Perkins, whose application for work in Indonesia had been rejected.

The following article brings a number of strands together that resulted in fresh advances for the Kingdom and for WEC.

'Hello, Kees,' cried Andrew (who was to beome God's Smuggler) as he burst into Kees Glas's room. 'I have just come by bike from the Hague (80 kms away). Who do you think I met there? An Englishman who speaks good Dutch and represents an interdenominational faith mission!'

'What mission does he belong to? And what in all the world is a "faith mission"?'

Andrew replied, 'Yes, Kees, I know it sounds crazy but according to this Englishman's story it seems to work. This mission, the Worldwide Evangelisation Crusade, sends people all over the world without guaranteeing their financial support. Each one trusts God personally to supply his needs. All I can say is that I found it tremendously impressive.'

Kees was more than interested – he had been exercised about mission for some time. He wrote to Jack Perkins, the 'Englishman who spoke good Dutch', and soon after went to the Missionary Training College of WEC in Glasgow – as Brother Andrew did a little later.

Eventually Norman was to intervene in Kees Glas's life – when he was a candidate at British headquarters. He was feeling drawn to Nepal, but at that time the country was closed to missions. Rubi had the vision for a new field in Korea and flung out the challenge to the candidates. No one responded.

But one day Rubi took Kees with him to a meeting in London and asked him to give his testimony. Kees told of God's apparent leading to Nepal via India. When he had finished Rubi stood up and announced, 'This young Dutchman won't go there; he will go to Korea.' Kees was nonplussed and the congregation looked at him in astonishment. Kees stuck to his guns and was accepted by WEC for work in India pending Nepal opening.

Back in Holland, Kees was disappointed when he heard that his visa application for India had been refused. Soon after he received a one-line letter from Norman Grubb.

Dear Kees.
Hallelujah! Everything is going to plan.
Yours,
Norman.

He sailed for Japan, en route for Korea some time later.

Another European who was 'hooked' by the WEC vision was
Wilhelm Bergling, the son of Swedish missionaries. At 20 he committed himself to the Lord and heard a call to missionary service.
Without any financial backing he went to Oslo to study under Prof
Hallesby. As long as Willie tithed gifts received the Lord supplied his
needs. When he withheld tithes he ran into financial difficulties. So he
learned the faith life there. After serving in China for nine years he
was unable to return because of the war. He read *After C T Studd,*
and was deeply impressed, and prayed for an opportunity to become acquainted with WEC.

His daughter gave him a booklet about taking positive action if
he felt led in a certain way. When he committed himself to going
to Britain God provided his fare and visa.

After visiting several WEC regional headquarters he returned
to London and confessed to Norman Grubb, 'I am still not quite
certain whether or not I am the right one to be WEC's representative in Scandinavia.' Grubb's comment was, 'Then you should
hurry up and become certain!'

Bergling asked for a sign. He had been cold in bed because of
insufficient blankets. 'Lord, I don't want to be cold another night. Do
something, as a seal I'm in your will being here.' But no one asked him
if he needed more. Before going to bed he visited the bathroom and
saw a cupboard he had never noticed before. He opened the door and
found a pile of blankets!

Willie was WEC's representative in Scandinavia for a number
of years.

1947 was a year that brought about a remarkable healing in the
relationship between WEC and the Unevangelised Fields Mission.

It was one of the outcomes of WEC being touched by the
Ruanda revival. Norman Grubb was brought to a new level of
brokenness before the Lord and was facing up to the 'horizontal'
implications of brokenness – being right in his relationship with
others.

The events surrounding the split in 1931 had cast a shadow over both WEC and UFM and Rubi felt the time had come to seek a reconciliation. On 26th July, 1947, he wrote to the then General Secretary of UFM, Mr Leonard Harris. Here are extracts from that letter:

My dear Len,

I was most interested to hear from John Whittle that you and a UFM party were in the Ruanda Camp at Keswick. God has been speaking to us much about revival in our midst through Ruanda and the two Africans who make their home with us. I know you will wholeheartedly agree with me that one of the bases of revival must be a true breaking down of all barriers at the Cross.

Now I want to confess that there has never been a consciousness in my heart of a true breaking down between us all since 1931. There is a certain level of brotherliness in the Lord but not an absolute melting down. I, for instance, always feel more a sense of rivalry and competition in my heart when I read of UFM news and doings than I do of true brotherly joy and love.

I believe many of you feel much the same. Indeed, although God has been speaking to me about approaching someone in the UFM for some long time, it is actually a remark in John Whittle's letter which leads me to write to you. He mentions your party being there, but also the sense of barrier between.

What God says to me is that if I want revival, it has to begin in me, and if I seek a melting down between us, I must take the first step; and this is especially so, because we were obviously 'the senior partner' of the 1931 split.

It would not be right for me to claim to voice the views of others of the older WECers who were in the work at that time, but I can voice my personal conviction. I believe that we were guilty before God of fighting about and defending minor points which should never have been made an issue between us. Although I have never had any personal difficulty about the DCD, and still do not have, yet I believe that Mr Studd and we did wrong in attempting to make the DCD something that we all must subscribe to. This stressing of it, I believe, to have been not in the Spirit.

Morphia is a more difficult point, because the actual taking of it was Mr Studd's personal affair. But I do believe that on the field there was undue pressure brought to bear on missionaries to agree to Mr Studd's taking it, and that was not right. There was also a time or two, I believe, (although I was not involved in this myself and so am not fully sure of my facts) in which morphia was obtained from doctors in Uganda and brought across without declaration. This, if so, ought, I also think, to be confessed as wrong.

I think these are the main points in which I feel that I from my point of view need to make an admission to you brethren that we did wrong, and thus were the major factor in causing the split.

I have no doubt in my own heart that I fully did God's will in standing by Mr Studd and the WEC in spite of these things; but I do want to put right, so far as I personally can, any measure in which I feel that we gave grounds for the split, and in which then and now, I still showed or show a bitterness.

I can only say that I most earnestly desire that melting down at the Cross which will really make us free and happy brethren in the Spirit with no shadow between.

Thank God for the personal fellowship in Christ which you and I have always had, and it makes me all the freer to write like this.

Ever yours in Christ,

Mr Harris replied on July 30th and the following are extracts from his letter:

My dear Norman,

It was kind of you to write so much from your heart, as you have done and as I read the letter, sorrow surged through my mind, as the old sore was reopened which caused us all so many tears, blood, and searching of heart. Let me assure you first of all, that the love and esteem I have always borne to you, still abides, and there has never been anything in my heart but love to you.

We too have been broken down at Keswick – as you say, that is the great need of us all, and had we been broken before it might have saved all the tears that flowed when brother was divided from brother.

I don't think the barrier existed at Keswick that Mr Whittle seems to have felt – if it did exist may God forgive us for such an unkind thing. There is a difference of opinion that may restrain the sense of fellowship, but that cannot be altered; but I am convinced we love you all in the Lord.

It was Christlike of you to write as you have done regarding the division. The years have taught us that when such division is about to break upon God's children it is better to be broken then, and with a broken heart we save intact true fellowship.

It is not easy to express what one feels on paper – it is always a dead formal way of expressing what one feels in the heart, but if I am able to say what I feel in as kindly a way as I can, there are one or two things I would like to say.

I have always felt that it would have been better if Mr Studd's life had never been published. As great as his sacrifice was, there were things towards the end of his life that would have been better had they been left to face a higher court than human judgement. The book, however much it seeks to give the call to modern youth to sacrifice, must cover sad patches of his life. As I have said, it is better to leave these matters until that awful day when each man shall hand in his accounts to God. I verily feel – though I should hate to wound you - that the book, when it runs out of its present edition should not be republished. His life, and our conception of it can then be put under the blood and cleansed away for ever, and I believe God would honour such a step.

I am not intending now to dwell on your part in that publication, for when we stand before Him, the matter will be judged, but I do feel that the sore would be greatly healed if the book ran through no further editions.

The time is short, and we cannot afford to fight any more over the matter but we can do what we ought to bring to birth a renewed spiritual fellowship. Maybe one day God may heal the breach, but it will take all heaven's grace to do it, but I for one do it here and now – forgive me for ever having told of what I know of C.T. and in the future, I will never mention it again to anyone by the grace of God.

I do pray that we may be led into deeper fellowship for a lost world that may soon have had its last chance to take Christ as Saviour.

May God strengthen you, guide you, and bless you, is the sincere prayer of your brother in Christ,

Leonard Harris.

Part of Norman's reply was as follows:

1st August, 1947.

My dear Len,

Thank you for your letter and the spirit in which it is written. I feel sure that with true brokenness at the Cross on both our sides, there is a place where the past can be put under the blood, leaving a free flow of fellowship between us. I believe at least that you and I are at that point. Maybe, that would be as far as we can go at present towards the larger melting down of barriers between us all, but maybe God means this as the first step towards it.

While I'm glad you freely and frankly state your point of view on some things, you will understand that I cannot see eye to eye on those practical points; but we can leave them together under the blood, and each walk forward in the light we are given to see.

To me, C.T's last days were not something to be mourned over. We who saw him go saw him live to his last breath for God and souls. He was always a man of immensely strong viewpoint, which was partly the rea-

son why many could not work with him, and he would go right through
with what he saw to be right. Thus to him the DCD was a recall to the
mission to full consecration, and the morphia a means for enabling him
to keep going with the Gospel to the end. Where I would differ from C.T.
would not be in the feeling that I was called to pass judgement on him in
these matters, but because I did feel that (without his realising it) he did
put too much pressure on others to express agreement. This was no new
thing in his latter days; he had, to my mind, always that tendency, even
from early CIM days.

When I wrote the biography, I had it out first with the Lord and felt
that I must faithfully speak of both these things – DCD and morphia –
and so I did (chps 20 and 22).

You might take me up on the one point that I did not mention that (I
believe), although the morphia was always supplied by doctors (Dr Cook
of Uganda, etc.) yet it was brought in on at least one occasion without
being declared. I don't know why, because, having been authorised by a
doctor, I presume it would have been passed in without any difficulty.
That again I must leave as between C.T. and the Lord. But I think you will
see from any biographer's point of view that it would not be my place to
raise such a matter in a book.

On the other hand the whole story of that outpoured life is a testimony to God's glory which I feel it has been my greatest privilege to
bring to the world in print. In doing so, I made no attempt to assess C.T's
character, but merely to state facts and use large quotations from his
own writings. The hundreds of testimonies to conversion and consecration which never cease coming to my knowledge are, I think, proof of
God's seal upon it. Also I feel that a man walking in the flesh would not
be God's agent for a great enduring work of the Spirit, yet today, branch-
ing out from his faith and obedience are our two missions reaching already about twenty unevangelised fields.

I would not expect you and the UFM brethren to see and agree to this
angle of things, but you have spoken from the heart and now I do believe,
and I think you do too, that we should leave the thing at the Cross and be
one in Christ in present-day fellowship.

Anyhow, thank God for that true love in Christ between us.

Yours in Him,
Norman Grubb.

CHAPTER 12

THE ENCOURAGER

John Whittle, who joined British WEC in 1937 and then moved over to USA in 1948, described what it was like to travel around with Norman during his tours there in the early fifties.

When Rubi wanted to do more extensive tours I began to work for him, the main objective being to find openings in churches and colleges and other Christian groups. I travelled with him for long periods and started to find out what a remarkable man he was and how very generous and thoughtful he was.

Some of the best responses came from big churches like the Presbyterian church in Hollywood. He also had contact with other large and influential Presbyterian churches, and although he was not an easy speaker to listen to, people wanted what he had to share.

He would tell a story and bring the challenge of the mission fields and how by faith WEC was opening up and getting results even in war time when everybody was retreating. He was determined to lead the advance into unreached areas. He would always explain the spiritual principles underlying these developments.

Bus and Marge Williams, presently living in Albuquerque, New Mexico, tell of meeting up with Rubi soon after finishing Bible college in USA. Marge commences:

Our first meeting with Rubi was in Southern California. My husband, Bus Williams, was just out of Bible college. We had three young children and besides having a job my husband was also pastoring a church in Pomona, California. Our hearts were open and hungry, seeking for reality. God was so good to bring into our lives people deep in the Lord so we were very much blessed. Rubi was one of these saints. When he came on the scene my husband had the joy of driving him to many of his meetings in Southern California. Pacific Palisades was one of them – a retreat for ministers who came from all over to hear this man. While Bus drove, Rubi was constantly talking. Bus was soaking it up. Needless to say, God was bringing us into a deeper commitment, deeper faith and trust, and finally, action. We left behind all worldly security and joined WEC. These people trusted God for everything from A to Z.

We left California with our little family to go to the Chicago head-quarters and just a month or so later we moved on to Fort Washington where property had been acquired for a national base.

Although he was international director of WEC, he was never too busy to invite you into his office. This was a blessing to us. Never too busy to help someone to the highest for Jesus.

It was during our days with WEC at Fort Washington that Bus en-quired of him one day, 'Rubi, I know some very special people have in-fluenced you, along with the Lord, concerning the truths you have been able to impart to us. I'd like to know who they are?' Rubi threw his head back and laughed and laughed, then replied, 'My dear Bus, you really do want to know, don't you! You're the first person in 25 years that has asked me such a question.' So he mentioned a few books that the US director had in his library. The US director at that time was Alfred Ruscoe. He said, 'You read these books and when I get back to England I will send you my treasured books by Jacob Boehme; but guard them with your life. They've already gone through the blitz.'

Sure enough, one day the treasured package arrived and Bus spent every spare moment reading and devouring these books. He quickly be-gan to understand what Rubi was getting at. Grubb's mind was so keen and alert, and sensitive in the knowledge of God, that the overflow touched so many lives, cascading on us all. Rubi was always pressing on, never looking back, always positive, sometimes controversial, but always stand-ing firm in the truths that God made real to him, speaking that word of faith, seeing beyond what the natural eye sees.

Bus continues:

Through Norman and our introduction to the writings of men like Jacob Boehme, William Law, Andrew Murray and others, I began to realise what Jesus was doing through us, for we are extensions of Jesus Christ in this world. It was through Norman that the reality of Romans 6-8 and our union with Christ's death, burial and resurrection became real. I would place special emphasis on the resurrection for this is the part that is usually missed. Knowing our union in His resurrection makes us able to walk in newness of life, indwelt by the Holy One, free from condemna-tion, overcoming all that is of the evil one and enjoying this life. Norman enabled me to understand what the scripture meant where it states that we are vessels, temples, members of His body, branches of the vine, therefore just containers. Perhaps the greatest thing, if one can place one truth ahead of another, is the freedom that is available to us all as we choose to walk in this wonderful relationship. It is a life of rest in Christ's total sufficiency within.

Over in Britain the same impact came through Norman's ministry. Wherever he went the Spirit used him to touch hearts and to change the direction of many lives. Here are the stories of a few in the UK who were influenced by him in the late forties.

Dorothy Barnes of Christian Literature Crusade remembers life as a candidate at WEC headquarters in Britain:

I arrived at WEC headquarters (19 Highland Road) at the end of September, 1949. There was no specific date for the intake of candidates and no formal course of training. Several applicants for WEC and CLC had been arriving since the end of the Bible college year, and we fitted in to the daily routine, doing practical work in the kitchen, the laundry and household cleaning.

It so happened that Norman Grubb had just returned from a trip overseas, and during my first weeks, he led morning prayers. As there were some twenty candidates, he decided to go through the *Four Pillars of WEC* and began with faith. As he sat with his Bible open on his knee and began to expound the scriptures and the principles of faith, I was enthralled and knew that this was the way God wanted me to live.

Through Rubi I learned that faith was simply believing what God said, and continuing to believe His promises, even when circumstances appeared to contradict them. Then, as always, whenever Rubi ministered, I felt that he did not just give a message, but he imparted spiritual truth. I felt that I had been fed and inspired, and built up in my faith. He was so humble and gracious, but he was forthright and would not hesitate to challenge anything which was not real. But he was very fair and would look for the best in everyone. Bessie Brierley once told me that, in a staff meeting, when Rubi was defending someone whom she felt was no good, she burst out, 'Oh Rubi, I do believe you would even see some good in the devil himself!' At that Rubi laughed heartily, and agreed.

On Monday mornings, domestic matters were reported at morning prayers. Pa Lewis, who was in charge of hostel catering supplies, announced the amount of money that had been received in gifts, and the amount spent on food. For several weeks these two amounts had tallied exactly. Pa Lewis was summoned to Rubi's office and asked to explain how this happened. Rubi's suspicions proved correct and Pa Lewis had to admit that he had made up the short-fall from a small retirement pension he received. He was forbidden to do so again and Rubi concluded '... and if God lets them all starve to death, I will bury them myself!'

One morning, in the Autumn of 1949, Rubi was leading morning prayers. He began by reading Judges 6 and shared how God had spoken to him about his forthcoming visit to the Congo field. For many years the

missionaries there had been praying for revival, and God had told him
that He was now going to bring spiritual revival through his ministry. His
response had been like that of Gideon, and he asked us to pray for him.

On the day of his departure he was due to leave for the airport about 6
am. I was one of six or seven women candidates housed in two rooms of
No 32 Highland Road, opposite the hostel. We got up extra early and
peered out into the dark street. When we saw Fred Anthony bring the car,
a small black Hillman, to the front of No 17, we crept downstairs and
clustered on the pavement to see Rubi off. He came down the steps,
looking very ordinary in a raincoat and trilby hat, and when he saw the
little group, gave a surprised and deprecating smile, then he said, 'Let's
have a word of prayer'. Removing his hat, he began to talk quietly to God,
and it seemed to me that heaven came down and glory shone around us.
Then Rubi said goodbye and got into the car.

Ray Oram of Bristol, who served with WEC and CLC for many
years, also remembers life at London headquarters at the same
time as Dorothy Barnes.

Norman would come down morning after morning for prayers and impart his teaching of scripture. I look back on my time under his ministry
as very foundational – the greatest blessing I've ever received. His teaching has stood me in good stead throughout my life and I think has deeply
affected my outlook on life and on the work that I've been able to do for
the Lord.

I suppose one aspect of his teaching was getting to know the will of
God. If we know the will of God we can pray in faith. He would go through
the Old Testament stories and characters and bring out teaching from
them. He showed how they laid hold of the promises of God, and if they
were rightly related to the Lord then they were in a position of power and
authority.

I remember one morning in particular; Norman was to go to the Congo
for a time of ministry. Of course we'd been much in prayer for this. He
came down and shared what the Holy Spirit had been saying to him. As I
watched, the perspiration broke out on his brow. He obviously had to
make a declaration of faith and, being the humble man that he was, found
this difficult to do. Nevertheless he was prepared to go out on a limb; he
said he felt that God's word to him was that revival would come through
his ministry there. And as I watched him I could see how difficult it was
for him to make this statement. He did go to the Congo and revival did
break out; there was much blessing.

Alastair Kennedy, who became deputy international secretary for WEC, describes several incidents in which Norman Grubb affected his life, starting in 1947.

I always found talk with him stimulating – he had spiritual priorities in everything he did. He didn't just react like an ordinary mortal, he was like a prophet – a man of God – trying to instill spiritual principles in all his workers.

The whole thrust of his life was a challenge to spiritual priorities, not just to look at things in the human and natural way but to look at supernatural realities. He was a man of faith and he constantly, just by his questions and his talk, challenged you to look and see what the implications were for your faith. That to me was a tremendous help. Also he was a man of tremendous vision; you were aware that he was looking at situations from a divine perspective. That was amazing to me. It taught us much about how we can be on the stretch for the Lord in every normal circumstance.

In my early days I looked up very much to Rubi. He was my role model. I felt very strongly that God was speaking to me through him. Then later there came one or two incidents where I had to doubt whether what he was saying was really God's will for me. That changed my attitude slightly. It made me a bit more analytical and balanced in my evaluation of him; he wasn't just a model – he was also God's messenger, but I had also to think out what it meant for me.

Let me outline three incidents where I had to evaluate his comments. The first was when, in 1947, I met Rubi when he was doing the Nationwide tour of meetings. I think it was in Exeter. I was still in the Army at that time but getting ready to be demobbed. I was thinking about my future and I went to see him after the meeting. (It was a tremendous meeting and I was greatly blessed by it.) I said to him, 'Do you think I should do a degree? Should I go to university?' He said, 'By no means, forget that. God's will has to come first. God has called you to the mission field: throw the world away and go crusading.' I accepted that and was convinced by it. I wouldn't be today but at that point I felt it must be God speaking to me. However when I went home and put this to my parents, my mother was very very upset and said, 'We've sacrificed quite a lot to get you a good education and you're going to throw that away. I don't think that's God's will for you. If you go down that road we'll put you out of the house.' I had to choose! Eventually, after prayer the Lord led me to go to university, but to do a shortened war degree.

Incident two was when I arrived as a candidate at Highland Road in 1952. I was on my way to Senegal. I felt very sure at that point that God had called me there. But I'd only been at headquarters a matter of two or three weeks when Rubi called me into his office and said, 'Alastair, I think you're making a mistake because we're desperately in need of someone to head up our school work in Zaire. We're looking for somebody with university training and teaching experience. Would you go there?' I said, 'Rubi, are you asking me to go to Zaire? Because if you, as my leader say I should go to Zaire, I won't have any alternative.' With that unmistakeable twinkle in his eye he said, 'You know me too well, Alastair, to believe that I would give you a command like that. I want you to find out God's will, so I think you should pray about it; but I cannot command you to do it.' I spent my whole candidate period praying about that until finally I was just convinced beyond any shadow of a doubt that his advice was not God's will for me.

The third incident was when I was on the point of sailing for Senegal, I came through headquarters and Rubi was there. I said, 'Rubi, I hope I can go to Senegal with your blessing even though I disregarded your advice.' He replied, 'Brother, I still think you're wrong.' However, there was still that twinkle in his eye. You could never take him too seriously because of his whimsical attitude.

I think one of his outstanding qualities was his ability to recognise a spirit of faith and vision – what we call the 'go-through spirit' in people. He knew how to find and motivate recruits to go all out for the Lord. He knew how to find people of tremendous enterprise and initiative, and stimulate them to give that to the Lord. WEC could have so easily just disappeared off the map of Christian things in 1931. It was under attack from every side and Rubi had the courage to stand firm on what he saw to be scriptural principles exemplified by C.T. Studd and to prevent the mission from just drifting into oblivion. He was able to turn disaster into victory. He did it by virtue of his faith and vision and he saw what the Lord could still do. So he picked up a man like Staniford and sent him off West Africa, and a man like Pat Symes and sent him to Colombia. He was a tremendous selector, motivator and inspirer of workers.

It was the authors' privilege to meet and become acquainted with Norman between 1947 and 1949. WEC was experimenting with a missionary training programme. A group of about a dozen students was living at the Glasgow headquarters and taking classes at the Evangelical Baptist Fellowship Bible College in town.

During these days Rubi made occasional visits to headquarters and his talks to us students had us enthralled. My wife and I felt called to WEC and thought originally of applying for service in India. But the Holy Spirit was checking us, and it was during one of Norman's visits that he said, 'I don't think God is wanting you in India in the near future; would you stay on in Glasgow to help your senior workers, the Rowbothams, for a while?' It was hard to accept this at first but eventually we knew it was right.

We did a shortened candidate course in London and Rubi must have sensed we were not adequately equipped spiritually for the task envisaged. So he wrote the following personal line to us:

7th August, 1949.

My dear Stewart and Marie,

You know my deep concern that the heart of the MTC (Missionary Training College) may be right, in such a way that God Himself may get hold of the students in His fulness. That is why I am so concerned about what will be our central teaching to them on the Holy Ghost. The rest – such as we discussed with Godfrey Buxton – is of great importance and value, but is only on the circumference. The heart is how the Holy Ghost will get through us in His fulness to the students, and later through the students to the world. That is why I have searched with you into the problem of the type of teaching (doctrinal) to be given them, and God has given me no clear answer on this.

But I am seeing more and more clearly now, although it may take time for others to see. I see that what God gave WEC in its founder, C.T.S., was not so much a doctrinal presentation of holiness or a spirit-filled life, but the sight before our eyes of the Holy Ghost in person living in and through a life on the altar. We saw amongst us one whose whole body was totally possessed by God, almost the very natural things in it burned up that it might be one sole channel of Christ to the lost. Our foundation was an intercessor in action, God coming through a man to the world; therefore I see that the foundation of each branch of WEC has to be just that, not a doctrine, but the Holy Ghost Himself seen coming to the world through a body on the altar.

I see that this is God's answer that I am seeking – YOU YOURSELVES.

Now I thank God, first of all, that you have evidenced in our midst in London a real openness to God; especially you, Stewart; Marie I naturally know less. And I think these are days of tremendous importance for you both, just because you are tender in spirit, faced with a commission which you feel too big for you. You have not found your feet in it yet; and are still fluid before the Lord (may you keep so) but all the more, therefore, these are moulding days for the Spirit in you. It is quite clear to me in the Spirit that God has you ready for the deep revelation of Himself in you, but that He has not yet done the work He seeks to do. That will come in His good time.

It was through Rees Howells in Swansea that God gave Ma Rubi and me our renewed commission and anointing at C.T.S's death in 1931. I had known all through the years in my spirit that God revealed the Holy Ghost as the indwelling Person and Intercessor there at the College, exactly as He seeks to be in and through us in WEC. Thus, when I went back for my first visit on returning from USA, I had an immediate confirmation of this in my soul, and as usual, God met with me again.

Now what I saw again was that this is the revelation of the Holy Ghost working through the members of His body, which is the real heart of the WEC position and message. This is C.T. all over again, and this is the heart I am seeking for our MTC. I feel sure, therefore, that some method should be found by which you two could go and have a time with Rees Howells. God must show how, for I don't see how it can come about in the present state of your programme.

I look in faith to a deep spiritual flow of unity and cooperation between MTC and Bible College of Wales, for they turn out men and women just as we long for them to be turned out for service, whereas we have the knowledge and experience of actually opening and developing fields. So I would ask you both to be before the Lord, ready and open for all that He may want to say to you in a link with the college in the future. God has to do His full work in you two, then and then only, is the MTC safe as a training place.

Much Love.

Yours in the Crusade,
Rubi.

The outcome of this was that we agreed to spend a month at the Bible College of Wales. It was a time of tremendous revelation, and towards the end of our stay I wrote Norman a letter of which these are extracts:

26th Aug, 1949.

One night Marie woke up and in the stillness and darkness the conception of the Holy Spirit as a Person – God Himself – broke in upon her. Last Tuesday I was on my knees about the whole business and Marie came in after having a chat with one of the girls here. She said that this girl was sure that I wasn't 'through' and that she had been praying for me all the previous night. It was then that I started to realise that God still had something to do in me. I went out to brush my teeth before going to bed, and as I was standing by the washbasin God met me. I have never known anything like it. I realised that up to that moment I had been living the life of consecrated self; He wanted to possess me. Something inside just seemed to crumple up and I asked Him to come in.

I got to bed at quarter to one and was in a daze – I couldn't see reason in it at all after the previous experiences of the new birth and sanctification. I got up at 6.30 next morning in the same kind of trance and lived in that right through the day. I cleared out of the college partly because I needed to be alone, and partly to leave Marie undisturbed because she was going through it too. I went to Cardiff but sat the whole way there and back in a daze. It seemed as if the old life was shattered – I could never go back to it; I felt as if I had been taken as a dry stick and broken in two. I had no desire for food – I missed lunch and tea and returned to the college at 6.30pm.

Mr Howells asked us in for prayer that night and we had a helpful time getting straightened out. It was then that I really and truly by faith and without feeling trusted God to make my body His temple.

We are just finding our feet in this new way. God has so much to teach us but having had a glimpse of such a life we know we could never go back to a 'normal' kind of experience.

We re-read your letter and it became clear as never before. We see now what you meant about the Person of the Holy Spirit.

Another who formed a close link with the Grubbs around this time, was Dr Helen Roseveare, now famous for her experiences in Zaire as a WEC missionary and for her subsequent writings and spoken ministry. She describes her links with Rubi:

I met Len Moules in 1949 when he was showing the film *Three Miles High*. This hooked me into WEC really. Len saw that I was in a very dicey situation at that particular time and invited me to WEC headquarters to nurse his sister-in-law, Edith Moules, in the last days of her illness. I was a medical student, two years from qualifying.

Instead of living as a candidate in the hostel Norman Grubb invited me to live in No. 17 Highland Road pretty well as his daughter. I had meals with them and lived in a room below them for two years. I became a close friend of his daughter, who at that time was a day student at Ridgclands Bible College.

As a student, I was going up daily to the West London hospital on my bicycle (I had no money). This was before I came into WEC as a candidate. During these days he really did treat me as a daughter. I can remember on one occasion we had prayers on a particular Sunday morning. (This was unusual as we nearly always avoided a clash with church times.) I was unable to put anything in the offering plate so at lunch time Norman said, 'Why didn't you put anything in the offering plate?' I said, 'I didn't have anything.' He replied, 'That isn't true.' I looked at him and he said, 'I know that yesterday you had an envelope in which you had a two and sixpenny book of stamps, and I know you went to the finance office and turned it in for cash. At least you have threepence tithe.' I said, 'But I needed that money. I went and bought a new tyre for my bicycle.' He said, 'You stole it from God.' End of conversation. I learnt some of my lessons in that sort of way.

He just took it for granted that I was going to go to the field with WEC. There was no question about that at all. But if it hadn't been for Rubi I doubt whether I would have joined, because WEC was too holy for me. There were a lot of candidates in those days from Emmanuel Bible College in Birkenhead. From the general conversation around the table I just knew they were all streets ahead of me spiritually and theologically. I felt so ignorant, I felt so out of it all. I just felt I wouldn't fit, but Norman Grubb said, 'You are one of us.'

At the end of candidate days I came up before the staff to be accepted. There was no question that 90% of the staff wanted to turn me down. (I learned this later.) They said I was bossy, that I always knew all the answers to everything, and that I never liked giving in to anybody else's opinion. Norman Grubb was in the chair at the meeting and said, 'Okay, but I don't agree. God can use that sort of a personality on the field if we'll trust God.' I came into WEC because Rubi had the courage to believe in the Lord Jesus in me, when neither I nor anybody else could see it.

He didn't insist that I do Bible training. Many missionary societies in those days were making the same mistake; they felt that medics had trained for so long and been Christian Union members for six years doing training courses with IVF so we did not need Bible School training as well. Missions were so desperate for doctors, their fear was if they put us into Bible School they might lose us. A great mistake. In some ways, medics need it more than others, because we've so concentrated on medicine to become doctors that we grew very little in spiritual things.

He was a great encourager. He encouraged people who were prepared to be loners, who were prepared to be flat out for the Lord, prepared to throw away everything. When everybody criticised them he'd back them up. He was the backer-up of the underdog.

He tended always to be able to catch on to what was the going concern. When I came into WEC, in the late forties early fifties, the great theme then was the Ruanda revival; he grasped the message of Ruanda to the extent that this was the only thing that mattered. He had a drive, an enthusiasm about him.

When I was a candidate he took morning prayers and he wouldn't let up on a thing and he wouldn't let us let up either!. When people stopped praying – we were praying at the time for Colombia, and the terrible suffering of Colombian missionaries – he would grip this and say, 'Come on, come on, we're not through yet.' He'd keep us going on our knees until suddenly there was a lift and everybody was through. He kept us at it. Prayer was real and God would lift our spirits when we touched the throne. He made these things real so that they were no longer just theory. Not just praying around, but praying through. He'd get on to one subject like a cat with a rat; he'd stick at it, hang in there; he taught us to persevere. He taught us about 'seeing Jesus running around in African bodies'. He taught us also to see Jesus running around in one another. 'Don't always be criticising the things that irritate you or annoy you or aren't right. See Jesus in every situation.' This was the sort of theme that came across to us candidates. He drummed into me, through those prayer meetings, the fact that when everything was against you, when the days were so dark that you couldn't see anything, then you just said, 'Okay, glory in Jesus; He's put me here for this very purpose.' He made this so real to us.

He continued to be a spiritual father to me when I was on the field. There's no question about that. He wrote to me every single month whether I answered or not. I mostly did answer although once or twice I didn't because I was uptight about something, or didn't agree with what he was suggesting. He'd write back one of his humorous letters, tongue in cheek, saying, 'I still love you even though you don't love me at the moment.' He fed me with books that probably are not usually read in WEC – the mystics of the 14th and 15th centuries. He got me on to Jacob Boehme. I had to read St John of the Cross, Theresa of Avila and other such books.

He was always moving one on spiritually. There was always a push to be striving for the top, to keep your vision clear, not to get bogged down in details. That would come through over and over again.

I shared very openly with him and he trusted me in a way that I sensed the people on the field were not perhaps willing to do. He encouraged me to believe in and trust the African. He was ahead of others in this. He had seen much earlier that we needed to hand over more to African leadership and to train Africans for it. He had caught that vision and he fed it to me.

He was a great lover of Jack Scholes, my field leader. I loved Jack Scholes with a deep, deep respect – one of the finest Christian men I've ever met, a meek man of God. Norman Grubb encouraged me to share with Jack and to trust Jack's vision, and he wrote to Jack Scholes and encouraged him to trust me as I sought to put Africans into leadership.

Eva France (née Duff) was a candidate in 1948. When Fred Anthony, Rubi's personal secretary, was away, she occasionally filled in for him. Her recollections are both insightful and amusing.

He would dictate and I would type. He would walk up and down the room as he thought and talked. I remember one of the things that really used to annoy me. I had had a very limited education but he used to upset me by starting his sentences with 'ands' and 'buts'. I remembered at school we were taught never to start sentences with conjunctions. This so annoyed me that one day I couldn't contain it any longer. I said, 'Can I ask you something?' He said, 'Yes.' I said, 'When I was at school, and that's a long time ago, I was always taught never to start my sentences with conjunctions, and here you are with your ands and buts.' He just threw his head back and laughed. 'Just a minute, Eva' and he walked over to his bookcase and opened a book. I remember him saying 'Look, if Macaulay can do it, I can do it!' That was lovely I thought, and I've never forgotten it.

Once, some of the candidates and I were deeply troubled over something that had happened at headquarters, so I decided to tell him. He took it in a surprised manner. I think it was a shock to him that this had occurred but having said that, he was gracious and humble and promised to attend to it, which he did. The whole matter was cleared up forthwith.

The Ruanda message about walking in the light really pervaded the mission at that time. I remember him saying to me, 'I'm sorry, Eva, that we treated you workers as servants instead of comrades.' That was his graciousness. It was beautiful. I think he was a most understanding, gentle sort of person. It was a privilege to work with him. In fact I didn't feel it was 'work' at all. It was fellowship!.

I never saw him angry once, even in the midst of sternness; yes, his face was set, but never once did I ever see him angry, or ruffled.

It was Christmas. I was down at Blueburn, in Devon, typing for him. I said to him, 'You've got a real passion for kipper paste, haven't you?' We were having marmalade on our toast and he would be having kipper paste, always eating kipper paste whenever there was the opportunity. He just wryly smiled, chuckled, and said, 'I don't really like it Eva, but it saves the marmalade for the others.' I've never forgotten that. I thought it was beautiful. Here he was eating this kipper paste pretending that he liked it and all the time he was considering others. It was wartime and marmalade was hard to find.

He said to me one day, 'Now when you get to the field Eva, there's one thing I want to say to you.' I said, 'What's that?' 'Don't let circumstances make you lose your bubble.' And I thought, 'What does he mean?' so I asked him and he said, 'Well, it's there.' He didn't explain. I found out later what he meant – my freedom and spontaneity in the Lord.

Coffee time was really the only opportunity to talk about personal things. We discussed Pentecostalism one day; he said that he'd never spoken in tongues but he took by faith the life of the Spirit and felt the Spirit was with him. We all knew that was so.

One Sunday he called on me and asked me to do some work for him. I said, 'Oh! I can't come today – it's Sunday.' 'Oh,' he said, 'you're a sabbatarian, are you?' I said, 'Well, I'm not used to working on Sunday.' He said, 'I'm used to working seven days a week for Jesus, Eva. Every day is the Lord's day to me.' I had a nice lecture. But the lovely thing was, he said, 'Right, I'll respect your position. You needn't come.'

CHAPTER 13

PING PONG WITH THE DEVIL

Mention has already been made of Norman's departure to Congo. This was indeed a wonderful journey for him as it took him to every part of that large field.

He was in his element. Back in Africa after twenty years, he found the Bangala language returning to him, and above all, he had the witness of the Spirit that God was going to bless his ministry.

The fruitfulness of that tour can be realised from these accounts which he afterwards penned:

> The first great event at Ibambi was the Christmas conference, a series of meetings held right through the Christmas weekend in a large open-air church, giving shelter to the crowds beneath a roofing of palm fronds spread over a framework of supporting poles. There must have been about 3,000 there from the neighbouring bush churches.
>
> I was most glad to find that the language in which I worked twenty years ago, Bangala, came back to me with great ease, although in this Ibambi area it had to be retranslated into Kibudu and Mayago. The main message God laid directly on me for all my tour was from 1 John 1: that the only thing which hinders the Christian from an overflowing life is sin; but often it is unrealised sin, for in the subtlety of our hearts we so often call things which are really sin by other names. But when we come to the light of God and are willing to walk in that light, sin is seen to be sin, however it may try to cloak itself. We cannot rid ourselves of sin or sinful habits, but we can be honest. We can recognise, acknowledge, confess with bended neck and broken hearts, for Jesus was broken by sin at Calvary that we might also 'break'.
>
> If we do, the same light which shines on sin shines on the precious blood (1 John 1:7) and we can know not only forgiveness but heart cleansing and deliverance: we can learn not only to come to the light but to walk in it by acknowledgement of the least deviation in thought, word and deed from the divine standard.
>
> Some of the testimonies at the conference were good to hear. The wife of the African leader, herself a leader among the women, told of her temper, revealed in the house with her husband, but never in public; how she tried to get the victory through prayer, but could not. Then one day,

when God was searching hearts in the Bible School, the Spirit said to her, 'When you cease being a hypocrite and admit to your fellow-believers what you really are, I will meet with you.' She did so and testified with a full heart before us all how the Spirit came to her in His fulness at that time and gave her a complete deliverance.

The spirit of deep conviction came upon many. In the Ibambi Conference about 300 were personally dealt with by the evangelists. A move of the Spirit began to be manifest about the third day, one of the elders saying, 'God is doing a great thing here.' They were up until 3 am dealing with souls.

At Wamba, on Monday morning, after the big Sunday meetings, the Spirit began to get the victory in hearts. About eighty came out that morning, increasing gradually to two hundred. They included several men for whom there had been much prayer lately, including the chief grumbler on the station, and his wife. Colin Buckley, in charge of the station, put off the church meetings that day so that the leaders could go right ahead in dealing with souls. Later, the leading elder, Samwele, came to say that God had done 'a mighty thing' among them. Christians they had thought were absolutely true, confessed to hidden sin, adulteries, lies, thefts, unpaid debts, hatreds and malice in the heart; one, a trader's man, was asking the Africans 200 francs for articles worth 100, and was pocketing the difference. The Christians were saying, 'God has indeed filled us full with His Spirit.'

At Lubutu the crowd packed the building, with many more standing outside and looking in over the low sidewalls. A party of burly goldminers had come in, lively bright Christians, whose consistent testimony in their rough life so impressed their white overseer that he gave them permission to make the two day journey. There were about twenty of them and they asked leave to stand and sing. This they did with great gusto, beating time with their hymnbooks on their hands. The Holy Ghost poured Himself out, and it was difficult to handle the flow. The first break came early, and from then onwards there was a stream. One afternoon and evening there were fifteen groups of souls being dealt with by men and women evangelists. Darkness came but still they continued. It was 11pm before the groups broke up.

At Malingwia we started by having a two day conference on the station with a packed church of about 500. The people listened intently to the messages and it was a joy to me to be able to speak in the old Bangala without interpretation. The Spirit worked in many hearts, and the leading elder, who with others dealt personally with each, said later to us that they were 'amazed' at what they heard. 'Hearts of stone had been broken,' he said, and we should weep if we knew what went on inside houses, when all appears well on the surface.

This elder himself, with his two brothers, is an outstanding trophy of grace and the firstfruits of the work. Great big fellows with open faces and hearty laughs, they told us how they were supposed to be Roman Catholic teachers yet had thirteen wives between them, and were often picked up drunk on the road. The Word first reached their hearts through a Scripture Gift Mission booklet *The Way of Salvation*, in Bangala, which was handed to them once when Mr Scholes was passing in his car. 'The Catholics,' he said, 'only showed us Christ with His legs crossed on a crucifix, but they never told us a word about the power of the blood.' Then he added, 'The officials beat us with a whip, but we went straight out and did the same things again; there was no change. But this wonderful gospel does what the white man's whip could never do!'

Others may disagree, but in the opinion of the writers the fifties and early sixties were the zenith of Norman Grubb's ministry. He had come through the restrictions and trials of the war years. His personal faith had deepened. His grasp of mission strategy was never better. His writing skills were sharper than ever before. Loyalty to his leadership and leadership style were unquestioned and the rate of growth of WEC in terms of new fields was at its maximum. The fields of Uruguay, Japan, Venezuela, Italy, Taiwan, Korea, Brazil, Viet Nam, Sumatra, Java, Gambia, Turkey, Chad, and Iraq were opened. Sending bases in France, Germany, Sweden, Holland, New Zealand and South Africa were established. New ministries such as the Australian MTC, SOON and BIENTOT, the free gospel newspapers, flourished.

The early fifties were memorable for Rubi's increasing linkage with North American WEC. Of course he realised the vast potential for missions there and he eagerly accepted invitations to visit and minister. However another factor pressed in upon him and that was the need to impress upon the USA and Canadian staff the absolute necessity of loyalty to the four pillars of WEC – faith, sacrifice, holiness and fellowship. It was in the last named area that considerable adjustments were needed and the USA staff invited the Grubbs over in 1950 to help them for a time.

Writing later about this move he said:

You will remember that I was asked to come out as director of North America in 1950. Ma Rubi and I came, but I never had any doubt that it was merely temporary, and that God was bringing the North American staff through the furnaces to fit them for an even greater ministry; for we never forget that this is God's great day for North America, and we must expect to see more for worldwide evangelisation from them than from anywhere else. I don't know what would have happened, when we came out in September '50, if God had not begun to teach us the way of walking in the light, and breaking at the cross as He kept showing us our individual need and sin. God did not give us a full solution and unity then, but He kept us broken enough to stand together and carry on until He did show His full way.

Rubi returned to Britain in 1951, mainly to write the biography of Rees Howells (see pages 162-163) and then was back in USA for the staff meetings in early '52.

About these he wrote:

I can only say that we are all thrilled at what God has done. The WEC (fellowship) with one heart and voice reappointed Rusiko (Alfred Ruscoe) to leadership. I think a new understanding of the balance between leaders and led is coming out more clearly. We called it at the conference 'dynamic leadership and democratic control', meaning that a leader must lead, but that final control must be the mind of the Christ through the whole fellowship. My! They can speak frankly and truly here, yet in the love of God. The staff here says what it thinks. We must find a place, all through WEC, where the sin of the fear of man is recognised and dealt with in us. I had the feeling of a healthy strong outspoken staff here now. The days of growing pains are over and the time of maturity and large expansion has come.

With Ruscoe's reappointment the staff proposed a new concept – the position of 'General Secretary' for Rubi, with a mandate to have an advisory role in the conduct of all WEC bases and fields. He wrote round concerning this:

When reappointing Rusiko, the staff here invited me to continue on an official basis with them as General Secretary, functioning between here and Britain. This gives me the right to investigate, advise, criticise (I trust in the right spirit) etc., but without authority. I am glad of this, as on earlier visits, I felt merely a visitor and was reluctant to be too outspoken, in case it was felt that I was interfering. Now I can feel part of them, as of Britain, with this right of a voice in things. The staff added a recommendation that other fields and home bases should regard me in the same light. Actually fields and bases do give me the privilege (or I take it!) of sticking quite a long nose into their affairs, by way of advice, questioning, etc. I think the point is that, being as wide-flung as we now are, already on twenty-five fields and eight home bases, there will gradually arise the need of some more coordination without red tape or over-all authority. Some have already mentioned feeling so isolated on their fields, as if WEC was hardly one solid unit at all. This is a point.

Also questions are beginning to arise which need sending around – almost the idea of a Leader's Council in action by letter. Thus, for instance, I have recently sent round from the British staff the suggestion of the triennial re-election of the leader (all replies so far, by the way, have been in favour). Then we shall be sending from this staff this matter of how to handle married candidates, and probably later a word on faith and mortgages. It might be good, if, being freed more now from direct responsibilities in Britain and here, I act as kind of coordinator and see if I can develop something along this line. So far, I suppose, these occasional circulars can be the nearest attempt at a coordinating news sheet. But to do this, I think I would need a word from the fields and home bases, such as USA has now given me. We might then make an arrangement by which any field which wanted to submit some suggestion to the whole of WEC, could do so by sending it to me and I will get it around.

Norman had always resisted the concept of bosses and servants, managers and managed, and his spirit did not easily accept this role. In fact to minimise the danger of WEC having an over-all 'boss' his next general circular spelt out the task as being very definitely advisory.

APPOINTMENT AS GENERAL SECRETARY

The last point in my previous circular concerned the proposition by the American home base, to which the British also agreed, that the time had come, with so many fields and home bases, for someone to act as a coordinator; and it was suggested that I be that – a kind of General Secretary.

In order to disperse any possible fears, may I make it clear that this position carries with it no authority whatsoever. It is only coordinating and advisory, It allows me to corrrespond with you all and discuss field and home matters (as I already do). It means also that I will channel around to you all the questions raised for decision, such as the above points; but I think such questions should be confined to anything raised by a field leader on behalf of his field or home base, and not merely by an individual.

Finally, as this is a new position in WEC, I would make it clear that it only continues subject to the three-year re-election, and that I claim no right to appoint a successor, and that there is no need for the post to continue at all, if later it does not appear to be of God. This is all said to insure against any feeling that the hidden hand of a dictator is creeping in!

The same letter is also memorable because of his clear statement on voting, which, to him was anathema.

We have never used the voting system in WEC, although I note that one or two fields have adopted it. *Principles and Practice* does say that in the event of a crisis, after a day of prayer a two-thirds vote can be final. But we do not believe that this is the highest way God has taught us of deciding things. We believe that a company should wait on God with full and free discussion, the oldest to the youngest being at liberty and encouraged to speak the truth from the heart according as they see it; then the decision should be according to the general 'sense' of the meeting. If obviously the overwhelming majority is for one decision, then probably that is the mind of the Spirit, and the one or two who don't agree should willingly place their conviction on the altar and go in with the others in hearty acceptance; but if there is quite a sizeable minority opposed, it would seem an indication that God's mind had not yet been revealed, and there should be a delay in making a decision; or even, if necessary, a postponement until next conference. At all costs we should seek so to be not only of one heart (which we are) but of one mind, that divisions or resignations following decisions become out of the question. God's Word plainly exhorts us to go on and through at all costs till we find the one mind as well as one heart (Phil. 1:27; 2:1, 11; 4:2; 1 Cor 1:10).

In all these matters, we can get terribly bound up by fiddling details of procedure. Let us keep as free and natural in the Spirit as we can, so that our so-called business meetings are more in the form of a family fellowship than a council of war.

As previously mentioned Norman returned to the UK in 1951 with a commission to write the biography of his friend and mentor, Rees Howells. This was not plain sailing.

Mr Howells had made some predictions regarding the course of World War II which did not eventuate. So while there was respect for the testimony of the Bible College of Wales and Mr Howells' spiritual perception, the confidence of the general Christian public had been eroded.

This in turn caused the British staff to try to put the brakes on Norman accepting this commission. But he would have none of it. The writers can remember the actual staff meeting in which he said, 'I'm going to write this biography even though I have to leave WEC to do so.' At that the staff capitulated.

Later, when writing to Roy Hession about this disagreement, Rubi wrote:

As to the Howells book, I think it is true that I would not go so far as you in accepting the voice of the fellowship as the final word. I believe that in the final issue we have to preserve our walk with God alone and our following of what appears to us to be His voice. I believe the Howells book will be an evidence of this. I haven't a shade of doubt – and I am a person who does have doubts – that I obeyed the Lord in this, and I believe a mighty blessing will go with it and that the Lord will manifestly seal it.

Dr Kingsley Priddy, a staff member of the Bible College of Wales, remembers Rubi coming to Swansea to write Mr Howells' biography:

My first period of close contact was when he came in '51 to write *Rees Howells – Intercessor.* He was with us for a few weeks then. The poor chap had a very hard time and said that he felt like Daniel in the den of lions!

The bulk of the material he had to work from comprised books of handwritten notes which secretaries had meticulously and diligently made of Rees Howells' meetings. Mary Henderson had carefully gone through all of these, cataloguing and indexing the references to each main event and period of his life.

The Spirit had given him the plan of the book but in putting flesh on the bones his idea was to let Rees Howells tell things in his own words. So his first manuscript consisted of great chunks of stuff taken out of the notes, which he linked together to make a continuous narrative. The result was a disaster! So he had another go, but this was not much better. He was still trying to hang on to Rees Howells' own words, only putting it all into the third person. We had to tell him that what was coming through was just not Rees Howells. At which point he said, 'Well, if that is the case I will just have to pack up and leave; because that is all I can do.'

But it was the Lord who had spoken to him and commissioned him to write this biography – we had not asked him to do it. I knew what he could do because I had read *C.T. Studd* so we urged him to be himself and write it in his own way, as he had done with *C.T. Studd*. It was then that he let out the stratagem the enemy had been using to prevent God's truth from coming through. Norman said, 'How can I, in my own words, talk about spiritual positions that I have never reached? He must be allowed to tell it himself in his own words.'

So I asked him how God had been able to make known all that He wanted us to know of the life and teaching of His own Son. If the Holy Spirit could give us everything we needed to know about the Lord Jesus through Matthew, Mark, etc., could He not make available all He wanted to, about a man, Rees Howells, through him? He had no answer to that and saw how he had been limiting the Holy Spirit. It seemed that the blockage was removed and, as we then worked with him, the Spirit gave him liberty and the ultimate work flowed from his pen. When we read that, we exclaimed, 'This is it!'

A unique characteristic of Rubi's ministry was his ability, indeed his passion, to hold on to and encourage workers who had unusual or unique gifts but were individualists and did not easily fit into the WEC team. At staff meetings dogfights often ensued with Rubi strongly backing the individual, and the staff declaring its conviction that this person would never have a fruitful ministry in WEC. One of these cases was Heini Germann (later Germann-Edey) whose ministry in Indonesia was crucial to WEC's expansion in that land. His story is intertwined with that of Harold Williams, a placid Australian team-man who was the key figure in the start of the work in Borneo.

Harold and his wife Alice had served for many years in Congo where Harold had been a right-hand man to Jack Harrison (who succeeded Studd) and Jack Scholes (who succeeded Harrison). They were on leave in Australia when they received a letter from Rubi asking them to consider assisting in the advance in Borneo (Kalimantan).

Indonesia (or the Netherlands East Indies as it was then) had always been one of WEC's targets from the days when Mrs Studd functioned as mission secretary in London.

It was not easy for the Williamses to give up Congo, but recognising the mission's need for a senior couple to lead the new advance, they agreed to go. With the co-operation of the Christian and Missionary Alliance acting as sponsor, permission was obtained from the Dutch government to enter Borneo.

The area where they commenced had practically no road system, the arteries of travel being the rivers. For several years the Williams' home was a primitive house-boat providing three bedrooms, a kitchen and bathroom, built upon a raft of large logs lashed together and tethered to the bank. These conditions almost cost Alice her life. She fell, unnoticed, into the deep water and, being unable to swim, would have lost her life if she had not been rescued at the last moment.

We leave the Williamses at this point to pick up the beginning of Heini Germann's pilgrimage to WEC. He came over from Switzerland to the WEC headquarters in London in order to learn English. His

vacated bedroom was occupied by David Batchelor, a young Scottish
WECer who was trying to establish a base for WEC on the Continent.
So, in a sense, Heini's home was the birthplace of WEC in Europe.

Heini fell in love with the mission's unorthodox methods, and also
with Agnes Edey, a new worker from Canada, who with Leona Passmore,
had hoped to go to Spanish Guinea. However, as only one visa was
forthcoming, this was given to Leona. The romance blossomed: Heini
completed the candidate course; they were married in Switzerland, and
were sent to Australia to await developments regarding entry to Indonesia. After spending over a year in the Sydney and Brisbane headquarters they finally reached Borneo.

If Rubi ever did have a 'blue-eyed boy' it was Heini. Full of creative
ideas, restless, unorthodox, with boundless energy for new projects, he
continually had Norman's enthusiastic unfettered backing. Often this
support flew in the face of opinions and advice from other missionaries.
But Rubi saw the tremendous possibilities for advancing the work
through this young tiro and wished that WEC was elastic and resilient
enough to contain him.

Thus when he suggested moving from Borneo to Sumatra in
1951 to pioneer a new field where no missions were working, it
was Rubi who backed him and Harold Williams who encouraged
him.

In 1953 he wanted to go on to Java, and again, against others'
advice, Rubi backed this new venture, as did Harold Williams.
This move turned out to be one of the most strategic factors in the
development of the work.

Heini ministered in one of the churches in Kediri and soon
came to see that a vast field of ministry could open up among the
Protestant churches – a legacy of the Dutch occupation. They
were traditional and orthodox but lacking in spiritual life and fer-
vour.

Such a policy ran contrary to the views of a number of new
American missionaries who had been trained in schools of a very
narrow conservative persuasion. But Norman totally backed the
Germann-Edeys, seeing the vast potential for the gospel and for
missions among such churches throughout the whole country.

When Heini suggested to Rubi, during his tour of Indonesia,
that he join up with the National Council of Churches he was all for it.
Although this organisation in America and Europe was liberal in its

theology, in Indonesia it was orthodox. Heini arranged for associate membership only, but even this opened many doors for effective ministry.

After the Germann-Edeys' furlough it was agreed that they be recognised as an 'extension department', separate from the church planting activities of WEC. This gave Heini the freedom, together with Pak Octavianus and Detmar Scheunemann, to commence the Bible Institute at Batu, East Java, which Rubi described as the most significant move for WEC since the revival in Congo.

Rubi was able to visit Java in 1954 after the conclusion of his Australian tour. He was amazed at what Heini was doing. His fertile brain, crusading spirit and strategic genius was leading him into all kinds of valuable 'sidelines'. He invited Scripture Union to co-operate. He established a link with Gospel Recordings. Over 900,000 records in 131 dialects were eventually distributed, along with thousands of gramophones. He contacted Moody Press who shipped thousands of tracts and books to him for distribution. He was also instrumental in the commencement of World Vision.

Heini drove Rubi around and one night stayed with a rich Chinese man who had been blessed by his ministry. Heini recollects:

He had a ping pong table. Rubi watched them, and the Chinese man said, 'Do you play ping pong?' Rubi said, 'Yes, I play ping pong – with the devil.'

CHAPTER 14

BROKENNESS AND OPENNESS

Honesty, humility and teachableness were three characteristics of Norman's life. They were factors which greatly attracted him to the Ruanda revival in E. Africa with its strong emphasis on brokenness (humility), openness (honesty) and challenge (readiness to bring a spiritual truth to another who needs it).

But there were other factors that pushed Norman towards the revival messages. He was deeply aware that WEC's 'strong suit' of absolute faith did not provide the answers to problems of interpersonal relationships. In field after field he had watched great men and women of faith pioneer new areas, commence a great work, yet flounder in defeat when they could not handle the succeeding wave of new workers. He sought an answer and found it in the Ruanda message.

After his 1949-50 tour of the Congo field he asked Jack Scholes to take him 500 miles over the mountains to the CMS work in Ruanda. Here he saw genuine fellowship, spontaneous joy and total honesty in confessing sin. He describes his own experience:

Brokenness is obedience; indeed is the simple outcome of obedience to the light. But for many of us the brokenness to which we are now referring, including openness before men, starts by being really costly. The reason is obvious. The walls of reserve and self-esteem have gone so high, probably without our ever realising it, that the first step into this brokenness is probably a big one. The walls of Jericho have to fall down flat! I certainly found that, and so have many others.

In my own case I suddenly found myself face to face in Central Africa with a brother whom I had met and disliked in England! I had disliked him only because he was too open for my taste, although I had not at that time traced the real cause of my dislike; I was not ready enough for the light in those days. But here I was in a revival company where dislike was only another word for hate which was faced and brought to the light as sin; and I was carefully pretending that I had brotherly love for a man whom in the white and black terms of 1 John, I 'hated'! It was then I found how high those walls of pride are. I just could not bring myself to admit in public that I had the sin of dislike against him, and equally the sin of hypocrisy against all my brethren in pretending that I did like him. As a senior visiting missionary, I could not let on that I had such a 'foolish' thing in my heart. But it was not foolish, it was sin, which crucified my Lord.

To say I could not bring it out was to deceive myself; I could, but I wouldn't, that was all. I had to learn obedience to the light. At last, after two days, under the constant inner compulsion of the Spirit, I just took the step of cold-blooded obedience, brought it into the light before the brother and all, and of course the blood reached me at once; there was the cleansing, the love of God in my heart, and the joy of the whole company. I love and honour that brother today. That is why the first step into brokenness is probably a big break.

He also recounts how he saw the brokenness/openness principles worked out in a church situation:

In Africa, in a formal Sunday morning service, I saw an interpreter who had been corrected in a mistaken interpretation by someone in the congregation, stand up five minutes later, as the service ended, to tell the whole congregation that God had dealt with him for having resentment and pride in his heart because he had been corrected. Not only did he have an immediate restoration of the joy of the Lord instead of carrying hardness and resentment about for a day, but the testimony released a moving of the Spirit among the people, who carried on with testimony and praise meetings in groups outside the building.

One final word about the way revival starts. It begins by one person who sees from God what it is to walk in the light. But to walk with Jesus like this involves also walking in the light with one another, horizontally as well as vertically, and that involves at least one other person. Of course, as one brother said to me, 'One would naturally start walking like that with the person nearest to you – husband and wife, brother and sister, friend and friend.' In other words, revival starts with two people being revived, and starts at home!

A confirmation of this can be seen in a message that Rubi later gave to the WEC staff at the Chicago headquarters during 1950. He lifts the curtain on his relationship with Pauline.

Pauline and I have been married thirty years, and during that time there have been big strains and battles. We are the exact opposites, I fast, she slow. I found that I had been judging her slowness as flesh, carnality, while I considered my quickness as spirituality. Only now have I discov-

ered that I have put her down for years as an appendage. Now this thing is
coming out into the light. My attitude had put her down, and she eventually accepted this which I judged her guilty of, and stayed under and in
the background. When this was brought out into the light, we saw that we
had both been guilty. My sin was putting her down and hers was that she
accepted it and slipped into passiveness. Now this has been put away we
are enjoying much greater fellowship than we have ever known before.

But, returning to the immediate impact of the revival on Rubi
during this African tour, his immediate thought was, 'How can we
get this message through to the whole WEC fellowship?' The answer
came to him – invite a team from Ruanda to come to the WEC headquarters in London. This was arranged. The writers were two of those
privileged to attend these sessions. We all arrived expecting some super
high-powered Keswick-style holiness messages. Instead we met these
humble African brothers just giving simple testimonies. In fact the first
thing they said was, 'We want to confess a failure on our part. This
morning we felt sorry for ourselves in this cold British weather, thousands of miles from our own warm country and our families. Then we
realised this was sin and asked the Lord to forgive us for not being
happy in His will.'

God used such a total honesty and openness to pierce our hearts and
make us realise what self-righteous hypocrites we were.

The first meeting ended. X moved purposefully over to Y and the
two sat down to get their relationship sorted out. Z headed off to the
telephone. Many went to their rooms and wrote letters seeking reconciliation.

Dr Helen Roseveare was a candidate living at WEC headquarters soon after Rubi's return from Ruanda and she describes his
ministry:

He spoke many times in morning prayers of the way of the cross, not
only in conversion, but also for the daily walk: 'keeping short accounts
with God', the immediate confession of sin as soon as conviction regis-
tered, listening to the still small voice of the Spirit, the quick claiming
of the cleansing of Christ's blood and renewal through forgiveness, the
restitution to any offended brother, the joy and happiness of walking in
the light. My heart was stirred. I wanted all God had for me. I began to
feel the sinfulness of pride and selfishness, lack of prayer burden, as
well as of exaggeration, or deceit or quick temper. The open way of sharing and fellowship became precious and vital.

The message of 'walking in the light' constantly came through not only in Rubi's teaching, but in his correspondence. To a lady missionary in a strongly Catholic country where the government was repressive and antagonistic he had this to say:

4th February, 1953.

Dear ....,

I was very glad to get your letter on Dec. 28. We very often think of you and pray for you. We constantly thank God for the courage and faithfulness He has given you.

It seems that in nearly all fields, especially one like yours, there is a hard sowing time. 'He that goeth forth and weepeth, bearing precious seed...' To a large extent nationals have actually to see Jesus in us, barriers have to go down, hearts be melted and confidence gained, and I believe that is only done by our steadfastly sticking to the job. You will 'doubtless come again rejoicing, bringing your sheaves with you.' How hard it was in Colombia. If there was one soul in a year, it was wonderful; and yet today they have a large staff and a liberty to preach now which you have not. So we will keep believing, and the Lord is going to do the same with you.

Perhaps the most important point is that you can keep working together. 'Brethren dwelling together in unity.' Isn't that the hardest battle on the field? We can escape our defeats at home. If one can't get on with another, one goes and finds fellowship elsewhere; you cannot, and it is a marvel of God's grace when missionaries do keep loving one another. I know no way except this walk in the light. If we are each willing to accept light from the other, to accept rebuke even though we don't see the point about ourselves, if we are willing to be the first to 'break' when we are conscious of hardness, rather than demand that the other breaks, then I believe unity is possible.

May God keep you like that. We do get on each other's nerves. Temperaments are so different. To suppress our ragged feelings doesn't help; it only leads to bondage and bad nerves. It is great when God gives grace for a frank expression of the thing that rubs us, and also a willingness to confess that even the feeling of being rubbed is itself a sin. We have proved this again in our conference. Getting things into the light has melted away so much.

With the end of the war in the Pacific, General MacArthur put out his famous plea for a thousand Protestant missionaries to come to Japan and spread the gospel. The church of Christ was not deaf to the appeal, and 2,000 evangelical missionaries poured in, nearly all members of interdenominational missions. No restrictions were placed upon their entry.

The first WEC workers to enter in 1950 were long-time members of the USA home base, Lon and Yvonne Fulton, who, though without direct missionary experience, at least had a thorough grasp of WEC principles and methods. After they had arrived on the field Norman wrote to them:

Feb 20th, 1950.

My dear Lon and Yvonne,

I heard with very great interest of your Japanese call. I trust I shall not be incurring the wrath of Rusiko in writing you, but as you will have some of our [British] 'lambs' too, it will be good to have direct touch with you. The points on my heart are these:

First, as you will know, Japan has a bad reputation [in the matter of] nerves. It is said to be the worst field for that. Humanly, I think that that would be against your going, Lon; but if it is God's call, then okay; but I think it will be necessary for you to have deliverance from God in a peculiar way so that He gives real continual victory in this, because you will realise that a leader has to be the example to the others, and always go a bit further than them, so it wouldn't do for you to lead the way in conking out physically or nervously! We shall stand with you in this. I think nerves very often have a spiritual basis (though not always) and it may be that now God has shown you His real call, you may be a new man in this direction also.

I hear that you have a vision of living more like the Japanese than many missionaries do. I would suggest to you, Lon, that you go very cautiously and humbly in this direction. A new worker can never really tell the best ways of living and working; the greatest need for a new worker is to be 'clothed with humility'. I believe you would make a very great mistake if you arrived there and gave any idea to the faithful folk of other missions that you had some 'better' way up your sleeve than theirs for approaching the people. I believe you will do far more for the glory of God and for WEC, if your contacts with other folks, as a beginner, are in a 100% teachable spirit. Be eager to learn and listen, and don't experiment with new ways until after a year or two, once you have your feet well into things. Remember again that you are the first representative of two groups, WEC and CLC, and we want to win our way as humble brethren with the older groups. This will not prevent us forging out on our own lines in God's good time. I personally question your outlook of living like the Japanese; it may be possible, but I note that on practically all our fields our original theoretical ideas on these lines get much moderated by experience.

Well now, folks, I must say, like Paul, 'Suffer the word of exhortation!' I feel the great advantage of your call is that God has matured you in our ranks; you really know WEC, and I know how much you have our fundamental principles on your hearts.

You will have the additional most delicate matter of all – the handling of young lives in the Spirit. I hear you passed through storms in Toronto but that God has taught you by means of them. The only thing I can say is that you will handle others [successfully] if the Spirit is handling you! Be the FIRST to break on all occasions, the first to apologise. A leader must lead in everything and that includes 'breaking' and humbling ourselves [before] our fellow-workers. We lead in truth if we lead in being constantly crucified.

1953 started with an important international conference held at the London headquarters. Differences of view point had emerged in the three major sending bases – Britain, North America and Australia and some felt that Rubi had overstepped his authority by trying to impose his views upon these bases, thereby denying a basic WEC principle that all fields and bases retain the right to determine their own programmes, within the guidelines of our *Principles and Practice*.

This was a large conference – between sixty and seventy being present. To it came the leaders from Australia (Arthur Davidson), USA (Alfred Ruscoe), Canada (Earle Frid) plus two senior workers from USA, Bob and Bess Butters. Quite a number of other field leaders were also present, so it was a crucial time.

After it was over Rubi wrote round to all the fields giving a full account, and again we can see his openness and humility as he admits that he himself has been part of the total problem:

12th January, 1953.
Dear Fellow-Crusaders,
You will all be awaiting news of our January conference which finished yesterday, taking a week instead of the ten days we had allowed for it.

The Lord gave wonderful victory right through. We knew His presence from the first day spent around Himself in worship, prayer and the Word – Sunday, Jan 4. Our thoughts were then centred on the pre-eminence of Christ in Colossians and that the one necessity throughout the conference was that we must 'hold the Head'; and that if we did so His pre-eminence would be known amongst us by a consciousness that we were drawing from the hidden treasures of His wisdom, and not coming to man-made decisions (chap 2). His hidden life would be manifested in a spirit of humility, meekness and forbearance – the Lamb Spirit – among us (chap 3). We were also given the thought that while we already had oneness of HEART, the need was impressed on the Philippian Church that they should have oneness of MIND, and in the Corinthian church that they should actually 'SPEAK the same thing'.

There were periods of wrestlings and travail during our discussions, as would be expected; but in each case, thank God, we came through to fulness of victory. I believe every member at the conference marvels at the unity, liberty, warmth of love, and unanimity of decision which were among us.

I think we may say that the basic issue of the conference was a homebase affair. That was particularly why Arthur Davidson and Rusiko had come to join us. Real adjustment was needed in our homebase relationships and understanding of each other. To a large extent that centred around myself. Every work of God has to pass out from a stage of paternalism to a functioning fellowship, yet with a proper place given to honouring those over us in the Lord. There is a balance between leadership and fellowship in the New Testament, and that has to be found and maintained among us. We three, therefore – Rusiko, Arthur and myself – had to come to a clear, harmonious and brotherly understanding in our relationships.

Just because the work has stemmed out from Britain, first to USA through Rusiko, and then from USA to Australia through Arthur (not forgetting of course the fine work of the council before that time), it has been easy for me to have a kind of paternal attitude towards 'the younger branches', and to exercise an influence that was sometimes overwhelming, without my realising it. This has often made it difficult, especially for Rusiko, to act freely, particularly because he was used in early days in Britain to a close tie with my leadership. But we are all certain that the very heart of the way God leads us as a Crusade is the autonomy of each field and homebase; therefore we founders and leaders have to learn the sometimes painful lessons of recognising the adulthood of our sons and daughters! 'Bringing up father' as Rusiko said! But God has been giving us all a teachable spirit this week, and we have all been learners at His feet and from one another, and I do accept what God has been showing me in this matter.

Having solved the problem of sending base relationships Norman's attention was arrested by news coming in from the mother field, Congo. Letters started to arrive telling of another 'tornado' of the Spirit sweeping through the WEC stations even more powerful than when he had been there a few years before.

At every centre the pattern was the same. From Opiengi came the report that as one of the missionaries was praying the Spirit came down in mighty power. People were filled and, indeed, drunk with the Spirit. No one had ever seen anything like this. The Power and presence of the Lord was awful indeed. Elders and evangelists were reeling about shouting 'I am filled, I am filled.' Some came up to a missionary and asked forgiveness for having been critical of him. As soon as forgiveness was granted they praised the Lord again with loud voices. Then they moved on to another and did the same thing.

At Lubutu while some were singing and praising, others came under strong conviction. They shook, fell to the ground, crying and shouting in an agony of spirit. The distress was indescribable. The shame of having to confess to adultery and hypocrisy was devastating, but not only did they acknowledge these gross sins but others such as spite, name-calling, bickering, murmuring, and discontent with their work and wages. A phrase became common among them – 'the whip of the Holy Spirit'. Hardly any slept that night. Those under conviction groaned and cried. Those who confessed and sensed forgiveness broke into singing.

From Ibambi the field leader wrote:

> The Holy Ghost came down in mighty power. We have never seen any-thing like it before. Words fail to describe it, but we know something now of what it must have been like on the day of Pentecost. As one prayed, another began to pray, and another, and then the whole congregation to-gether. Such a noise, as they poured out their souls in prayer and praise to God! Men, women, boys and girls were just drunk with the Spirit, many shaking beyond their control, others throwing themselves on the floor, some leaning, some standing. One man danced about exhorting them to fear God and not hide sin, but his voice was soon drowned in the hubbub. We just stood there amazed, but were not afraid, as we knew the Spirit was working. We just walked about among them, seeking to help where we could, though it was impossible to make oneself heard. If this had not been of God, it would have been terrible, as they were beyond all human control. Although many threw themselves about, or rather were thrown down, yet none was hurt.

Egbita had the reputation of being, spiritually, the hardest and least responsive station, but God mightily dealt with 200 women who had gathered for their annual conference. One by one, they took off their earrings, beads, bangles and all kinds of jewellery, brought them out and flung them into a hat, which was soon filled and finally thrown into a deep pit.

There was deep concern among the missionaries that husbands and wives should go through together, because the average African couple has little of love and homelife. The fruits of that were seen on Thursday which was the 'glory day' in the meetings. Wives and husbands stood on the platform weeping together with arms around each other. Others were testifying together to the great joy and love God had given, as they had broken unitedly before Him. One woman stood with her husband saying 'Now I love my husband like a child', for love of children is great, but love for husbands much less common.

In the book *This is That* Norman skilfully analysed the conditions necessary for revival:

1. The floods have been poured out on prepared ground. People have had it driven home to them with all the authority of Scripture that repentance towards God, in the completed sense of renunciation of all sin, must precede a living faith toward our Lord Jesus Christ. The Holy Ghost has come to a people who can recognise sin as sin.

2. There was a prepared missionary body. Unless He first had His missionary servants walking so closely to Him, how could they have stood the sight of these consuming fires of which they have been witness? There have been confessions and breakings, meltings and revival among the missionaries too. When these terrible convictions have come like a tornado on the churches, the missionaries have been able to recognise them as the holy fire of God. It has required discernment and steadiness. None but the pure in heart, poised in the Spirit, could have welcomed the reality of such emotional upheavals and seen calmly and clearly through the contortions, cryings, fallings, jumpings and dances, to the pure stream of the Spirit flowing beneath.

3. The revival spread through the revived, life transmitting life. It is not sermons on revival, but personal revival in the speaker, expounded from Scripture and illustrated in life and testimony, that transmits revival. We transmit what we are, not what we say.

CHAPTER 15

THE OVERFLOW

Later in 1953 Rubi embarked upon one of his most extensive tours; it took him to Australia, New Zealand, Indonesia, Japan and India.

If one characteristic of this tour stood out more than any other it was his concern to see lives enriched rather than WEC promoted. Indeed, the truth is that in God's hands he became a channel for individual revival in many places.

One of these was the island of Tasmania where a real move of the Spirit occurred – a move that in God's own time was to lead to the commencement of WEC's second Missionary Training College.

Colin Haynes and his wife, Nora, had joined WEC in 1945 and for the four years prior to Norman's visit had been the mission's representatives in Tasmania.

Here is Colin's account:

In April, 1945, my wife Nora and I entered WEC headquarters in Sydney. During the nine months there we enjoyed fellowship with the staff and other candidates (one of whom is now my second wife, Evelyn, née Parish). The fellowship and, especially, the reading of Grubb's *Touching the Invisible* and *The Law of Faith* really baptised us into WEC and revolutionised my life. I learned how to pray effectively and walk by faith.

In 1949 we were asked to represent WEC in Tasmania. The highlight of those years was the visit in 1953 of N.P. Grubb, now known to us as Rubi. It was my privilege to arrange his itinerary in north Victoria and Tasmania and travel with him. After years of reading his books now I was living with him and feasting on his teaching.

At this time Rubi concentrated on revival as outlined in his wonderful booklet *Continuous Revival*. Most meetings were with small groups and there was a very warm response.

The ministry was not to promote WEC but to bring light and love to the body of Christ. You were not left with a consciousness of Norman Grubb but of the Holy Spirit's message to your heart.

In Launceston a prominent Christian said to me, 'This teaching in *Touching the Invisible* on "almighty meekness" is ridiculous and impossible to practise.' I said, 'Would you like to speak with Mr Grubb about it?' I arranged a meeting and after my friend had poured out his heart

Rubi quietly replied, 'Yes, it's a long time since I wrote that and if I were to write it again I would probably express it a little differently.' Jack was thrilled that Norman Grubb had admitted this. What the dear man didn't realise was that he had just had a demonstration of 'almighty meekness'.

After the visit five of us who had been so blessed started a prayer meeting for revival. As we prayed and witnessed to the work of the Holy Spirit, God added to our numbers until about seventy were meeting regularly; lives were blessed and transformed, and others were touched all around Tasmania and beyond. The heart of the message was our union with Christ.

Then God laid it upon our hearts to have our own WEC College where these truths could be taught to those preparing for missionary service – not just a Bible College, as there were already a number of those in Australia, but to train recruits in the principles of faith and victorious living.

These principles as taught to us by Rubi now came into operation. As we prayed we were led to a property called *Tolarno* with forty acres of land. We had no money but by faith claimed it and finally it was bought. This property at St Leonards is now the home of the WEC Missionary Training College.

All the money except £200 came from Tasmanians who had been blessed through Rubi's visit and teaching. Several donors gave all they had and one old saint gave £10 which she had saved in case of sickness; it was all she had in the bank.

One man since said to me, 'Col, I have travelled all over the world to centres of revival but never found anything to compare with what God did here in Tasmania.'

A similar work of the Spirit took place during Rubi's New Zealand tour that followed Australia. Rubi wrote this account for the British WEC magazine:

I have just finished a wonderful two months' visit to New Zealand. My difficulty is to compress all the things I would like to say within reasonable limits! The welcome I received, first from the Council and friends in Auckland (although, alas, bad weather prevented the plane from Sydney arriving in time for the welcome tea, chaired by Mr R.A. Laidlaw, with about 130 present), and then from the Lord's people of all denominations throughout the dominion, exceeded anything I have known elsewhere. One would have thought some important people had arrived in each town, instead of Alex Thorne and myself, 'the whippersnapper and the worm', as we once called ourselves from a Youth for Christ platform, and then found it in the headlines of a paper!

The tour could not have been more comprehensive in the time allowed. I think it was the most perfectly organised and the smoothest I have ever known. 'Kiwi' of Spanish Guinea – Alec Thorne – had done the organising, arranging the meetings in places which had asked for them. We travelled almost daily, except for weekends, visiting thirty-two cities and towns, and the normal strain of such travelling was wholly removed by going round in the lovely new Vauxhall car with which the Lord had provided him. This also gave us wonderful opportunity for long heart-to-heart talks on all WEC affairs, and on the Lord's personal leadings in our own lives. They were precious times of constant refreshment, joy, and heart unity; just once or twice when Satan touched either of us with a spot of annoyance or something like that, we proved the blessedness of walking in the light with the Lord and with one another. This gave us a testimony to pass on in the meetings. The Lord led Kiwi to take all expenses of the tour by faith without touching mission funds, and He most bountifully provided.

The Lord has His people here in every place. There is no revival, there never has been yet in the dominion; but there are those who love and serve Him, witness for Him and take their share in world evangelisation. I was particularly impressed with the Brethren and the Baptists. I found the Brethren very much more 'open' for fellowship than in some countries. Some of our best meetings were Saturday afternoons and evenings in Brethren halls. All through the tour we felt it our commission not to 'talk WEC' or 'push WEC', but to give His word as given to us, usually on the Person of the Holy Spirit in our lives, and the kind of things that He does in and through common people when He is free to have His own way, and on the cleansed daily 'walk with Jesus', as in the little booklet *Continuous Revival*. There was a large number of open indications of His definite work in lives, a touch of revival in one college group, and other testimonies such as this one from a young minister, who is now offering for a foreign field with WEC: 'There has been a work of God done in this town, and although there has not been any mass revival, many have come to the Lord for cleansing and are walking in the light. In the church where I am the pastor there has been a breaking down and a confessing... My own testimony is that not since the day I was converted have I known to such an extent the witness of the Spirit in my heart...'

Space prohibits a mention of all of Rubi's journeys around this time, however the following account given by Ken Roundhill of his visit to Japan is worth telling.

I have a pleasant memory of his visit to Japan in the early 50s. He was the main speaker at a summer conference for missionaries at Karuizawa.

His major theme had to do with the privileges of being in Christ – our union with Him. This must have been the early days of Rubi's special interest in that truth. His joy and conviction relating to the subject was, I tell you, very moving and was a tremendous blessing to me at the time. It made me want to stand tall and revel in all the privileges of being blood-bought. One incident during those meetings I will not forget. He was speaking about the blood of Christ and just at that moment a missionary decided to take a flash photograph of him. Rubi stopped and said very sternly indeed, 'How dare you take a photo of me while I'm talking about the blood of the Lord Jesus!' You can imagine just how small that missionary felt – deservedly so!

During that same series of meetings another great blessing was Rubi's willingness to share frankly just how the Lord had dealt with him over issues in human relationships that pointed up his frailty and humanness. Confession like that from the pulpit is not all that common, but it gave tremendous thrust to all the points he made – even if he did talk so fast!

Norman was also able to include a visit to India. He had a special interest in this land for many years dating back to the early thirties when Dr Wilf Morris pioneered a new work in the Nepal border. Wilf and Nancy had a very close relationship with Norman and Pauline. The following testimonies take up from the earlier encounters with the Grubbs, mentioned in chapter 6.

Wilfred records:

In 1934, I commenced my missionary life by spending a year at the CMS hospital in Quetta in order to gain surgical experience. During that time, Rubi was a constant inspiration to me; hardly a month passed without an interchange of letters. Considering his many other commitments this was quite remarkable.

The following year, by which time I had moved to Kohat, he sent out a prayer letter stating that WEC was looking for a place to start work on the Nepal border. At the same time, Dr Katherine Harbord, an independent missionary who had pioneered work there, had to go to England for an operation. She sent me a telegram: 'Nautanwa on the Nepal border needs a medical missionary. Will you come?' I went, and, using the medical and surgical equipment she had left behind, took up the work.

Rubi was very strong on us adopting Indian customs, clothes and food. I was distressed about this. As a doctor I knew the risks which people at home were not aware of – risks not just to myself but to future Crusaders. Eventually Rubi persuaded me and I gave in. I chose the Muslim garb which I had worn on the Frontier. But in Nautanwa there were Muslims,

Hindus and Nepalis and herein lay the crux of the problem – dress was related to religion. Once Rubi realised this, conformity in dress was dropped as impracticable. Two new recruits joined me and by the end of a fortnight both were on their backs with enteric. I nursed them for three or four days, at the same time running the dispensary, and then I went down too. All three of us were stranded, seriously ill, in Nautanwa. All this had to be conveyed to Rubi – a swift and dramatic result of ignoring Western hygiene!

Nancy comments:

It was fortunate that Dr Harbord was in London. After leaving hospital, she was able to meet with Rubi and Ma Rubi to discuss India. She was able to bring many aspects to their notice and warn them that Crusaders could not go altogether Indian – eating uncooked food from the bazaar, or living as outcasts. This could result in death! She suggested that we choose a sensible middle status, such as that of a village post-master, and not that of the outcasts. Her advice was followed, and we arranged to live in a simple village house with earthen floors.

Wilf continues:

Rubi wisely consulted a well-known missionary statesman, Alexander McLeish, of the World Dominion Press, as to areas to be targetted by this new WEC field. He suggested to Rubi that it would be good to start a hills-and-plains work in order to reduce the health risk to workers who would otherwise have to live continuously in the very unhealthy, malarial environment of the North Indian plains. In the meantime, after earnest prayer, I consulted an experienced American missionary on the subject. He too advised that we start a hills-and-plains work. I wrote to Rubi to put the suggestion to him and my letter crossed with one from him giving identical guidance. What a confirmation!

Rubi was an enthusiast and once he had seen something by faith he would go for it. By contrast, I saw the local difficulties and opportunities. Therefore, there had to be a degree of mutual acceptance. I found Rubi very understanding and willing for adjustments.

Nancy continues:

When I went out, the WEC rule was that marriage was not permissible until both had been on the field for two years. We accepted this although we had already been separated for three years. I reached India in March 1937, and in July, after conversation with Dr Harbord, Rubi wrote saying he realised that it was not a good thing for several young men and women to be without chaperones. He therefore advised our early marriage. We did not argue!

Wilf describes events fourteen years later:

When we came home at the end of 1951, we were under a cloud over the question of our leadership. Rubi was very understanding. His faith in us never diminished. He always believed the best and stood for that. I appreciated this all through our relationship with him. I failed many times but he would not concentrate on failures, always having faith that I would do better and eventually come through. In our relationship there was never any break at all. This was very wonderful because we needed all the support we could get at that time.

I always remember him saying, relative to another field where they were having serious leadership problems, 'What did Jesus do when the waters were rough? He walked on them. I'm walking in faith in that situation.' That's the line he took with us – he was walking by faith that the Holy Spirit was in control and it would all work out in God's time and way. He was always very positive.

Nancy writes about their return to India:

On our return in 1953, we were invited by an outstanding God-anointed Indian leader, Brother Bakht Singh, to stay at his headquarters in Hyderabad.

But, relative to this, I must refer back first to the time in 1941 when we WECers were waiting on the Lord with deep concern for our future ministry. This prayer was laid on our hearts: 'Lord, we don't want more "mission"; we are ready to lose our WEC label, but we want to see an Indian church raised up with the spirit and power of early WEC.'

As we fellowshipped with the believers at Hyderabad Wilfred and I looked at one another and said, 'This is it: this is WEC in Indian dress.' We felt so at home. The language was the same: 'getting through for this', 'getting through for that', 'trusting the Lord here', 'trusting for provision there', and our hearts were very much knit with them. At that time, we stayed for three months but there were to be many visits in the following years as we responded to Bakht Singh's invitations to minister to related assemblies in many parts of India.

Wilf adds:

It was during our first period with Bakht Singh that Norman Grubb made his visit to India. After his arrival the three of us had a meal together –

Bakht Singh, Norman and myself. I was absolutely astonished at Norman's behaviour because he seemed so passive, so meek, so utterly humble before this Indian leader. I had the impression that he was almost in depression. I asked myself, 'What's the matter with Rubi? This is not like him! No faith, verve or assurance!' Periodically I tried to prod him on issues, but he wouldn't respond. But the outcome was that his attitude enabled Bakht Singh to get over many of his prejudices about Western missions. Here was the leader of one of the largest showing a meek spirit, sitting there almost as a learner or disciple!

Later it became obvious that the reason that Bakht Singh opened up to ministry by WECers lay in Norman's attitude. Previously Bakht Singh had had some very big problems with some societies but Norman Grubb was so different.

When he was invited to speak at meetings there was a real stirring of the Spirit among the people. They told us that they felt freed by his ministry, which was really lovely.

Because his heart was so big Rubi was always very positive about WECers working with these assemblies. Two of those who did so were Geoff and Blanche Abbiss. The latter gained Bakht Singh's confidence and started off the whole Daily Vacation Bible School ministry which, incidentally, is still flourishing. Steve and Daphne Jacobs also had a very helpful influence as they started the Bible Correspondence Courses within the movement. Several other lady WECers laboured for years and were greatly appreciated.

Rubi wrote appreciatively of his time in India:

Most outstanding of all was my week with beloved and mighty Brother Bakht Singh at Madras and Hyderabad, where I spoke twice a day to an assembly of about 800. In the evenings, and between meetings I had hours of fellowship with him and one or two of his co-workers such as Dr Angus Kinnear, plus, of course, Doc and Nancy Morris. It was indeed a time in heavenly places, both in the meetings and in personal fellowship.

In retrospect however, it must be said that not all WECers have continued happily with the assemblies, possibly because they felt that the Eastern leadership style was too autocratic for Westerners.

Norman was able to visit nearly all the WEC stations in India. Jac and Helen Dyck, Canadian missionaries on the Nepal border describe his visit and tell of a later family tragedy:

When Norman was scheduled to visit us we told our servant that the 'Big Boss' was coming so we wanted everything just so! He worked hard and got the place just right. But afterwards he said, 'The Big Shot? He's so gentle and humble.' That was his impression. He worked that out himself. We thought that was beautiful, and true!

We had seen little fruit during the first term. But then in the second term we had started Bible Correspondence Courses and they were going like hot cakes. So we shared with Rubi how few converts we had seen in India, just some here and some there. He had been in Africa and had seen thousands coming to the Lord but he said, 'I don't think that they are any more devoted than you are.' That was an encouragement to us. There was no rebuke for lack of fruit.

Another instance of his thoughtfulness was much later in 1958 when we had had to come home with Lois, who had hydrocephalus. We finally managed to make an arrangement to take Lois home because the hospital couldn't keep her any longer. When we arrived in Philadelphia Rubi was very gracious, and we thank the Lord for him. Marie Dinnen and I took Lois to the hospital and two doctors examined the child. They said she could be saved physically but there was no point because her mind was gone. I remember that there was no bill, and was later told that Rubi had taken care of it personally. He was a great blessing to us and I'm sure to so many – his lifestyle, his testimony, and his message.

Beth Allinger from Canada and Elaine Crane of Australia had a unique ministry among Nepali people in Shillong, Assam. A good work had been built up, with 25-30 believers, but the leaders of the United Provinces field were very concerned about these two ladies being 'out on a limb' and separate from the care and fellowship of their field.

But they had resisted leaving because a national brother, who showed much promise, needed their encouragement and counsel.

They were apprehensive regarding how Rubi might view their situation. He came, took some meetings (speaking through an interpreter) and then gave his verdict. 'You girls are in the right place. This is where God wants you. You stay on and continue the work.' Beth and Elaine noted how well he fitted in, considering the primitive conditions in which they lived and worked.

And Ken and Cecily Booth were members of the Himalayan field when Rubi visited in 1953. Ken writes:

To meet him in person was memorable. He carried an air of authority and he quickly responded to fellowship particularly when getting on to issues of the Word of God and the ways of God manifest in the human heart. I first met him in India in 1953. He acted as father of the bride to Edith Shingler (née Seager). His hearing wasn't good and he gave the impression of being shy and withdrawn at times. His manner of speaking was somewhat staccato, running his words together in bursts. But he was a deep thinker and often made outlandish statements in order to produce some reaction. He would then say, 'Good, now I know what you are thinking!'

One humorous situation occurred during Rubi's time with us at the Himalayan field conference. There was to be a public session and Rubi said to us all, 'There's one thing I can't stand and that is WECers going to sleep when I'm speaking. So if you are going to sleep please don't come'; to which our leader Len Moules' response to us was, 'Don't you dare!' However whilst Rubi was speaking there came loud snoring! A cautious appraisal revealed Len's old dog sound asleep under the grand piano. Rubi's consternation was turned to guffaws of loud laughing, much to Len's great relief!

CHAPTER 16

THE FIRST TO DIE

The mid-fifties were characterised by extremely limited financial support for WEC in Britain. Rubi sent round the following letter as an encouragement to the missionaries and as a partial explanation as to why 'WEC is always poor'.

I feel it on my heart to write to you all about our British financial situation, and its effect. We cannot give any particular reason why general funds should have been specially short over the past two years or so, and certainly much less than we humanly would like to see going to the fields. All missions seem to have been in the same condition. Now this does not affect us in our central stand of faith in God alone; we know by God's grace how to be abased, as well as very occasionally how to abound! Our eye is single upon Him, and so our bodies are full of light, whether we have little or plenty. We know no second causes. If we have plenty, God sends the plenty. If we starve, God starves us. So we are praising the Lord anyhow.

But shortage does raise certain points concerning the use of the little God sends us. And here, first of all, I would point out that I think there is one clear reason why it has always been God's will to keep us on a tight-rope financially. It is because we have not hesitated, by God's grace, you on the fields and we at home, to go right forward with our commission to 'preach the gospel to every creature'. As a consequence, you all keep urging us to send out reinforcements, and we believe it right to do so. It is the constant increase of reinforcements which has a good deal to do with our tight corners in finance. When we look at the increase of our funds these twenty four years, we see that we have gone from about £5,000 in 1931 to over £100,000 all told this year; but we have equally gone up in our numbers. As well, the price of everything has increased tremendously.

So you see that we are voluntarily paying the price in our 'poverty' for our refusal to stop spreading out with the gospel, while there are still the millions in darkness. We may say, 'Why does not God send us more anyhow?' I can't tell. I can only say that all these twenty four years in which I have been at the home end, it has always been on a financial tightrope, though on occasions it is a little more ample than others. Therefore, I cannot say with any confidence that it will change. It may do so in

God's goodness, but I really think that it is the price we are honoured to pay in carrying our cross for a lost world. If we stop sending out new recruits, we probably could build up more funds for you and the existing work; but we should be straightly disobedient to God as we did so. Requests for reinforcements come from you all, as you can see by the list recently sent to you; you all say the same! Even since that list went out, we have had additional calls for twenty four for Congo, (medicals and teachers, besides evangelists), and maybe 100 for the new area being surveyed in Central India.

So I solemnly warn new recruits that they come to a mission which is probably nearer the poverty line for Christ's sake than any other. I tell them that we don't say that other missions, who take care to provide more by thinning down their intake of recruits, are wrong; but merely that God has called us otherwise. And I urge the young folks to feel free to go to another group, if they would be happier there.

My own opinion is that we shall always appear on an unsound financial basis to the world, and to much of the church. We shall always appear weak and foolish, and open to the criticism: 'Why do you talk so much of faith and yet have so little?' The truth really is that for Christ's sake we stretch and stretch what we do have to cover so much. I believe it is the glory of the Cross for us, so long as our faith-elastic can take the stretching without coming to breaking point! And it won't, for it is the blessed faith of the Son of God within us.

Relative to this challenge to faith, Brian Woodford, WEC's International Training and Resources Secretary remembers Rubi's teaching during candidate days:

One of the keys was his determination to allow God to deal with people individually. He was a great individualist. He expected workers to get their guidance direct from God. That actually allowed for expansion because it multiplied the resources and usefulness of others. He cultivated and encouraged faith in others. I would say he had a kind of loose authority. He expected people to have a hold on God equal to that which he had himself, and if you didn't, his very being challenged you to get there.

He believed that God was constantly leading and that there was a real possibility in every situation of finding God's will. Everybody recognised an anointing in Rubi, and expected him to lead us into God's will as a fellowship.

I think another thing in his leadership style was his humility. That came through very much in fellowship decision making. Rubi didn't come across as someone who had the answer, he came across as someone who challenged us to find the answer, including candidates. Everyone was free to speak up. He was humble. Where there were disagreements he didn't come across as brash. And I think his holiness stood out on the practical level. He walked in peace, as far as one could tell, even when there were pressures around him. He sought to walk in the presence of the Lord.

I was attracted by the principles that I saw in action and I wanted to get into that lifestyle. There was a humility, an openness to others, and a simple lifestyle, just getting along with the basics.

How should the director of an interdenominational mission handle criticisms and challenges from denominations in the home countries? Some of Norman's replies to such confrontations reveal him at his best. Here are two. The first is from a Pentecostal pastor querying WEC's attitude to the movement and raising some pertinent issues. The second is from the secretary of a large denomination who felt that WEC's influence was divisive. Names have been omitted for obvious reasons.

Dear Brother,
Greetings in the Name of the Lord Jesus Christ!
There are some of my people who are interested in the Worldwide Evangelisation Crusade, but from your literature and other members of the WEC we are not quite clear on certain points of your teaching in regard to Pentecost. Would you be kind enough to make a clear statement with regard to your attitude to the Pentecostal teaching?

1. Do you believe and teach that the baptism of the Holy Ghost is received as at Pentecost, and the evidence of that baptism is the speaking with other tongues, as in Acts 2:4?

2. Should Pentecostal believers be accepted by you for missionary work, who believed in, and had the baptism of the Holy Ghost as such, would they be free to preach and teach that the baptism of the Holy Ghost has been received, only when evidenced by the speaking with other tongues?

3. Would such a Pentecostal believer, baptised with the Holy Ghost, speaking with other tongues, and possessing the gifts of the Spirit, any of the nine (tongues, interpretation, prophecy, healing, etc), be free to exercise such gifts in WEC meetings and also on their respective mission fields and encourage their fellow believers, along with the natives, to do the same?

I would be very grateful to receive your answer in a straightforward statement concerning these points that have been raised. I have never been able to have a satisfactory answer from any member of WEC although questions have been asked me many times by other interested friends also. Trusting to hear from you as soon as possible.

Norman replied:

Dear Brother,

Thank you for your letter. I appreciate your writing in a straightforward manner, and asking these fair questions.

We believe that, according to the emphasis of the New Testament, the Baptiser is more important than the method by which He baptises a believer. We believe that this mighty Third Person of the Trinity comes into the heart of the believer at regeneration, and reveals Christ to him and in him, so that we may speak either of the Spirit in me or Christ in me.

We next believe that, as the believer has the eyes of his understanding enlightened, and is obedient to what he is shown, he enters by faith and experience into a sanctified as well as justified relationship to Christ. He discovers he needs to be crucified and risen with Christ, and as he appropriates this relationship by faith, the Spirit bears witness to him that his heart is purified, and Galatians 2:20 becomes his daily experience.

Thirdly, we believe that the Spirit in him is the Enduer with power from on high for service and witness, and that, just as he has been brought to know and experience salvation and sanctification by the Spirit, so he is also brought to know by inner witness, that this same Person is in him to be 'mighty towards others' through Him (Gal 2:8).

If the Spirit manifests Himself to any by the speaking with tongues, or by giving him any of the other gifts, we praise God; but we do not say that speaking with tongues is the necessary evidence of the baptism of the Spirit. As a consequence, any who holds the conviction that speaking with tongues is the necessary evidence, and that they must lead believers through to that exact experience, would not be happy in our ranks.

Any particular gift is of minor importance compared with the necessity of us all together growing up into Him in all things. We have a number like this in our ranks.

We believe in the full freedom of the Lord's people to use all gifts of the Spirit given them, and for that reason to call ourselves an interdenominational society. But it is fair to say that in a society as large as ours, with so many differing viewpoints of doctrine and experience, our members naturally use discretion in stressing any particular point. In the question of tongues, for instance, I have never heard any of our workers speak with tongues in our meetings, although a number use this gift in private worship (1Cor 14:27).

I hope this clears the points you raise. We seek fellowship with all God's people. We believe that God gives different revelations and experiences of the Holy Ghost to different groups of His people, and that He expects them to be true to their convictions. We believe that for this reason there will always be a place in the one body for variety, and that all the emphases together – Brethren, Holiness, Pentecostal, etc., – approximate to the perfect man in Christ (Eph 4:13). Where groups of believers are called strongly to stress their particular emphasis, then let them stand together in doing so, though with a larger charity to all. For ourselves, we feel called to a middle position which can contain around the one centre, Jesus Christ, all who feel called to preach HIM to those who have never heard, without too great stress on points of convictions which may be divisive; and God seems graciously to have prospered us so far in this way.

May God greatly bless you in your ministry,

Yours in Christ,

A denominational secretary wrote:

Dear Brother,

We have a situation in some of our churches that has caused us some concern. Certain of our churches have had frequent visits from representatives of your mission and unfortunately their activities in the cases we have in mind have created divisions among the members of the churches and unhappy situations have resulted.

We would hasten to assure you that we are in sympathy with the aims and the purpose of WEC. We have no objections at all to WEC representatives having access to our churches. As a matter of fact, missions like your own receive a considerable amount of support from them.

This is our problem however – in churches where prayer groups have been established by your representatives the groups have become, by their attitudes and their emphasis upon certain matters of opinion, isolated from the general work of the local church. This has often resulted in divided aims and loyalties, and there has been a consequent division and some ill-feeling between members. One feature of the problem is an unwillingness to tolerate any different point of view on certain aspects of Biblical truths and behaviour. We would add that it is not so much the rightness or the wrongness of the beliefs that we are concerned about, but rather the spirit that judges and would exclude any different opinions.

We are writing to you as the world leader of the mission feeling that these suggestions could help:

1. That in the establishment of groups in churches their purpose be kept in mind – i.e. to enlist support and create interest in mission field.

2. That they should never become, as has been the case, groups fostering any particular theological position or emphasis.

3. We feel that your representatives should encourage always a strong sense of loyalty to the local church. It is vital (and you would agree) that the witness of the local church should never be weakened by movements within its own fellowship. All Christians need to feel a sense of responsibility to the church, for after all it is the divinely appointed channel of presenting the gospel to the world.

We have written, not only because of our experience, but because we believe that these situations are out of harmony with the spirit of your organisation.

Sincere Christian greetings.

Norman's answer was;

Dear Brother,

Your letter of June 24th reached me today. Many thanks. I am glad that you have brought this matter to our attention. I think it can be a helpful word to us through all our home bases and regional headquarters, and I shall send a copy of your letter around to them.

I wholly agree with the points in your letter, and it is our desire and aim to work in exactly these relationships with all the churches of Christ in all denominations which are true to the Word of God. We foreign missionaries are only representatives of the churches of Christ; and we interdenominational missions, because we have no special group of home churches standing behind us, are in a special degree grateful to and appreciative of churches that open their doors to us; so we must be the very ones who take every care, not to disrupt, but to add to the fellowship and ministry of these churches. This is our clear and definite policy.

As you say, we each have our particular emphases on the life and ministry in the Spirit; I suppose ours comes under the four headings: sacrifice, faith, holiness and fellowship. But anything which is not held in deep humility for our own shortcomings, and appreciation of the measure of the Spirit in others, is certainly not in the Spirit. I grieve, therefore, to hear that you can point to some groups who are in contact with us or form WEC prayer fellowships, but are critical of their fellow believers, and divisive. I can only assure you, and I know I speak for all my co-workers at WEC home bases, that we stand four-square for integration with the churches and continued fellowship with them, and against censoriousness or separation. The only exception might be a group in a modernistic or worldly church. But even then, we would strongly advocate that these believers stand fast as humble witnesses to Christ in their churches, and only move out, if they have most definite leadings from the Spirit to do so.

I am immediately sending a copy of your letter and my reply to our general secretary in your country. I know he and I hold the same viewpoint as I have outlined above. But he can only deal with instances of this if there are known cases where a word of exhortation is needed. Doubtless he will get in personal touch with you.

Finally, I would again assure you of our agreement with what you say; but if you feel that there are still points to be raised which are not settled by this reply, or any further action we might take, please feel fully free to write me. It is only to the glory of God that we should wholly stand together, the churches who represent Christ in the home lands, and we who are their representatives on the foreign fields.

Sincerely yours in Christ,

As fields began to be fruitful and as national churches started to develop, Norman applied his mind to the whole issue of mission strategy. In 1953 he put out a 'round robin' letter to field leaders in particular and to all crusaders in general.

1. NATIONAL CHURCHES TO INCREASE, MISSIONS TO DECREASE

Now the era of world nationalism has arrived. All nations and countries are feeling and beginning to claim their rights to their independence, and we who treasure our own liberties and independence must gladly recognise their rights to the same. This has its immediate repercussion on 'foreign missions', which inevitably have the flavour of foreign dominations or influence, even though we don't intend it. We must expect, therefore, a rapid increase of your national churches, and an equal diminution in the acceptability, influence and even existence of foreign missions.

Now with these general thoughts, I want to consider with you whether we are going far enough or rapidly enough or daringly enough in the absorption of the foreign mission into the young churches, in transferring leadership from ourselves to them, in becoming as it were the hidden fertiliser in the rich young soil. I believe this is an essential part of the way of the cross for us missionaries. 'They must increase, we decrease.'

2. TRAINING OF NATIONALS

I think it is a great matter for praise that God is laying on our hearts on all fields the necessity of Bible training for the nationals. Following on from the first Bible School founded by Harri in the Congo, and then the one in Colombia, there has now been the start of Bible Schools in Liberia, Portuguese Guinea and Ivory Coast. Congo has built its work on that firm foundation – for the wives as well as the husbands; and I believe we should be equally strong and firm in not passing out of the schools any about whom we have any doubt not merely about their Biblical knowledge, but also about their having the fire of the Holy Ghost and the truly sanctified heart and life; far better hold them back indefinitely or remove them from the school than send out unsanctified material.

But concerning all these schools, in addition to the importance of them being in existence, I want again to raise the consideration as to how they can be wholly the church's school, and the mission's. Obviously no set suggestions could cover the various stages of growth in our various fields, but don't you think that we should have this objective clearly in mind not in the distant future, but in the near present? And that control should be in the church's hands (which would also include the missionaries as members of the churches), even to the point of the selection of the teaching personnel? To this end, should not steps be taken from the beginning to include responsible nationals on some committee of control, at least leading on to full control by the church?

3. WORSHIP AND MINISTRY IN NATIONAL CHURCHES
Another subject of which I suggest that we all make a further careful study, as we are now growing into maturity on several of our fields, is the method of worship and ministry used in our churches. I have a fear that we are slipping into a 'normal' form of 'conducting services', copied from the common method to which we are used at home. But are we carefully enough making sure that it is as near as possible to the New Testament way?

I already mentioned in a previous letter our careless and unscriptural way of talking of our places of worship as 'churches'. Even using the expression 'the house of God', I believe, sows a false seed. God dwelleth not in temples made with hands, and I believe we should teach our young churches that there is no such thing as a 'sacred building', but only sacred human temples of flesh and blood given over to Him. We should adopt some such name as 'house of prayer' (which is also Scriptural). I believe this is important in view of the apostasy, not only in Rome but in plenty of Protestant denominations, of linking the presence of God with a building or with outward forms.

Then in the conduct of our services or meetings, do we not tend to put all the emphasis on the leader or preacher rather than on the congregation? But in the New Testament it was on the congregation – 1 Corinthians 14:26-33. I suggest that our young churches should be trained to give free expression to the movings of the Spirit in their hearts by testimony, prayer, etc., and that this should always be a part of our Sunday morning meetings, or any meeting. Mr Studd used to do it by opening each meeting for free prayer, and to this I believe we ought to add free fellowship. Then the ministry of the Word can follow, as of course it always should. But I believe our danger spot is in allowing our meetings to become 'one man shows', where the pastor does all, and the people just sit and share publicly in nothing except the hymns. The early church 'continued in the apostle's doctrine and fellowship, and in breaking of bread, and in prayers' (Acts 2:42). This, coupled with the 1 Corinthians 14 statement, seems to me to imply a congregation taking active part, as well as being taught the Word (doctrine).

4. THE LORD'S SUPPER

That brings in also the question of the Lord's supper. Don't you think that from the beginning we should get as near as we can to the Scriptural use and method in this part of the church's worship, which has caused so much controversy and produced so much heresy through the centuries? To start with I am sure we will all agree that it is the Lord's supper, and is therefore the simple privilege of all who are His to share in it with Him and one another, with the least possible intrusion of human leadership or 'priesthood'. Therefore, for instance, we would think that the idea of one selected person 'administering the sacrament' quite unscriptural. Everything should be done to eliminate any idea or method which seems to teach a young church that this is a form of worship which can take place only when the missionary or evangelist or pastor is there to 'conduct' it. It is the Lord's supper and the communion of the Body of Christ. Must we not then be most careful to teach the churches and demonstrate in action that it is their united 'breaking of bread'? Personally I think that the Brethren are nearest here to the New Testament in having the breaking of bread each Sunday morning, and in their method of having it with no man in a prominent position.

5. LOCAL CHURCH STRUCTURE

It seems to be, therefore, that the nearest we can get to Scripture is the independent local church with its own elders and deacons, and with some of these brethren (and 'sisters' who can 'prophesy') being able to minister the Word, having had some short training in this to help them. The local church should be an active fellowship where all freely take part and the varied gifts of the Spirit in the members are exercised. Beyond this, there are full-time trained evangelists and pastors, who can give their whole time to a ministry among churches and in evangelistic activities for the starting of new churches. Finally, there are overseers who co-operate with the missionaries as their co-workers, just as Timothy and Titus did with Paul, in general oversight of full-time paid evangelists or pastors.

6. FINANCE

There is also the problem of the payment of full-time workers. Personally I only wish that the faith principle could be maintained in the indigenous church. It seems to me far healthier than the regular salary and the constant danger of wanting more security, larger increases, etc. It seems to be the way Jesus and the disciples lived, and I presume also Paul and his company. They lived by what God sent them. But perhaps that is not possible as a normal church principle. The point then arises, should a local church (or group of churches) pay their own evangelist? If so, we soon get the inequalities of a rich and attractive district in which to minister, and a poor and unattractive one. We soon get that horrible pursuit of the good and comfortable things of life which can run right through a denomination. The alternative seems to be some sort of pooling of church gifts and an equalised salary for all. Who can say which is the wisest method? The faith principle is the highest, I believe, according to Jesus' own words in Matthew 6. If there is a chance of maintaining that in the national churches, praise the Lord. If not, we have to choose between a local church (or group of churches) supporting according to their ability any full-time worker who ministers to them (which would seem to me to be the next most Scriptural method) or alternatively, pooling all church contributions and having an equal distribution between all the full-time workers, which, though it gives equality, may take away from the spirit of voluntary faith and sacrifice, and also may give a dangerous power to a committee which distributes the funds.

During 1956 the Holy Spirit did a remarkable work in the WEC churches of Portuguese Guinea (now Guinea Bissau). The acting leader at the time – Michael Tarrant – shared freely with Norman about these events and particularly on the manifestations of the Spirit. The wisdom of Norman's replies is worth noting.

It has been a great thrill to learn of the public manifestation of God in W. Africa, similar to what happened in Congo, and I am most interested to know you held back from interfering in situations which might have shocked you, had you not read how the Congo churches went through the same.

May the Lord come through more and more mightily upon you. May it not be just one touch, but continual breakings and meltings and cleansings and fillings, whether with the emotional scenes or without.

I was interested in the case of the brother who spoke in an unknown tongue. There is no doubt that God has come upon His people in these ways since the day of Pentecost. If such experiences just open the heart and mouth wider to love Jesus and testify to Him, not glorying in experience, but in Jesus Himself and they are accompanied with the humility which equally sees Jesus in others to whom He has not come with like experiences, then they can be a means by which the Lord glorifies Himself through His servants. But they also contain the danger that those who have the experience think they have some special virtue, and trust in it, and glory in it, and don't think others are right unless they have also had it. Watch against this. Keep yourself steady, and your fellow workers, and the church members. We all enjoy an emotional and releasing experience; therefore we ourselves are tempted to feel these who have not had such experiences ought to have them. No, this is off beam, and leads to division in the body. We have Jesus, we have the Person who is the power. Let us recognise Him by faith in all His fulness in us, let us centre together in Him, and let us all go on together showing Him forth according to the gifts given us, praising God with those who have special outward manifestations of Him in their lives, but also equally rejoicing in His indwelling those to whom He has not come in such outward ways. Keep that balance, and we are safe.

In a second letter Rubi gives further guidance on the question of tongues:

Thank you for your further long letter of May 20. I was most glad to get it with all the details. It is this kind of letter which lets us get in to the problems on the ground floor. I think you must obviously take a firm stand at this time on the tongues question, even if it is costly. It looks as if ultimately it may head up in a split, with some going along with the position that tongues is the only sign of baptism. Our stand is on Jesus manifesting Himself above all as in 1 Corinthians 1:24 by meekness,

humility and love. It is quite a tight-rope to walk, on the one hand acknowledging that tongues is a gift of the Spirit, given for edification in
personal worship, and for use with interpretation in believers' meetings,
yet on the other hand, it is not THE sign of the Spirit. He is in all believers, magnifying Jesus through them, producing His fruits, and leading
them all to the appropriation of faith by which they recognise that they
have been crucified with Christ and He lives in them according to Galatians 2:20. He is also in them as the Giver of power to witness and serve.
His gifts are by no means confined to the spectacular ones which are the
least, but all those listed in Ephesians 4 and Romans 12 and 1 Corinthians 12. Our centre is always and only Christ dwelling in our hearts by
faith, and we are one with all in whom He is formed. May the Lord enable
you to keep the church, members, elders and missionaries Christ-centred in this.

CHAPTER 17

FINGER IN MANY PIES

While our commission does not include giving a full account of Norman's ministries beyond WEC it would be remiss not to give some indication of the diverse groups to which he related and the many who were blessed by his visionary and teaching input. This chapter will reveal something of the extent of his influence.

Before his application to WEC in 1919 he played a pivotal role in the founding of InterVarsity Fellowship. In *Intercession in Action* he gives an account of his links with this group. This is reproduced through kind permission of Zerubbabel Inc.

I had two weeks left of what would be my final term at Trinity College. It was as if the Spirit 'came on me', as in the Acts of the Apostles. I had a strong inner compulsion to spend those last weeks in calling on all the men with whom I was acquainted there or in other colleges. Likely it would be the last time we should meet on earth, and I wanted to have a final word with them. So I did just that.

One by one, I called on them in their rooms. These were not the normal students of college age, but returnees from the war – sophisticated and mainly ex-officers of various ranks. But I spoke boldly.

The results were phenomenal for those days, though very different from the present thrilling responses in the student world. About sixteen took various steps in accepting and committing their lives to Christ. This was 'news' among our CICCU[1] friends, and they asked me to meet with them and tell more about it. I did, and as I did, once again that inner voice spoke clearly to me. 'Should not every university and college in Britain, and then in the world, have some kind of union of Christian students like the CICCU?'

Might it not be possible, even before I sailed for the Congo, to arrange some get-together where some of us in the CICCU could meet with some from other universities? I turned to two of my special friends – Clarence Foster, later Secretary of the Keswick Convention, and Leslie Sutton, who later joined us in Congo – and asked if they would meet me in Leslie's room in Queens. Even in these last weeks before Christmas,

---

[1] Cambridge Inter-Collegiate Christian Union

could they get the loan of a hall in London and ask others from Oxford and London and Durham Universities to join us in a first InterVarsity Conference? They agreed, and about sixty of us gathered.

What I only dimly realised then was that this was the birth of a world-wide movement in the colleges of the world. What actually happened was that it was agreed upon to have an annual InterVarsity Conference (IVC). This then became the beginnings of the InterVarsity Fellowship (IVF).

Dr. Douglas Johnson gave up his medical profession to become the first Secretary, and really developer, of what is now so strongly established all over Britain. Dr. Howard Guinness did the same in Canada and Australia, as did Stacey Woods in the USA under the title of IVCF (Inter-Varsity Christian Fellowship).

Now throughout the colleges of every nation, students gather under the title of InterVarsity Fellowship of Evangelical Unions (IVFEU). Many thousands of students have been brought to Christ and built up in the Word and Spirit these sixty five years, since we had that first Inter-Varsity Conference in London in 1919!

* * *

Mention has been made of Rubi's crucial role in the commencement of the Christian Literature Crusade, under the leadership of Kenneth and Bessie Adams. This led to a lifelong friendship in which the courses of the two missions and their leaders' lives were closely intertwined.

In 1947 an invitation from the North American staff of WEC went to Ken to come over for an exploratory visit.

Norman writes in *Leap of Faith:*

> It did not take Ken long to sense the challenge of this great continent with its potential in personnel, prayer and funds.

When Ken returned to England and gave his report to the annual CLC staff conference, all agreed that the Adams should be released for two years (longer if necessary) to develop CLC in USA and Canada. God certainly blessed this decision and it was four years later that WEC and CLC, through Ken's initiative, were to make a combined move that had enormous implications for the future. Norman tells the story in *Leap of Faith.*

> The finding of Camp Hill, Fort Washington, Pa, and the establishing of a WEC/CLC headquarters in North America was another romance of faith. Ken, along with others, went to inspect the property. Here is his account:

We went to look at the place on Thanksgiving afternoon, 1951. It certainly was a mess. The majority felt convinced that this place was unsuitable, so serious was the damage caused by vandalism. My reaction was more favourable. I went through every room, including the dark and dismal basement which stretched from one end of the large house to the other. Then as I looked across the grounds and saw the other stone buildings (about six in all) I felt there were 'possibilities' here in spite of their poor condition. We made inquiry through the real estate agent and found that the asking price was $150,000 for twenty four acres and the buildings! That seemed to be the end of that.

Rubi continues:

In a neighbouring district is a remarkable work of faith called Christ's Home, where difficult children are entrusted by the authorities to the care and education of its devoted workers. They are wholly a work of faith, members of a German-American community whose deep roots reach back to the piety and spirituality of those same communities in their fatherland. Many generous gifts of furnishings and produce have been shared with the Crusade from time to time by these dear friends as God has prospered them. Shortly after this visit of inspection to Camp Hill, one of the CLC workers spent a weekend at Christ's Home and, in course of conversation, learned that the owner of Camp Hill was known to several. A contact was made, and the owner expressed much interest when she found that the Crusade operated on a similar basis of faith.

Ken Adams takes up the story.

We boldly asked her for the whole sixty seven acres, with the thought of selling off some of the land. I asked what her rock-bottom price would be. After a moment of thought she made a remarkable offer. 'You are doing a good work,' she said, 'and as it is like Christ's Home to which I feel very attracted, I will let you have everything for $65,000.'

Then followed a series of 'miracles' that resulted in WEC and CLC obtaining joint ownership of the property: a further reduction in the purchase price of $5,000, the encroachment of a new expressway on to the property, with appropriate compensation, the contractor's desire to purchase 'fill' from the site for the construction of the roadway, gifts from friends, and a large anonymous donation of $35,000 for renovations.

The Grubb family moved to USA in 1952 and took up residence in the WEC section, but some years later Ken Adams took the initiative to provide ground within the CLC area for a permanent home for their latter years.

Ken and Rubi kept up a constant flow of correspondence over many years, Rubi continually backing Ken in the development of literature centres overseas. Here is just one example:

December 21, 1965

My dear Ken,

I was very grateful that you had passed on to me a copy of your Bangkok personal letter of September 17 together with the notes on the constitution. I can only say that I am just thrilled all the time at the greatness of the purposes of God blossoming out through you and CLC. This is just the kind of thing I saw in embryo when we started, and all you've presented to the CLC for the expanding future in these notes and comments is like you moving out again into a fresh, new era for CLC worldwide. How wholly I am with you. God always planned for you to become what you are now becoming, and I can only be so thankful for the personal way He has led you and Bessie through many rough passages (and that's where we're really made) into your present maturity and leadership, and your growing staff with you. How I thank God too that you have had your Bessie with you in all this, with her tender loving spirit enveloping us all, and how God is blessing your girls too. You are, indeed, blessed. I heard how the devil also had an incidental dig at your ribs, or at least Bessie's ribs, in your automobile accident. Thank God you can still both go forward.

Rubi's interest in and support of CLC was intense and he constantly called on the parent mission to make sacrifices in order to see CLC advance.

Ken and Bessie Adams' daughter, Marge Almack (who with her husband are now part of the leadership team in CLC, USA) reflects on the Grubbs:

My parents had a deep respect for Norman and Pauline, and that rubbed off on me too. I loved them as people, I loved them for their love for my mum and dad, I loved them because of the visionary man that he was and the way he inspired mum and dad, and for the way he stood by them when they went through some really deep waters. Norman was there for them; Pauline was there. They helped my folks in all sorts of ways.

***

At the end of the fifties a young seminarian was just finishing his course
and with his wife, was thinking of a future pastorate. However he had a
burden for missions and because of his interest in Israel was actually
leading a Bible study for some Jewish Christians in Westchester, N.Y.
He tells his own story:

I decided to explore every possible avenue. Having met a few missionaries associated with the Worldwide Evangelisation Crusade, and having
been impressed with their dedication, I felt led to check out the possibilities there. One afternoon Dede and I left the children with friends and
drove down to the WEC headquarters at Fort Washington, Pennsylvania,
just outside Philadelphia.

Driving along the banks of the Schuylkill River, we turned up the steep,
winding road on the mountain behind the Christian Literature Crusade
headquarters where Dr. Norman Grubb, head of the WEC, lived with his
wife. Mrs Grubb, daughter of famed missionary, C.T. Studd, met us at the
door of the apartment and ushered us into Dr. Grubb's study.

He was expecting us and offered us a scat at the far end of the room,
apart from his cluttered desk and typewriter where he had produced so
many books that had blessed the Christian world. Advanced in years and
yet still active and healthy, he settled in an easy chair and listened to my
presentation. Obviously, however, he had no leading from the Lord that I
was to come as a missionary with WEC.

'Here we are,' I said impatiently, 'my wife is a graduate nurse, I have
a law degree and will soon graduate from seminary, and we're both volunteering to go as missionaries. What would you like for us to do?'

'There's far more to missions than simply volunteering,' he said in
his English accent. 'You have to be called.' 'But we're desperate,' I said,
'we'll do anything God wants us to do.'

'Even though you are both eminently qualified, it would be wrong for
WEC to accept you as missionaries if God has other plans. We would, in
essence, be standing in the way of God.'

'But it seems a tragic waste for us to just sit around twiddling our
thumbs,' I argued futilely. 'It would be a far bigger tragedy for you to get
into something God has not called you into,' he said kindly. 'For us to
make a place for you in WEC just to make you happy would be a mistake.
In fact, we have a place where you and your wife could serve right now.
We need men and women like you, but only if God has called you specifically.'

I got up and walked up and down the room, careful not to bump into
the various artifacts that crowded his desks and shelves. 'But the Bible
says, "Go ye into all the world and preach the gospel to every creature,"
and I have assumed that is my call to missions.'

'No, no,' Dr. Grubb said, clasping his hands in front of him, his white moustache bristling. 'God's written Word is the *general* guide to his people; but remember, Pat, the Spirit gives the guidance, not the Book.'

Dr. Grubb got up from his chair and put his arm around my shoulders, signalling it was time for us to go. 'God calls all His people to go into the world and preach the Gospel to every creature. Now it's up to you to wait on the specific direction. I sense His call to you will be in ways quite different from any others in the past.'

We walked to the door and stood on the concrete stoop. The huge trees towered above the house, and the wall of greenery shut out most of the sound of the busy traffic on the turnpike in the valley below. 'I believe God has great things in store for you in the near future. Wait on Him and pray. One day you will thank Him that WEC did not stand in the way by taking you on as missionaries.'

That young man was Pat Robertson of the 700 Club who, soon after that interview in 1961, commenced a radio and TV ministry that was to spread all over the world as the Christian Broadcasting Network. (We are grateful to Pat for permission to use this account from his book *Shout It from the Housetops*.)

***

In the mid fifties Norman met with a group of keen folk in Manhattan, New York. He established a close link with Irving Harris, Bruce Larson and other leaders. He was greatly drawn to the warm free vital outlook of 'Faith at Work'.

Again his catalyst ministry was evident: Norman suggested that they opened up on the West Coast and then the South, where Rubi had numerous contacts. He even arranged for a team to visit England where they were warmly welcomed by Rubi's friends.

Norman wrote appreciatively in a personal circular:

Faith at Work is spreading widely and rapidly over this country. Its emphasis is bringing the challenge of personal committal to Christ to church members largely of the older denominations, through participation on a group fellowship level. Teams of lay folks go for weekends to churches, conducting fellowships in homes, and leaving behind them continuing house groups as part of normal church life. Many ministers and churches open widely to this, because it does not draw from them, but brings life to them. The larger FAW conferences which we hold in ever-increasing numbers about the country are on the same sharing basis, with workshops on specific problems of Christian living and witness.

* * *

Another group with whom he had very close links was International Christian Leadership founded by Abram Vereide. Converted as a lad in Norway, he emigrated to USA and commenced a work for God among leaders in Seattle, WA. Norman was invited to speak at a breakfast meeting organised by Vereide and this was the commencement of a life-long friendship.

When Vereide moved to Washington DC and commenced a strategic work amongst Congressmen and Senators, Norman was often asked to address groups of these influential people.

The yearly climax of events in International Christian Leadership was a presidential prayer breakfast attended by the nation's leaders. Rubi wrote about this in 1963:

> I have been greatly privileged to work in close co-operation with International Christian Leadership which aims at bringing Christ to leaders in all walks of life. I wrote the life of its founder, Abram Vereide, last year under the title of *Modern Viking*. He has been a friend of mine for years; and it has been one of God's original ways to take a Norwegian immigrant from the sheepfolds of Norway and make him the one to start the weekly prayer breakfasts in Senate and Congress, leading on to the Annual Presidential Prayer Breakfast attended by 1,000 of the nation's leaders, the President and Vice President, Cabinet, House of Representatives, Supreme Court, Pentagon, etc. President Kennedy has attended each year. It is no milk and water message that is given, but the clear word: 'Ye must be born again'. I have attended the last five of them, leading a pre-breakfast prayer meeting for about 80-100, mostly men, and was due to present a copy of the book to the President last year; but, as Presidents do, he came a few minutes late, so that the book had to be given him privately afterwards.

* * *

The following extracts of letters from other strong evangelical groups in USA indicate something of the impact of Norman's ministry.

WORLD VISION

April 11, 1963

Dr. Norman Grubb
Worldwide Evangelisation Crusade
P.O. Box A
Fort Washington, Pennsylvania

Dear Norman,
I meant it when I said that your ministry helped me personally a great deal. I
wish I could have attended more of the meetings when you spoke. Your coming at the same time our board meeting was scheduled made this impossible.
However, reports from the staff indicate that God has really spoken through
you to the great benefit and inspiration of all of us here in World Vision.

Gratefully,
Bob Pierce,
President.

THOMAS ROAD BAPTIST CHURCH

August 20, 1962

Dear Bro. Grubb,
This is to confirm the dates you mentioned in January, to minister here at
the church. Please plan to give us the Sunday, as well as the Monday and
Tuesday. This is an answer to prayer. Your last visit has been a great blessing
to us.

The Lord is truly working in these past weeks. Many souls have come to
know the Lord, and Christians are being stirred. Last night, our prayer rooms
were filled to capacity. Praise the Lord.

Sincerely in Christ,
Jerry Falwell.

INTERNATIONAL CHRISTIAN LEADERSHIP

August 20, 1962

Dear Mr Grubb,
This is just to let you know that we are thinking about you and praying for
you. How thankful we all are for all that you have come to mean to us. Your
life has been a constant source of inspiration and encouragement to many of
us, and especially to me.

We are looking forward to your being down this way again and trust it
will be sometime soon.

As always,
Doug Coe.

Another who was linked to International Christian Leadership and who was influenced by Norman, was Wallace Haines, who held the office of 'Associate Secretary General' of ICL. Wallace fulfilled in Europe a similar role to Abram Vereide in Washington. Based in Paris, he conducted a ministry among political leaders as well as having links with European royalty.

He writes about Norman:

I think he taught me more than anyone the principles of discipleship and the truth of 'Christ in you' (which would come up in every letter he wrote to me). While there were many reasons in my personal background for me having doubts and fears about this ministry, he always encouraged me, and I think, thought of me as Vereide's spiritual and idealogical successor.

In England I had close contact with Lord Caldecote and George Thomas, Speaker of the House of Commons, and in Paris we had a large villa as a 'Fellowship House', to which Norman would come and minister.

Norman and I had a mutual interest in the Christ-centred mystics, especially Jacob Boehme, William Law and St. John of the Cross.

He eschewed Pantheism and would have none of it. He was soaked in the Word, but not a diehard fundamentalist. He sought truth wherever he could find it, always testing what he found by the Word and the faithful inner light of the Holy Spirit.

CHAPTER 18

THE FINAL STRETCH WITHIN WEC

In 1956 the decision was made that, for a number of reasons, Norman and Pauline should be released from Britain in order to take a leadership role in N. American WEC.

Len and Iris Moules, who had been leading the Himalayan field in India, were appointed to succeed them in Britain. Len, with his several years of army officer experience in World War II, was a gifted man both in ministry and administration, and it wasn't long before the new broom was sweeping clean.

Iris Moules recalls encountering some on-going problem situations. She says:

Rubi was so taken up with the wider picture that he had not concentrated on nitty-gritty administrative details. Of course his strength was vision. He was always concerned for advance, and this meant being strong in faith. He was head and shoulders above us all in that regard. As long as he knew what God's will was, he would go for it. The thing I liked most about him was his openness, his frankness; he was so down to earth in his vision and in his communication of it. He was so approachable.

In Len's mind, administration was very much to the fore. He was the first one to introduce keeping minutes of staff meetings. (Often he would attend a staff meeting only to find that everybody had their own interpretation of what was decided at the previous one. This had to be stopped!)

When the decision was reached about Len taking over, Rubi spent a month with him going over the task. I feel he had a great grip on things and what was happening. He understood people's situations and seemed to be able to take up anything that was happening at any time. But I would not say he was a pastoral type in the modern sense. We were so challenged to be crusaders that we didn't look for that. I suppose he was a bit like Garibaldi who gave his soldiers red shirts so they wouldn't see the blood from their wounds. I think that was our attitude, you didn't look at your wounds, you got on with the fight.

We had a picture of the head of Christ – I can't remember the title or the artist – and Norman would say, 'Take that thing down; it's an insipid looking thing, that's not my Jesus.'

These final years of active service within WEC in N America, 1957-66, were probably the most difficult for Norman and Pauline. A multiplicity of factors contributed to this.

Firstly the N. American staff did not have the familiarity with his teaching that the British staff had.

Secondly, tension continued between the WEC and CLC. The Grubbs aligned themselves sympathetically with the latter. Of course they had consistently backed and encouraged the leaders, Ken and Bessie Adams since 1941 and felt strongly that WEC's responsibility was to support the offspring mission totally. They saw no problem in the fact that CLCers could attend WEC staff meetings ('Aren't we all one?') yet CLC conducted their own staff meetings apart from WEC ('We have a special function!'). The WECers felt, quite naturally, that this was unfair – CLC, it seemed, was autonomous, but WEC wasn't! Only the Grubbs and a few senior WECers supported this arrangement, but to newer, younger WEC staff it was an inexplicable anomaly. The issue was not settled until 1964 at a meeting of WEC's Consultative Council at Camp Hill.

The third difficulty was the demands on his time as International Secretary, and the fact that the popularity of his teaching ministry took him all over USA for more than half his time. These two factors resulted in a feeling amongst Camp Hill WEC residents that he was not getting to grips with WEC affairs.

By the late fifties it was decided that N. American WEC should be led by an executive committee of seven men chosen by the staff. Rubi was thus released from the administrative demands of national affairs and freed to develop his teaching role, as well as continue what he called his 'WEC watchdog' task as General Secretary – a task which he did not see as major since it was essentially advisory.

But WEC had been growing internationally by leaps and bounds and the small consultative group with whom he shared correspondence (leaders of UK, NZ, USA and Australia) felt that an international conference of leaders should be called in 1961 to deal with a number of important issues and to make strategic decisions regarding future directions for the mission.

It turned out to be indeed a watershed event and had important implications for future development. Describing it sometime later Norman wrote:

In 1961 we had the first leaders' conference in our history, at Kilcreggan, the lovely house and 30 acres of ground given us in Scotland for a conference centre. Sixty of us gathered for four weeks from all parts of the world, all leaders. The thrill to me was to see the younger generation arising and taking on the same principles upon which the Crusade was founded by C.T. Studd – sacrifice, faith, holiness and fellowship. There was a marvellous unity through those weeks, as we looked back and saw the expansion to a staff of nearing 1000, in forty mission fields, nine home bases (in sending countries), in the two Crusades which have been born of the one, WEC and Christian Literature Crusade. I was asked to write and have completed a small brochure on these four principles, their meaning and function in our ministry, called *The Four Pillars of WEC*.

It was at this conference that Leslie Brierley presented the 'Nineteen point programme'. It was a survey of areas in need of missionary occupation: Brazil (south and inland), Senegal (Jola tribe), Gambia, Portuguese Guinea (Moslem groups), Mauretania, Chad (central and west), Mozambique, Tunisia, Libya, Somalia, Arabian Peninsula (by 'tentmaking' ministry), Borneo (Ketapang), Thailand (Uttradit), Turkey, Iran, East Timor, Cambodia (NE), France (50 cities), and Sardinia. Leslie was appointed WEC's first International Survey and Research Secretary.

It was then that the term 'General Secretary' was changed to 'International Secretary', and a Consultative Council set up to assist and advise Norman Grubb in his role. The members were to be the leaders of the five large sending bases – UK, USA, Australia, NZ and one of the three European sending countries (Germany, Switzerland, or Netherlands)..

In 1963 – the jubilee of C.T. Studd's going to the heart of Africa – the Grubbs wrote a personal circular which included these paragraphs:

The only field I would have space to mention is Congo. We express joy at the Congo churches' attitude in their season of fiery trial. If ever we were thankful that C.T. Studd laid no superficial foundations, and was never content with nominal profession, it was these days; for Christ had come to live in many Africans, and so the transition was not from missionary to African, but from Christ in the one to Christ in the other. The Congolese churches quietly assumed their responsibilities, in fullness of brotherhood with the missionaries, and have been going forward, as appreciative as ever of all the help we can still give them.

I spend more than half my time away from home and WEC affairs, because the open doors and invitations take me all over this country and Canada with the 'Christ in you' truth. So many know justification as an inner realisation, but not unification, not having come to the conscious-ness of the unity by the faith which substantiates a fact, in which He is my other self (the best way I can interpret Paul's 'nevertheless I live, yet not I, but Christ lives in me'); yet the paradox remains that within this unity is the duality (the little i and the big I), and our little 'i' is the means of the self-manifestation of the I AM. Marvellous.

I have put this in writing through three previous books, *The Law of Faith, The Liberating Secret,* and *The Deep Things of God*; but God seems to have given a clarity beyond any of the others in the most recent – *God Unlimited.* I am having very many evidences that it is bringing light to readers more than any of the others. Around the country, whether to large congregations, or in very many cases these days, to house groups, I find myself 'compelled' to stick to this one line which meets the needs of hearts.

Pauline is about the same, never too fit, but she carries all the bur-dens of our family life, giving herself wholly to the bringing up of our two grandchildren, Paul's Sandra 15 and Nicky 13, and so freely giving me for my wandering life. She is our backbone – we have been married 44 years. How good God has been to me. Our daughter, Pris, is with us. Our youngest son, Daniel, teaches high school in Michigan. He got his BA at Wheaton, MA in teaching at Duke University, one of the best uni-versities in the south, and now his MA in English literature at the Univer-sity of Michigan, another of the first class universities of this country. They have accepted him to study for his PhD. But God is now speaking to him about the ministry, probably Episcopalian, as he feels he should give his years to bringing Christ rather than English literature to people. We say amen indeed. Our eldest son, Paul, is in England. We did not hear from him for several years, but we are thankful we are now in touch and he tells us of his life.

As the years pass how thankful we are for the family of God every-where and the fellowship in Christ we find everywhere, with old friends in England and Europe, and many new ones in this country where we love to be. God has also been good to us in the gift of a home. Our old friend, Mrs Henry Woods of Atlantic City, who first got in touch with us years back for permission to put out a 20,000 gift edition of *C.T. Studd* for students, died last year. She left a generous gift to the work, and also her house for us. We sold this and are going to build a four bedroom house on the CLC grounds here, by their kind welcome.

Our loving greetings in Christ to you all.

In the same year he wrote round to the members of the Consultative Council ('C.C.'):

That brings me to a proposition that I think we might consider. The Kilcreggan conference in 1961 was really the beginning of a new era in WEC – practically the first stage in the start of a third generation. We might take it that we move into this era in a full sense when I move out in two years' time. I would therefore like to suggest that it might be good even now to consider a meeting of the CC either in Britain or in USA in 1965, when the appointment of a new International Secretary will be made, and the 'Holy Cow' cease to moo!. You might be considering this. Meanwhile I will continue to 'moo' vigorously as being of the older generation, reminding us all of our original principles and in that way perhaps help to mould us into our right God-planned shape as a functioning CC – advisors forever, but never bossing!

At this gathering Rubi resigned from the position of International Secretary and Len Moules took over. However, the Consultative Council (renamed the Co-ordinating Council) felt that he should remain a member.

In reviewing this meeting Norman wrote a letter to all members of WEC. Here are some of the paragraphs:

Dec 23, 1965

Dear WECers Worldwide,
The time has now come to inform you of the outcome of our triennial election.
    1. INTERNATIONAL SECRETARY – I am most thankful to say that there is a unanimity in confirming Len Moules as the Lord's choice to take over from January 1, 1966.
    I received communications to this effect from thirty one fields and homebases.
    2. MY CONTINUING AS A MEMBER OF THE COORDINATING COUNCIL – I'm grateful to have received a confirmation of this from all of you, again with no dissenting voice.
    Leadership in WEC is where God has built it and put it through these years – at the level of the field and homebase workers' fellowships. These other over-all appointments are to have the lightest possible touch among us, for coordination, inspiration, consultation, investigation if some point appears to need questioning, and the pointing forward to our ever-enlarging world commission. The International Secretary is what his name implies, a secretary, and not a leader, and I claim the right to say that, because it was I who first made the proposition, about ten years ago when we were revising the *P's and P* in London, that there was need for a

'General Secretary' as coordinator. And then at Kilcreggan five years ago, the name for convenience was changed to International Secretary; so I can assure you that I know what I am talking about when I say that the advisory status of the IS has been a fixed principle from its inception, and I now pass it on to Len on that basis, knowing how much one in heart and mind he is with me on this.

This is my last letter to you as International Secretary, and it comes with the deepest thankfulness for God's great grace through these thirty five years. We were compelled to take on at the home end after Studd was glorified on July 16, 1931. There were only the thirty five in the Congo and Ma Rubi and I in Britain. But we were given one clear guidance at that time, which has stood the test of time – that I was not to accept the position of President to which Mr Studd had appointed me, but to be secretary at home, with the Congo field autonomous in its field affairs. From this has grown our whole chain of autonomous fields and homebases.

I should, indeed, lay down my secretaryship with concern if I felt that our great expansion in size had weakened our convictions on our basic principles. But thank God that is not so, and the recent international conference was one proof of it. It is a great thing that we are workers together in an organism where we can be sure that those who take on from us continue building on the same foundations.

Of course, ceasing to be a secretary does not mean ceasing to be a WECer. That is why I'm thankful to continue on the CC; and with plenty of health still, by God's grace, in mind and body, I shall continue, as the Lord supplies the energy, to move about this country in many speaking engagements, and in writing.

If I said one final word of warning on our organisational level, it would be that we should all beware of any infringements of autonomy on a personal level as much as on a field or homebase level. There can be a fellowship dictatorship as much as an individual one, and I believe our aim should be, as it was with C.T. Studd, to give all possible liberty to each other, after we are through our recruit stage, each to fulfil the commission God has given us. Certainly there must be a place in a cooperating fellowship for necessary interaction, but wherever possible let it be through the individual and fellowship together finding the Lord's plan, rather than the one imposing it upon the other.

So we continue together, thank God, for the gospel to the world, and the only retirement we know is upwards.

Yours rejoicing, and commending Len and Iris to God's enabling grace along with you all,

Ever yours in the Crusade,

Jock Purves, for so many years deputy British leader under Rubi, wrote the following appreciation at this time:

Norman Grubb this month relinquishes, at his request, the post of International Secretary of the Crusade to make way for a younger man, our own British leader, Mr Len Moules.

In 1957 they went from us in British WEC to take part in our North American work. I was one of a number of fellow Crusaders and friends at Waterloo Station, London, wishing them godspeed. We stood around chatting for a time before the singing of gospel and missionary hymns and choruses, then prayer to the God who watches over our going out and coming in. With no apparent context of conversation, Pauline Grubb said to me, 'Zeal is not enough, Jock; love is.' I shall never forget it – it was a word from the Lord.

In writing of Mr and Mrs Grubb, whom I have personally known for forty years, zeal and love, and love with zeal exemplify their character and work. In these qualities they have lived their lives to God, to us, their fellows, and to earth's utmost bounds in the cause of Christ.

The first time I saw Norman Grubb was in 1925 when, on arrival back from the Congo, he came to the Missionary Training Colony to speak to us candidates training for various parts of the world. The MTC, founded by Alfred Buxton, co-pioneer in the Congo with C.T. Studd, had in it the unique genius of the Spirit by which the Crusade itself was founded. I had a thought of him then which is more true to me now than ever – 'That man has the marks of the cross of Christ about him.'

At C.T's request they had returned to London to help in this side of things to be known so well to us by their Congolese names, Rubi and Ma Rubi, and were here when C.T. was glorified in 1931. A crisis had been pending and it came leaving about thirty of us in the Congo and one or two of us at home. We touched rockbottom but found it Rockbottom.

Out of the crisis the Unevangelised Fields Mission was formed, greatly honoured and blessed of the Lord in their extensive work in various lands. In the recent Congo sufferings most of the roll of the honoured dead were of the UFM. We who remained as the WEC felt ourselves to be utter nobodies. But we certainly had God-given leaders, Norman and Pauline Grubb. The missionaries in the Congo, led by the young Jack and Mollie Harrison, told us that should we at home give up, they would go on! We told God that we too would go on together with our leaders and assisted by Colonel and Mrs Munro. If He wanted to finish us, He must do so.

Many of God's people were against us and told us so in no uncertain ways. Mr Grubb said to me one morning, 'I'm half afraid to open the mail!' We had very little personal provision either, being at one time on

bread and cheese for a fortnight. I went out on meetings to return at
Christmas to find Mr and Mrs Grubb humbly eating a bread pudding; they
had no tea, and tea is a favourite drink in British WEC! Someone had
kindly given them a Christmas tree for the children. Norman laughed
heartily saying, 'And we haven't got a bean to put anything on it.'

The lounge of No. 17 Highland Road, the original house bought by
C.T. Studd, became a power-place of prayer, intercession and faith. The
pictures on the walls were maps. We knelt in their world context, or sat;
we stood or lay on our faces wrestling with God in prayer. Led by Norman Grubb for hours each day, we went over the exploits of Old Testament prophets and New Testament apostles. We believed in miracles –
those of the Word of God and of miracles in the work. One young man
who applied to us said one morning, 'But you surely don't believe that
the iron swam, do you?' 'Oh yes, we do,' said Rubi, 'Our bread and butter
depends on it!' That same man did worthy work for the Master. Did some
of us become too enthusiastic?

What a healthy strengthening mind was that of Ma Rubi on many matters. I remember when I was engaged to be married. WEC workers were
asked to have a two year term of engagement. My life partner and I were
requested to do three years by Mr Grubb 'seeing we were at the home-
end', he said. We did. Our ring had not cost a great deal but we agreed to
sell it for the funds of the Crusade. I must admit I got a little fainthearted
when near the pawnbroker's! The WEC has always been a family, and
when Mrs Grubb saw my wife's ringless finger she kindly said, 'Where is
your ring?' She was told that I had it. 'Why?' 'To sell for money for the
mission.' Ma Rubi laughed heartily. 'Oh dear,' she said smiling sweetly,
'we surely haven't come to this. You get it back.' My wife did, and still
has it.

In 1935 Norman Grubb took ill. I was recalled from Birmingham to
deputise for him. What kind of illness? I testified at the time and do so
now, it was the illness of a man wrestling with God. Away from us for a
time, he returned, as his Master did, from the lone place of trial, with the
Spirit of the Lord upon him. The Lord gathered around the Grubbs men
and women of like spirit who have maintained the work as it was founded
by the Studds and established by Norman and Pauline.

Many books have flowed from Norman Grubb's pen. The life-story
of our founder, C.T. Studd is a missionary classic. How we prayed over
that while he was writing it! How God has blessed his writings on missionary administration and practice, on Bible principles and Christian
living, his editing of others' books, his unseen share in yet others, his
forewords and his articles!

Everyone has not always agreed with what they said and did. They
have not been without their confessed mistakes and failures. They may,

looking back, think that there are things they would now do differently. This humility of mind has always appealed to us. The love of Christ has given a graciousness, a large-mindedness, and a loving understanding. Out of this costly dedication to Him they have been quick to advance in the knowledge of Calvary. We, the led, have followed with praiseful and thankful hearts for we have seen in them the mind and marks of The Leader, Christ Jesus.

Ken Adams, International Director of Christian Literature Crusade wrote:

I first met Norman P. Grubb in 1932. He was speaking at a missionary rally in the tiny hamlet of Shopland in Essex, England. Frankly, I cannot remember much of his spoken message. I do recall, vividly, the impression that meeting made upon me as a young man.

The missionary society Studd founded was in a storm of criticism. Predictions ran high that before too long the whole thing would come to nought. To most it was a gloomy picture, but not to Norman P. Grubb, the newly-appointed General Secretary of the Worldwide Evangelisation Crusade.

Here was a man full of compassion. He spoke with deep feeling and warm understanding of people and situations he knew intimately. From his personal knowledge of Africa and his wide general knowledge of the overall missionary situation he spoke convincingly of the 'unfinished task'.

Here stood a man of conviction. Clearly he believed that the church's responsibility was to reach every corner of the unevangelised world and he spoke as though he also believed the task could be completed within the foreseeable future. His optimism was contagious; his vision seemed to engulf the whole world.

Nearly ten years later I met Norman again. That interview proved to be the turning point for this literature ministry. Some of us feel that in this moment there shone through one of the most remarkable shafts of God-inspired revelation and light of his whole vision-filled career. As we shared the 'problem' of our sincere interest in linking with the Crusade and yet our involvement in the literature work the flash of inspiration came – there was no need to leave one ministry and join another, link them together!. This immediately witnessed to our hearts though the full implication of what this could mean was by no means fully grasped or understood ... but from that moment we were 'on course' in the full will and purpose of God.

Norman Grubb has stood unflinchingly with us down the years, for in that moment a relationship and friendship was born that has weathered the storms and pressures any growing work of God must experience. It is to him, as God's human messenger, we have turned for counsel and guidance and it is from his never-daunted spirit of unwavering faith we have learned some of the secrets of spiritual greatness.

Under God, Norman has surely made his mark upon his day and generation. Through his many books and articles and his constant public ministry he has led thousands into a new Christian vitality, but the two Crusades (which adminstratively function quite independently) will remain living testimonies to his long and faithful ministry.

We do say a big 'thank you' to God and to Norman Grubb – and in no small measure also to his loyal wife, Pauline –for their unstinting spiritual and practical contribution to the Christian Literature Crusade and to so many of us on a personal level.

CHAPTER 19

MEASURE OF THE MAN

What made Norman 'great'?

Certain characteristics are immediately obvious – his dynamic faith, his passionate devotion to Jesus, his visionary leadership. All of which are evidenced in the preceding chapters.

But there were other traits and giftings, not so immediately obvious, that made him unique.

One was impatience. Not petulent impatience, but a holy impatience, evidenced by a divine restlessness concerning the accomplishment of God-given vision. He simply could not let go or give up. He had to pursue the target – whether it was the occupation of new fields, or the raising up of home base centres, or a target figure in recruitment – he was constantly laying the vision before the public in talks and magazine articles, or suggesting some relevant course of action in letters to fellow workers.

It revealed itself in his leadership of prayer times. A lull in the prayer sequence only stirred him further to exhort participants to give voice to their faith, so that ultimately a position of confident expectancy could be reached.

Of course there was a downside to this and as he became older and more convinced than ever about the truths he felt God had uniquely commissioned him to share, he found it difficult to deal with people who, though sympathetic, could not go all the way with him. Both within WEC ranks and in interaction with other groups such as Union Life Ministries he often felt tempted to display this impatience by simply walking out of discussions. In his usual frankness and humility he writes about it:

> I have the besetting sin of too much hastiness, and there have been times when I should have stayed put and didn't, and I need more of God's restraining grace in this respect. At the same time some of it has been purposed, and I still don't know how better I could demonstrate my stand as International Secretary against something unconstitutional.

Another unique quality was his capacity for minimising the failings of others. A favourite phrase that he often used when describing an area of failure in a worker was, 'It's only mist on the mountain.' The mountain, of course, was all the positive attitudes and gifts in a person. To the beleaguered housewife battling waves of condemnation for her inadequacies he would say, 'That's not the real you, my dear. You're a way beyond that.'

His consuming passion was the recognition of Jesus in one another. All else shrank into insignificance. He shone at this when defending individualistic workers from the justifiable criticism of team members. He was quick to exonerate, insightful at highlighting their achievements and totally reticent when apportioning blame.

Scanning letter after letter we find, usually around paragraph two or three, a peon of praise for the addressee and his or her magnificent contribution to the work.

He was totally positive with everyone, even to those who undermined him behind his back.

Testimony after testimony can be shared about workers who have gone into his study totally defeated, ready to resign, seeing their problems as gigantic, only to emerge an hour later, ready to take a new step of faith in utter reliance on the One within, about Whom Norman had gently ministered. Someone has said, 'You go in a worm and you come out a giant.'

A third and interesting facet was his capacity to be a lover of WEC and yet to ignore it completely. He was convinced that God had given the patterns for government, development and maintenance. He would defend these principles with the last ounce of his being, but he simply wasn't interested in defending WEC or even promoting it. If we were to have a graph of the amount of energy devoted to advancing the mission it would start high (but not very high), for the early years and gravitate down to nil at the other end.

His supreme ministry was liberating those in bondage through the truth of the freedom and fulness that there is in Christ.

Ask those who sat in his meetings in the sixties and seventies and they will not remember much of WEC's ministries and strategies. They will remember the impact of the man himself and his message of release and fulness awaiting those who would recognise their union with Christ in His death, resurrection and ascension.

Another intriguing aspect of his value-system was his regard, yes, his fascination with the ministry of the Holy Spirit, and the freedom that this brings to an individual's ministry.

One can remember a personal chat in which we were reviewing some of the current movings of the Spirit. He stopped for a moment and then, with reflection said, 'Stewart, go for the Spirit. Identify yourself with those who are moving with God in the things of the Spirit, no matter what others say, or what it costs you.'

This predilection for the ways of the Spirit meant that he was much misunderstood by mainline evangelicals, particularly in North America. He was ahead of his time, because he was moving with God and sensitive to what the Spirit was doing.

As with other aspects of his character, this had some unique spin-offs. Structure, organisation, rules and regulations were anathema to him. Even our own Principles and Practice he held lightly, and had little time for those who pressed for legalistic conformity. He was against minute-taking.

He once wrote:

> Our real aim must be to help people to learn a steady walk with God. When we are in the light, we don't see Principles and Practices (sic) because we are immersed in walking with Him. When we walk in darkness, then we feel the bite of Ps and P, because the law is for the lawless; and our experience is that when folk are in that state, they will anyhow find ways round any written code. Life can only be in the Spirit, not in the letter.

He hated anything that savoured of domination on the part of leaders and subservience on the part of followers. In fact he refused to work on a manager/managed basis. Why? Because we all had the Spirit, and the only criterion needed was sensitivity to *Him* rather than man-made regulations or decisions.

The same conviction led him to scrap heavy-handed regulatory committees. WECers were quite capable of handling their own affairs. Why? Because they had the Spirit, of course. He had total confidence in the Spirit within, and of course he delighted in C.T. Studd's ideal 'committee' – Father, Son and Holy Spirit.

This trust in the Spirit led him to take enormous risks in the sending of inexperienced workers into new situations. Of course there were the odd mishaps, but by and large this recognition of the Spirit-in-others paid off with dramatic developments throughout the world.

A further spin-off was his reputation among fellow-workers. If he obviously trusted *them* surely they could trust *him*; so there was an enormous *allegiance factor* in the mission. He was far more than a chief executive officer. He was a father, big brother, counsellor, confidante, encourager, and correspondent to hundreds both inside WEC and beyond.

He was the ultimate realist. He could not stomach spiritual theories that did not accord with fact. He could not agree with what he called the 'dog-eat-dog' theory of the two-natures in the believer. Once he had moved into the Galatians 2:20 experience he knew the reality of deliverance, and the power of the indwelling Christ.

This factor also enabled him to release workers to find a sphere of service in keeping with their gifting; he saw no need for constant consultation or reporting. WECers to this very day have a huge degree of freedom in the development of their ministry. Indeed some feel it gives scope for 'crass individualsim' as one senior leader has described it.

Another angle on Norman's thrust for reality was his honesty about himself. The Ruanda message touched this cord in his nature and he responded magnificently as readers of *Continuous Revival* will see. The writer quizzed him on one occasion. 'Rubi, is it always victory, triumph, joy in overcoming?' 'Stewart,' he said, 'I usually just get through by the skin of my teeth.'

This sense of reality dominated his prayer life. Why pray for something if you haven't discovered whether it's God's will? He would only go to prayer once that issue was settled. And then 'prayer' to him became a matter of assuring the Lord that he was expecting and counting on the answer. His Bible said, 'According to your *faith* be it unto you', so to him the key was the strong assertion of trust, not a wallowing in uncertainty.

Was Norman an extremist? Undoubtedly.

Even before reaching Congo he had an innate Holy-Spirit-inspired trust that led him to concepts, ideals, visions, practical goals that were well beyond the scope of the average Christian. When blessing attended the under-graduate meeting of the Cambridge Christian Union it was Norman who came up with the idea of such a union in every British university. It was he who urged Howard Guinness to undertake a tour of Canada to promote the same vision.

And of course his close relationship to C.T. Studd – an extremist

among extremists – thoroughly ignited a fuse that was already smoul-
dering. Although Norman could not agree with many steps that C.T.
took, he went wholly with him in spiritual values like total surrender to
the will of Jesus, and extreme sacrifice where necessary to accomplish
it. How else could he have endured these long stays in Congo, alone, as
a young married man? And these long tours of Amazonia, Canada,
Australia, New Zealand, etc.

He was criticised because his extreme views on sacrificial service took him away from Pauline and the children during the very years
he was most needed. But for him – unlike today's values in Christian
service – work came before family, and he never flinched in putting
Kingdom demands in front of his personal and family needs.

Nevertheless he constantly affirmed Pauline and praised God for
her steadiness and wise counsel, acknowledging that his own adventur-
ous spirit needed her steadying influence. In the foreword to *Yes I am*
he writes: 'Where should I have been without her through these many
years?' Undoubtedly her sacrificial spirit, her unwillingness to hinder
Norman's activities, made it possible for him to give virtually his total
life to the mission.

Although not within the scope of this book, mention must be
made of his doctrinal views, which, many said became extreme.

Most problems arose from Norman's extremist streak – namely
his desire to shock those of normal views by overstating a point,
as a device to make them thoroughly examine where they really
stood. He never considered himself a heretic; he simply wanted to
penetrate the body of Gospel truth deeper than the average person
in order to clarify and confirm truths that most people held in a
general kind of way. He often said 'The devil is God's tool' – a
jarring concept, yet not without Biblical foundation. 'No independent self' – not difficult to accept after reading Ephesians 2:1-13. 'I
am Jesus in His Norman form' – quite a natural progression from
Galatians 2:20. Neil Anderson in *Victory over the Darkness* says virtually the same thing but in a more acceptable form. 'Since you are in
Christ, His divine nature constitutes your core essence.'

It is abundantly clear that those who had an intimate acquaint-
ance with Norman and his spoken messages, and were not pres-
sured from other sources, seldom had major problems; these mostly
arose with those who did not know him intimately and took some of his
statements in isolation.

He was extreme in his love for other extremists. When he saw a WECer willing to go to any lengths for Jesus – like Bessie Brierley when she left her child behind to go alone to seek a visa for Portuguese Guinea – he backed her to the hilt and poured himself out in letters to her, encouraging her to go ahead.

What a series of vivid contrasts we end up with when we try to summarise the character of Norman Grubb!

Imperious, yet totally humble. Impatient, yet time-forgetting in personal dealings. Visionary and dynamic, yet willing to let others take the lead. Zealous for the growth of mission, yet indefensive when it came to protecting it. Quick to encourage and facilitate others but slow to interfere when the going became tough for them. Expert in delineating the way of holiness, yet reticent to condemn sin in individuals. Passionate in his desire to see Christ formed in people, yet totally unconcerned about the corporate body of believers – the church, about which he had very little to say.

God be praised for such a servant of Jesus – multi-gifted, many-faceted, a conundrum to some, but in life and ministry a veritable cascade of blessing to thousands!

CHAPTER 20

EVALUATIONS

WEC's DEBT TO NORMAN GRUBB

Studd was like a military or colonial pioneer, concerned for new territory, new ideas, catching the public imagination, but Grubb had to take over when the work was at its lowest ebb, and his was more an application of the biblical principle of faith, of injecting others and building a committed fellowship. If there hadn't been a Norman Grubb, what Studd started would have collapsed and not been revived. So I look upon him in many ways, if not the founder, then certainly the builder of WEC.

Neil Rowe

He taught us to have the courage to stand by the vision that God gave us. 'God gave Moses a vision to take the people to the promised land but he never told Moses there were going to be ten plagues.' I can remember him saying that in prayers, and he gave us this vision to stick to what God had given through thick and thin. Stickability was the key – he had no time for people who were wishy-washy. As a mission we owe a tremendous lot to him, not only the mission, but as a worldwide Christian community.

Helen Roseveare

Probably his biggest contribution was the tremendous faith that God had put in his heart after he met Rees Howells. That was his strong point. He spoke about it a lot in meetings.

Then, he set about changing the style of the original WEC. It had been the usual sort of missionary headquarters up until 1931; it seemed to recruit and send out missionaries from the upper classes. Norman Grubb turned it around. He saw that the Spirit of God could use the ordinary working class people in the same way. That's how some of us came in. I was just an ordinary working class lad from the north, without much education, having left school at fourteen.

Leslie Brierley

Many beautiful things were put into WEC by C.T. Studd – that daring for Jesus, that going for it, that commitment, that sacrifice. But Norman added further daring and faith and a willingness to take risks. Also, our fellowship structure and the way we govern ourselves is almost unique in missions. I know it came out of a reaction to what happened around C.T's death but yet it has stood us in good stead. Having worked within several other missions, coming into WEC has been an enormous exhilaration – a release really. I don't know whether WECers appreciate what we do owe to Norman in giving us this freedom. Today, any WECer can contribute to decision making, to the direction of the way things go.

Patrick Johnstone

Rubi got his guidance from God and went for it. He did not look to the right hand or to the left hand. He did not check out what other missions were doing and saying. He took the view that God has given us a job – worldwide evangelisation – so that was our commission. He felt we should look out those places that need evangelising, find out God's way to get there and get the job done. That single-eyed approach and that whole-hearted devotion – these were the big things that I learned from Norman Grubb.

Ken Getty

WEC is what it is today because of Rubi. We wouldn't have the present shape of WEC if it wasn't for him. He's been the biggest single influence of anyone on WEC. I suppose it wouldn't have started without C.T. but apart from that, Rubi was the one who shaped WEC. In terms of organisation, fellowship decision-making, the autonomy of fields, the loose organisational relationships rather than a legalistic structure – all these were very important. The ethos of WEC, as enshrined in our four pillars, comes from Rubi.

Brian Woodford

He and Ma Rubi were the ones who began the sending base, so we owe them a great deal for the way they set that up on a faith basis. That's been a unique thing in WEC, and still is.

We learned the faith principle from them but we also learned community life – sharing and praying together. Everyone came into the meetings and shared what was going on. We learned we were part of a family and not just an organisation. That's something very unique about WEC, and it has carried over on to the fields.

Joanne Major

HIS ATTITUDE TO THE CHURCH

There wasn't very much emphasis on going to church or being linked with a church, or taking part in church activities. He saw WEC fellowship as the church and didn't really look beyond it. Nevertheless, I think it was a weakness. He allowed, and even encouraged fields to develop without any unified church or doctrinal position. I came up against that problem much later in Africa, and it's still taking us a long time to rectify.

Neil Rowe

All I did in Africa was to help individuals come to put their trust in Jesus. And I certainly didn't understand anything about building up a church. We had a 'church' where we all came together and worshipped the Lord but that was a sort of 'spin off'. The total thrust was evangelism, to bring people to Jesus. I am horrified at how totally ignorant I was of that side of things. The concept of the church had never got through to me. If you don't have a church you can't send out missionaries, and with a weak idea of the church we never caught that vision. We never thought them capable as baby born-again Christians.

Helen Roseveare

I think his attitude to the church was part of his rejection of organisational structures. If you look at Acts Paul was much more than an evangelist. He was a church builder all the way. Obviously today we've moved into the whole field of ecclesiology because it's so vital to the future of our work. It may almost be a reflection of Rubi's attitude that today one of the big problems we face in our church is that it's so strong on initial evangelism, and so weak on building up Christians.

Alastair Kennedy

He was not a church man. He did not have a concept of the church as a body. His outlook was, 'Where does it say in the Bible "plant churches"?' Maybe there's a throwback to his Quakerism. However, the whole idea of the church was a missing factor. The fellowship perspective that he believed in and practised was not comparable to the New Testament church.

Ken Getty

In the fifties he wrote round to our churches suggesting quite a bit of church organisation, so he did have a concern for the church and he began to see the need for structure. But I think he was so non-denominational, he so sensed that Christian unity was an individual issue, that he did not see it as a corporate concept. It was a unity because you loved the Lord and I loved the Lord.

Brian Woodford

HIS RELATIONSHIPS
To me, generally he was a patient, and tolerant man. On odd occasions he could be otherwise. Generally speaking, he was also a humble man; but there was the time when he manifested a stubborn attitude. I have known him to walk out of a meeting! He stood for openness; but at times he was too open for some, betraying their confidence. I never knew him other than honest; and he was most persevering. He could be imperious at times. A leader to him was a man who SAW, not necessarily an administrative man, or manager. He was not completely impartial in his judgement, and perhaps at times lacked a little discernment. However, he was not generally lacking in wisdom. He handled people graciously, concerned for them to find fulfilment in the will of God.

John Lewis

He handled me, who everybody said was a strong person and didn't always agree with others, with the loving care of a father who was prepared to see Jesus always, almost to an extreme. He had a love relationship with Jesus the rest of us found very hard to follow, and this took over from clarity of vision when, perhaps, he should have rebuked. That fact may explain why he didn't grip situations. There are those that would say he simply couldn't confront people. He loved, and he believed we all ought to love one another, which of course is Scriptural. He took this to the 'nth' degree.

Helen Roseveare

He was stimulating and sometimes disturbing with his direct questions. He loved mingling with people, being with people, writing personal letters. Even shortly before his death we received short notes, scrappy little notes, but beautifully expressive of his care for individuals. He was a carer, very much a lover of people, even people who didn't agree with him, yet that affection came over in a wonderful way. He had a tremendous caring ability for individuals. I don't think of Rubi as a teacher, building solid Scriptural knowledge into people, I think he was more of an inspirational conference speaker who sparked loyalty, faith, excitement.

Alastair Kennedy

Norman was in hospital; it was the time that he had a broken bone, and he was in a room with one other man. Mrs Gloria Nyheim and her husband visited the hospital room where he was, or they met somebody who did (I'm not quite sure which it was) but the story was that his roommate was tremendously impressed with him. He remarked on his joy and victory and happy spirit. He was so touched that he became a Christian before he left the company of Norman. His family was so impressed! The key was Rubi's personality and attitude.

Hester Withey, USA

I typed for Rubi. I didn't take dictation or anything. I just took it right on the typewriter. That's the way he dictated. If you made mistakes he didn't like you to stop to make corrections. I had to sneak them in later. I think he was considerate. I never felt pressed, pushed. He was always thoughtful. He was always thankful.

Mildred McCadden, USA Secretary

The first link we had with Rubi was when we were home on furlough in 1955. He had a meeting in Vancouver and then visited us in Maple Ridge at which time we showed him our slides of Burkino Faso. He commented, 'Excellent'.

Rubi was an encourager. His remark 'I haven't seen such good slides...' was an encouragement to us as we were just starting out on deputation. To think that he would take time to see them – it showed a real heart interest. Each furlough we would visit Camp Hill and go down to see Rubi. Each time he showed such a keenness in the Burkino Faso field. He asked specific questions about the work and the people. We were amazed that he would remember so much. We were always struck by his capacity to remember details about our field.

Clarence and Lucille Knapp

HIS LEADERSHIP STYLE
Rubi was able to inculcate a tremendous sense of loyalty to WEC. He taught us 'WEC is us, we are WEC'. He often referred to the fact that 'we're all in this together'. Even the latest recruit was given the chance to speak. That is a tremendous social strength and that came from Rubi's time as leader. He made people feel they could speak up, and he would take note of what they said, even though they were just new candidates.

Alastair Kennedy

I, of course, never worked under Rubi as leader, so I can only look back and see the effects of what he did. He always tended to favour the unusual, the underdog or the lone ranger who had a vision. And of course it often led to the most amazing developments, like in Indonesia with the Bible School in Batu and so on. So I can see that when he supported a new vision which was of God, he didn't allow it to get stifled. But often it just cut across all the lines of communication and existing structures. So there were positives and negatives; but there was that sense of excitement about him that I loved. He was prepared to take on new challenges.

Patrick Johnstone

Rubi set people free and encouraged them along the lines of their gifts. And he was willing to take risks. Whereas people saw problems, he saw opportunities and he sought to capitalise on those and keep things moving. He didn't get bogged down by problems. In fact, sometimes one felt he might have done better to spend a little more time resolving them. But there again, that is his uniqueness. He could see if you're spending time resolving problems you're not moving forward. The main thing, he said, was to keep on moving. He seemed to be undisturbed by problems or setbacks. He expounds this perception in his article *The Adventure of Adversity*. It was a great help to many.

Ken Getty

HIS GREATEST STRENGTHS

I admire him for his loving tenacity in teaching 'Christ in you', year after year, whether we took it or not. By and large I think we in WEC didn't, and I think that was always a source of great grief to him, but he never gave up and I think he always did it in a spirit of love. So I would say his greatest strengths were his loving tenacity and secondly, his ability to keep us to revealed principles, mainly, of course, the four pillars.

Neil Rowe

I think one of his greatest strengths was his ability to recognise spiritual strength in people, and to give them freedom to develop their ministry and gifts. Another great quality was his ability to inspire and motivate young people, to inject the principles of C.T. Studd into individuals so that people went out really aflame with sacrifice, faith, and so on. He had this knack of letting people launch out when they had a big vision. He would say, 'Get going for God and God will lead you. We'll back you up with prayer. We've got no finance to give you but God will give you all you need.' That ability to motivate people was tremendous.

Alastair Kennedy

I think there were many times when people disagreed with him. Some didn't agree with his writing of my father's biography. But once he knew that he had the mind of the Spirit, he was unflinching. He wouldn't be influenced by others. If he thought it was something from the Spirit he saw that it was done.

Samuel Howells, Swansea

His life and his words were a living tapestry of quoting Scriptures and translating them into real life. He was so very encouraging. Here we were, only young Christians (I'd been born again five years before) and he says 'Your fellowship is so refreshing.' Can you imagine what it meant as a young Christian to get a word like that? Then he said, 'There is an eternal freshness in the One inside, isn't there?' He would give you this encouragement and point you to the One inside.

Irl, my husband, came through for the Lord and the two of us were then one in spirit. He was at that time working on his doctorate at the University of Pennsylvania. We were so impressed with the work of

WEC – how the people lived and the emphasis on missions. Of course our association and relationship with Norman made a deep impression; so we thought: 'This is it; we're going to sell everything, go to the mission field. That's it!' We had two small children at the time and so we went to Norman and said, 'Guess what, we're going to sell everything and go to the mission field.' He said, 'Oh no you're not.' Here he was – the leader of this big mission and was putting us off! He said, 'You can reach people that our missionaries can't reach, so you just stay right where you are.' You can imagine our reaction. We thought it was strange. I went home and was reading the Scripture where Jesus meets the man who had many evil spirits. After the Lord cast all the demons out he said to him, 'You go back home and tell your friends that the Lord has had mercy on you.'

Lois Duling, Philadelphia

HIS WEAKNESSES
There were those that might consider he was a workaholic; and this led to him being somewhat of a recluse. I must accept there was a problem along such lines for many but I always found him approachable.

John Lewis

Rubi could be intolerant. For instance, we arranged a nice meeting when he was coming through to Beaverton, Oregon, where we lived. We had quite a nice home there and we arranged a very good meeting. We had a doctor friend whom we loved very much although he was different. He was original in his approach to things, as Norman was in some ways, and they didn't agree in this meeting. Norman got up and walked out; he went upstairs and stayed there, and never came back! That's the kind of thing that would happen. He was a great 'walker-outer'. This has been the one thing that has marred the clarity of his testimony. If he was opposed he just withdrew, politely.

John Whittle

I think one of his weaknesses was an impatience with structure. Perhaps it was born out of the early days – the division in WEC and also the way C.T. was handled by the home committee when he was in Africa. (They virtually disowned him.) I think he acquired a distrust of strong structures so he tended to play down things like boards, committees and so on; it was just the consensus of the fellowship that counted. Now I think we still stand by these principles to some extent, but I feel that at times Rubi was very impatient with corporate decisions, probably as a reaction to what had happened in the past.

He tended to be a maverick in his opinions. He had such a depth in God that he could say things that were right for him but a disaster for a new convert. I think if he'd had to do a bit more solid building up of believers he might have been a bit more restrained in some of his statements.

Alastair Kennedy

I feel that he gave the wrong impression to some people, especially those who weren't mature. I can remember in one of his meetings he got up and said, 'I got up and read the newspaper before breakfast, you know.' He kind of implied that prayer and Bible reading wasn't necessary. I could see what he was trying to get over, that we needed to get away from bondage, but it gave the wrong impression to other people. The same with not attending church. I think that set a bad example because we are told not to forsake the assembling of ourselves together.

Agnes Germann-Edey

As far as I know Rubi had no one close as an equal with whom he could consult – somebody who would stand up and challenge him when challenge was needed. We did on one or two occasions but we were thirty years younger! However he took it. He never kicked us. In other words, it would have been a wonderful blessing if he had had some really close partners.

Heini Germann-Edey

HIS MINISTRY

When my wife and I moved over to Canada and had a WEC meeting in Vancouver, Norman Grubb and John Whittle used to visit at least twice a year. I used to be involved in getting meetings for him in different churches around Vancouver. His best meetings were when he sat down like a father and wanted to just talk, in a home situation, with a dozen or twenty people. That was what he enjoyed most, the fellowship with people. His voice was not the best voice for going through a PA system

– he spoke very rapidly. People used to enjoy him but he was very hard
to follow because of his voice problem.

Peter Guest

I was a student at Birmingham Bible Institute. Brash Bonsall, the
principal, announced that Norman Grubb was coming. He said,
'He's a man of God. Write down every word he utters.' He came
and spoke to the student body for about fifteen or twenty minutes.
It had a real impact on us all at that time.

Hubert Mitchell, Wales

When I was converted at university I became part of the Christian
Union, and a member told me that Norman Grubb was going to speak
at the WEC headquarters in Bristol, which wasn't that far away from
the university. So I went along and heard him. I think he must
have spoken for about an hour and a half, and he's one of the
people I have met in my early Christian life that I could listen to, non-
stop, for a long time. I was so impressed. I can't remember what he
said but I do know it made a very deep impact on me.

Patrick Johnstone

I had just graduated from Glasgow University and was invited to hear
Norman Grubb speak at the Scottish headquarters of WEC. I don't
know if someone had tipped him off, but he spent a lot of his time
contrasting academic attainment with spiritual power. I remember him
saying, 'Men die, by degrees.' This intrigued me – in fact it haunted me
– and I knew this man had a set of values that I needed to come to
terms with. It also attracted me to WEC, which I joined three years
later after graduating from Bible College.

Stewart Dinnen

I found his ministry tremendously stimulating. I can still remember one meeting in Glasgow where he'd spoken all afternoon. We'd
had two long sessions and then it came to about seven o'clock at
night and he got up and said, 'That's it folks' but nobody moved.
'Do you want me to go on again?' He went on for another hour
just simply opening his Bible again. It was just continuous. I think
he was talking on the life of Abraham and it just flowed through
him, also Moses, and the principle of death to self – that was one of his
great themes.

He certainly had a tremendous affection for people. I don't know to what extent he was a counsellor; he was more an exhorter. I don't think his gift was sitting listening to people. His gift was more talking to them, challenging them, making them feel good about going on with the Lord.

Alastair Kennedy

His public ministry in early days was fundamental to the future of WEC. We took the largest halls in the cities and towns of the UK and had a bishop, or someone like that, to take the chair. We usually filled the hall for these Faith in Action meetings.

His teaching ministry was marred, as was his public ministry, by the rate at which he spoke. He also failed to simplify things sufficiently, or perhaps to accommodate what he shared to the level of most evangelicals.

John Lewis

ADMINISTRATION

I personally don't think that he had the administrative gifts to be a good International Secretary. I think he had many many other gifts but I don't think that was his main area of gifting. That's why I think Len Moules played a vital role in sharpening up structures, and in defining things better through *P's and P.* I think Rubi liked to leave things fuzzy because he was strongly committed to this principle that God can speak through anyone and you have to remain free to follow the behest of the Spirit whatever He says. I think Len brought in the idea of strategy, planning and administrative structures, and I'm glad Rubi went along with it. I think he had to swallow pretty hard but I think he accepted it and saw the importance of it. As we know, the mission has grown so big we need structure now. We can't do without it.

Alastair Kennedy

When it came to the time when he wanted to hand over the task of International Secretary he made light of the job. He said to Len, 'There is really nothing to it.' In fact he expected us to take that responsibility and the British leadership as well, so we carried both jobs for seven years. As Len said, neither job could be done properly because each was more than one man could carry.

He was a visionary, whereas others of us had to deal with the nitty

gritty issues and work through situations that he had considered of
lesser importance.

Iris Moules

He was not always willing to discuss some problems. In my early
days as a candidate and first few years on the staff, there were
obviously growing problems at headquarters, much of it caused
by his absence. I don't think Rubi was willing to grasp the nettle.
He was very big in spirit, willing to let people have a lot of latitude but I
think he must have known that that doesn't always work because it can
also cause division.

Neil Rowe

I think it wasn't his particular gift to develop structures. It was his
gift to get things started and keep things moving. I suppose to
some extent it was the question of the difference between the wine
and the wine skin. There is no point having a wine skin if you
don't have the wine. So it was part of the whole progression of
WEC. He built into people who in turn could develop ministries.
He kept this forward perspective.

Ken Getty

ON HIS WRITINGS

I started with *Touching the Invisible*. I suppose I've only really
read extracts from other books like *Rees Howells*. But this little
booklet had so much about faith and the technique of faith. There's one
wee phrase: 'Faith in adversity makes the serpent swallow itself.' So
much hinges on the faith that the Lord enables us to exercise in situations.

Margaret Copeland, N. Ireland

God has singly blessed his life of *C.T. Studd*. It has been in continuous publication for many years. It has been translated into a
lot of languages, and large numbers of people, including myself,
have been called into missionary work through that book. As I've
travelled around to other missions throughout the world I'm amazed
at the number of people, especially older people, who have said this
was the book that got them going.

Neil Rowe

My wife, Lois, in an attempt to reach me for the Lord played on one of my weaknesses – reading. I was in graduate school at the time and I had a doctoral exam coming up in two days. When I sat down to study one evening when she was out I found she had left a copy of *Rees Howells – Intercessor* on the table. Well, I picked it up out of casual curiosity and began to read it; I became so engrossed that I spent the whole evening reading about the experiences of this Welshman. Sometime later I realised I had 'wasted' all my study time and hadn't had a chance to prepare properly for the exam. The next night, the night before the exam, when I sat down to study I prayed and asked the Lord to guide my study because I was feeling under some pressure now. This was the first time I had ever prayed about an ordinary life situation.

I had a big thick organics chemistry text book that I leafed through for about two hours, so you know how much of it I really read, just a paragraph here and a page there. The next morning when I went to the three-hour exam, they handed us four or five single-spaced typewritten pages of questions. I quickly read through them and I almost fell off my chair! It was so amazing: I had specifically studied every question on that exam the night before. It was some time after that I began going to the Faith at Work meetings with Lois where I again met Norman and other Christian speakers. I came to an awareness that God was real. Christ was alive and I could have contact with him.

This all really began because of my reading of *Rees Howells*.

Dr Irl Duling

One of the things that was most helpful to us was his little leaflet *The Adventure of Adversity*. When we found ourselves confronted with a problem that arose out of Carol's condition (cerebral palsy), that was a wonderful help to us. I think that set the course for the way we dealt with it all the years we had her. She lived to be almost 32.

His teaching in *Touching the Invisible* was a big help to us – getting God's mind then going forth by faith. For instance, when we set off to start the children's home at Three Hills, Alberta, we walked out with virtually nothing; it was a real venture of faith. We had a pressure cooker, some pillows and a table cloth or two, and we set off to build a three-storey house with twenty-two rooms! The Lord first of all gave us the land and then we were given a gift of $500 which was enough to buy the cement for the foundations. Herb did that and we had no money to go any further but when the cement was dry we received a gift of $1000 from Toronto. From there on it just grew.

Marion Congo

My first knowledge of Norman Grubb was when, shortly after the death of C.T. Studd, a box arrived at our church; I was in my early teens then. Inside were twenty or more copies of the book *C.T. Studd*, the story of his life. These were sent for free loan to anyone who wanted a copy. If I'd had to buy a book at that time I'd never have had it. And I might never have gone to the mission field. I received a copy, read it and was hooked. That was really the beginning of my association with the mission, and much developed out of that in later years when I became a missionary with CLC in Japan.

Ray Oram

I didn't really start reading Norman's books until I was in Africa; they then became very formative in my life. I was desperate for a deeper walk with God, and of course that was the time of the beginning of the charismatic movement and all the challenges about the gifts of the Spirit. The way Rubi put it in his books like *God Unlimited* had such a deep impact on me; they freed me up from the bondage of thinking that I had to look for tongues. I wanted everything God had for me, and Rubi just showed me freedom in Jesus – knowing the life of Jesus within, without it having to be stereotyped. So in my own spiritual life there was that profound impact.

But then when I was in Rhodesia (Zimbabwe) I was part of an organisation which was heirarchical in structure and quite paternalistic towards the Africans. When I read some of his books about the development of WEC in the thirties and about the fellowship principles and how to get guidance, this was a new world to me. So I began to apply those truths to the running of our team. (Generally our Africans would say, 'Well, you're the leader; you must say what we must do', and if things went wrong they would complain 'Well, you made us come down this track.') I thought, 'This can't go on,' and seeing the basic truth of getting through to God about what we should do, and knowing by consensus and the witness of the Spirit, I tried to get our African brothers and sisters to work in this way too. It took some time, but it came, and it really built a fellowship level that transformed the work, and enabled national leaders to develop in a natural way. The whole fellowship basis was given to us by Rubi.

Patrick Johnstone

EPILOGUE

The end of Norman Grubb's leadership of WEC was certainly not the end of his ministry. Indeed it would be fair to say that the laying down of mission responsibilities simply opened the door to a much wider sphere of service that took him to all parts of the USA and Canada and led to a spiritual impact on individuals and groups that was incalculable.

From 1966 almost to the end of his life, in 1993, he accepted invitations to give Bible-teaching, usually in homes, to small groups of individuals who had read his books or had otherwise come into contact with his unique presentations of Biblical truth.

This epilogue is a brief attempt to encapsulate a few of the features that were characteristic of these twenty seven years.

One of these was that, though distant from mission field activities, his concern for WEC and its workers never diminished. A veritable cascade of letters poured from his office to leaders, missionaries, bases, fields and ministries, lovingly encouraging them yet fearlessly challenging anything that he felt was a deviation from first principles.

Another issue which we have to face in all honesty was his tendency to overstate truths that he saw were crucially important to any disciple who wanted to go deeper with the Lord. He freely acknowledged that he was an extremist in everything he did and the result was that while many who knew him intimately were not perturbed, others saw his teaching as dangerous and even heretical.

On the other hand, it must be acknowledged that the main thrust of his teaching – the 'Christ-in-you' emphasis – brought new and joyful liberty to many who had been subject to shallow teaching with its emphasis on a list of 'do's and don'ts'.

Yet another feature can be easily recognised. Having moved out of the authority structure of the mission and from the pressure of initiating strategies that required greater and greater resources, his previous strong emphasis on meeting together and waiting on God for direction and supply virtually ceased and a rather more restful attitude took its place. It became his habit, borne possibly out of a vast experience of proving God, to assume God's willingness to supply and guide rather than wait upon Him in prayer. He would say 'I don't like this "ask-ask-ask"! I just "take-take-take".' Intercession took on a different meaning – not prayer to the Lord but the whole man in action ministering to humanity in its spiritual need.

We cannot pass the year 1966 without covering a sad event that was to lead to a severance of official ties between the Grubbs and the N. American WEC staff.

Some of the senior men were disturbed by statements in two of Norman's recent books, *The Spontaneous You* and his autobiography, *Once Caught, No Escape*. They felt that there were a number of passages that contained serious flaws of doctrine. They also queried his 'soft' attitude to theologians like Barth, Brunner and John Robinson, and groups such as the Oxford Group and Camp Farthest Out. Numerous attempts to persuade Norman to sit down quietly with a committee of American WEC leaders were unsuccessful and the outcome was simply that they agreed to Norman going his way and the mission pursuing its commission, no public announcement being made concerning this break.

Other bases such as Britain and Australia were far less edgy about Norman's writings. He wrote to the American staff remonstrating:

Being heart and soul in our WEC calling I take an active part in the Co-ordinating Council and keep in touch with various strategic activities. I had a wonderful welcome at Bulstrode (the British HQ) when the leader, Robert Mackey, said he was so sorry I could not be with them for their staff meetings. He asked me, if I make a return visit, to put aside several days for sharing the things of the Spirit with staff and recruits.

Regarding the committee who investigated his teaching he wrote:

I greatly respect and am thankful for all convictions and presentations of truth by these brethren and maybe many or most of you. Probably you are more right than I and certainly God-blessed. So I have no difficulty loving, honouring, accepting without controversy the Biblical positions you hold and messages you give. But I have to say for myself that what I have put in these books and the message I give I cannot change one iota, but rather keep emphasising more emphatically. In addition it is just a fact that I have a continual stream of testimonies by letter or word of mouth, after every meeting, amounting to hundreds, if not thousands, whose lives have been changed and for whom Christ has become their Centre through what they have read in these books or heard me say.

I watch over the souls of those with whom I keep in touch (as the writer of the Hebrews said we should); my job is the continual increase of Christ living and being glorified in these lives [so that] they become reproducers of others.

I think that very probably you have a more balanced overall point of view than mine, for I have always been an extremist and specialist, so I have no difficulty in working with you. But I also must go as God leads.

Was Norman exaggerating when he wrote that 'hundreds, even thousands' were blessed through his ministry? It is, of course, impossible to calculate, but anecdotal evidence abounds all over USA and Canada to confirm the fact that God used his message to bring release and blessing into a huge number of lives.

Perhaps a few excerpts from testimonies will suffice.

Mrs. Lois Duling of West Chester, PA. writes:

After coming to know Norman we began to read his books. His emphasis on Galatians 2:20 changed my life completely – just to know that it wasn't me, it was Christ in me that was doing all this, and that I was just a container for the Lord Jesus – it was totally liberating. I was to be His hands and feet and be free in the Spirit, not bound up by performance requirements.

Dr. John Bunting, a surgeon of Louisville, KY, writes:

It was Norman who showed me the wonderful mystery 'Christ in you the hope of glory.' I had to come to a point where I was ready to admit that I could not do anything. Once I saw it I began to live by faith, truly and utterly cast upon the Lord. My guilt had been condemning me for years but when I finally gave up and said, 'It's not I but Christ' that was the point when I started to come free. The major problem disappeared as I started to move with the Lord. It was miraculous. Norman was so influential at that time, not that he sat down and talked a lot to me, but he pointed the way, and the Holy Spirit was able to lead me into these precious truths such as Colossians 3:3, 'Your life is hidden with Christ in God.'

Bill Volkman of Chicago, in his book *The Wink of Faith* recalls:

The two and a half hours I spent with Norman Grubb on the afternoon of May 22, 1974 turned out to be the most significant divine appoinment of my life. Oddly enough I can't remember much of what he said, but the 'replaced life' he talked about was evidently a *total Gospel* for him. This was the first time I had met someone who really knew the meaning of life.

Later that night as I reflected on my encounter with Norman Grubb I breathed a sigh of relief. I knew that that day was to be a turning point in my life. My new understanding would enable me to exchange my 'obedience of works' for 'obedience of faith' (Rom. 2:5; 16:26).

I started to read Norman's book *The Deep Things of God*. Early in it he refers to this verse in Colossians, 'The mystery once hidden, now made manifest, is Christ in you, the hope of glory.' The mystery of the gospel is simply that the Spirit of Christ lives within you and is your only hope of successful living. The really good news is not just the historical fact that Jesus died on the cross for my sins, but that because a *replacement* of gods has taken place, a union has resulted. Your spirit and the Spirit of Christ have become one.

In the late seventies Norman's searching mind continued to explore the parameters of his favourite theme, *Union with Christ*, and about this time some became disturbed about an over-emphasis in his writings. He would write about an 'inner knowing' of Christ in us *as us*, 'as our total reality', and would freely use the phrase that he was, in effect, 'Christ in his Norman form'. Phil Booth, leader of Radio Worldwide (a branch of WEC) wrote to him:

> I cannot find 'Christ as me' in Scripture. The body is one with the Head and the Head with the body, but they are two. I am created a new creation IN Christ, not created Christ. I was dead but made alive IN Christ. My new weak born-again self is the means of expressing Him, but not Him. I cannot BE Him, or He would not be interceding for me. I cannot sit 'with' Him in glory (Eph. 2) if I AM Him. You cannot have union of one person. You can have two people who so live that one is the expression of the other – me of Christ to the world, Christ of me before the throne. But this does not make us one person.

Many in WEC, like Phil Booth, had deep reservations, yet others who knew Grubb intimately were not disturbed feeling that he was merely, in a kind of mischievous way, overstating some truths simply to make his hearers and readers waken up to the truths they had just vaguely accepted.

Bill Volkman – who had started *Union Life* magazine as a vehicle for publishing Norman's teaching – eventually felt unable to go along with Norman's later thrusts and withdrew his support.

Ken Getty, former director of WEC in Canada, sums up the situation:

Because he was original in his thinking and didn't run with the crowd, he had his own agenda, so consequently his theological perspective wasn't normal. If he had been so positioned to interact with others then he might have modified his statements somewhat. He spoke always in extreme terms. That was his strength and that was his weakness; he overstated his position to shock us. If C.T. Studd's strength and weakness was intensity, Norman Grubb's was seeing things completely from one angle. Some of us feel there is such a thing as biblical balance.

Dr. Helen Roseveare writes:

I used to get *Union Life* magazine. I would go through every single phrase and write in the margin the Scriptures that I felt contradicted what was written. I challenged him face to face over all this. Sometimes he would say, 'Well, you know what I mean' and I would say, 'That's not good enough, Rubi. *I* know what you mean, what matters is whether other people know what God is saying'.

The authors, when compiling *Summit Living*, (a book of daily readings from Norman's writings) felt a restraint about quoting from his last two books – *Who Am I?*, and *Yes I Am*. He was not happy about this and offered an alternative: he would write sections specially for the last few weeks, giving his latest theological views. We discouraged him from doing this.

Others shared their disquiet but any remonstration seemed to produce in Norman an even deeper determination to pursue the line on which he had embarked. His Irish blood was not conducive to compromise.

1981 brought a dark shadow over Norman's life. After a long period of debilitating illness, Pauline, his wife, passed into the presence of the Lord on September 16th. Just a few months prior to this, when writing the preface to his latest book, *Yes I Am*, he remarked:

This book has its background in the sixty years since Pauline, my precious wife, and I married and went to Congo together. Pauline, though now physically weak and unable to get about, lies in bed, resting in the Lord. Where should I have been without her through these many years?

Elsewhere in his letters and other writings he always extolled Pauline's steadiness and wisdom, recognising her astute, analytical mind and her ability to evaluate people far more accurately than he. She often, he said, would counsel restraint when he, in his impetuous way, would tend to rush in.

However, the parting, though painful, did nothing to interrupt Norman's constant itinerant ministry.

We turn now to examine Norman's links with WEC during the seventies and eighties. The mission of course continued to expand, membership increasing, new fields being added, and national churches being raised up.

With well over a thousand in membership there was a growing need for regular international conferences where leaders could meet, develop new strategies and sort out the inevitable problems that would arise in a fast-growing organisation. Norman was always invited to these and he never refused to come to any of them.

In 1984, at a leaders' conference in Kilcreggan, Scotland, he reviewed WEC's allegiance to some of its basic principles:

Now the first thing I must say is that I come among you with the fulness of joy. Because, after my sixty-five years as a WECer, from the year Pauline and I joined C.T. Studd in the heart of Africa right up to today, I do not believe that in essentials we have deviated from living out our God-given 'four pillars'.

SACRIFICE

The pillar of sacrifice I am not going to question, though our ways of living on a sacrifical level vary with the outer changing circumstances of our world. I wholly believe the same readiness to live at the same level of outer material identification with the precious people to whom we are called to bring Christ, is as much ours today as when C.T. reached the Congo, where he first built his 'Buckingham Palace' on the banks of the Welle River at Niangara for eight pounds.

Incidentally, this principle of living simply and solely by what He leads His people to give us, does keep us on the apostolic level of simple living because we are responsible for the right use of the sacrificial gifts of His people.

HOLINESS

It is here that I have a burning concern, and I cannot see signs of this taking the outstanding precedence among us which the Holy Spirit evidently meant and means it to take. I express this by the term holiness, not some particular interpretation of how the sanctified and empowered life is experienced and lived, but 'wholeness' – of God's people being 'wholly' what they have been redeemed for – to be in Christ.

Put in our WEC terms, I am saying that our founder, C.T. Studd, was a commissioned pioneer, by no means merely of the precious blood that cleanses sinners, but of the Holy Spirit who fills them. Studd was a burning preacher of holiness. He ate and drank both the blood and the Spirit. His famous statement of purpose was: 'Lord, we are out here to see Jesus Christ running around in black bodies!' Outer forms meant so little to him.

Now frankly, I don't 'catch' this kind of holiness coming out of the accounts given of the workings of God from our fields. Nor do I find this emphasis standing out as an essential for our new recruits, or see the passionate urge to transmit this total gospel to those to whom they are sent. The field letters are full of 'so many baptised' (who cares, unless that has plainly meant experience of the baptism of inner union of Rom. 6?). And our considerations are centred round church-planting – but never a mention of Holy Spirit-planting in the lives of the church members. And in our prepared reports, even for such as this confer-ence, very few references are made to the ONLY REAL PURPOSE of our HIGH CALLING which is to do what Paul called 'present every man PERFECT in Christ Jesus' (Col. 1:28).

Here I will go further for just a few minutes, for this one reason. All of us WECers know, and probably also affirm in our own lives as our reality by grace, Galatians 2:20. I hope so! But I have taken a radical stance for which I still get into trouble, even among WECers. I suppose I go further than many 'victorious teachers and writers'. To me the true significance is that He, the Spirit, in making Christ an inner reality to us, lays the emphasis on HIS taking over of us, rather than on OUR main-taining that 'taken-over' relationship. Quite simply, the emphasis is that He is now the 'Real One' in me, and it is **not** 'in', in the sense of two in a link between each other, but the two who have become **one**. In other words, it is the 'in' in the true Spirit meaning as found in 1 Corinthians 6:17: 'He who is joined to the Lord is one spirit'.

Do we transmit this to our new brethren? Although I believe and certainly hope that all we WECers inwardly know our 'Christ in you' reality, I have no present evidence that this so possesses us individually that we must get it to our peoples. Will you take this now to your hearts during these weeks?

ACHIEVING FAITH

This now takes me to our next distinctive – achieving faith. I think we have remained largely faithful to this pillar. Certainly on the level of the Lord supplying our funds, without appeals to man. But I also think that when it comes to being the regular God-given basis for finding the mind of the Lord, and moving into achieving faith for specific objectives, on the Hebrew 11 pattern, there is room for wider application among us.

By this distinctive form of reproducing faith I mean (as seen in the recorded lives of the Bible men-of-faith), quite a different thing from the normal prayer meetings, and the information sheets supplied to them. I would call it more a 'say-so' rather than a 'pray-so' activity. The simple fact is that the WEC and CLC of today have been solely built and expanded on 'say-so' words of faith.

WEC does emphasise prayer, as does the Bible, in the sense of constantly 'making mention' and bringing before the Lord the various pressing needs. But here again I would say that the distinctive of WEC, God-given, is not general praying, but the creative, reproductive faith.

But is this our normal way of approaching, handling, and solving our needs, problems and challenges worldwide in our WEC of today? I am not sure that it is. But if not believed in, and regularly practised on all fields as well as sending bases by our leadership, as being truly God's way right through the Scripture records, it will evidently not be the essential way of faith in operation in the life of our churches. That is the very reason why I still say that it is a specialised pillar of WEC, and needs therefore to be taught and practised as such.

CONCLUSION

Maybe this is my last word to all my beloved co-WECers worldwide, after my privileged 65 years, when Pauline and I joined C.T. Studd. It is a last word with greatness of joy, that by God's enabling, we WECers are pursuing our privileged calling on those same 'old paths' laid down by the Spirit, through our human founder, and yet, at the same time, applying a rub or two of polish to the sparkling steel of our drawn swords for worldwide evangelisation until He comes.

With the appointment of Dr. Dietrich (Dieter) Kuhl as International Secretary of WEC in 1987 a fairly voluminous correspondence developed between him and Norman. Dieter's gracious style comes through, and it is obvious that he very much respected Norman, yet sought to have a moderating influence over his pronouncements which in the eyes of most WECers were becoming somewhat extreme.

Here is Norman's reply to Dieter's letter stating that it would probably be unwise for Norman to circulate a pamphlet to all WEC leaders written by one of his protagonists, Ms. Jackie Ginn.

5/10/89

My dear Dieter,

I am greatly thrilled and intrigued because you don't throw me out, though you warn that I go too far [in my support of] Jackie Ginn's statement at the end of her pamphlet – 'I can trust myself.' You say if I send round statements of that kind for Intercon '90 (International Conference, 1990) they will cause controversy. Yes, I see what you say, and I suppose it is a fact that I have always had this extremist tendency, precisely as both C.T. Studd and Rees Howells had. They both died outcasts [as far as] the evangelical church is concerned. I have been told that my biography of C.T. Studd 'turned a maniac into a saint!'

The joke is that these two biographies remain best sellers! Both went too far, C.T. with his DCD leaflet and taking morphine, Rees Howells with his public celebration of the destruction of Hitler and Mussolini just as Hitler was seizing Holland and Belgium and France, with Britain in danger! But look today at the amazing spread of the gospel worldwide, which is what Rees Howells said God would do! It seems to have paid off, backing these men!

So you see my problem, Dieter. It seems that the Spirit backs these extremists either despite or because of their extremes.

You mention about the Ginn statement 'Trust yourself'. But if taken in its context it follows [right on] from the picture of our 'I' joined to His 'I'. Yes, yes, yes, we trust ourselves because we know that is trusting him in me. We do say with Caleb 'We are well able.'

You see, Dieter, I have deeply mourned these years when our WEC has spoken hesitatingly of ourselves as 'poor weak things' [instead of] saying, 'When I am weak, THEN AM I STRONG'. I hate these ditherings in our magazine about poor WECers coming home for a 'well-earned rest' and we flood our fields with half-baked crusaders who fully intend, after about ten years, to turn their backs on the fields for the sake of the children's education.

So, I remain 'crazy', beloved Dieter, yet rejoicing at the new spark of faith-in-action brought to our last Intercon, and now a new invasion of our missing Holiness pillar this year by you. All glory! It is not for me, the old Methuselah, to disrupt the wonderful new ways of the Spirit through you. So, I love you, Dieter and am thrilled at your loving tolerance of me. So go ahead and bring our loved modern WEC back to a clear strong holiness emphasis which discards that awful dog-eat-dog two nature lie and replaces it with a bold affirmation of the Spirit of life having cast out that lying spirit of sin and death (Rom. 8).

What was WEC's attitude to Norman in view of his extreme statements? Around this time the Co-ordinating Council produced the following statement:

STATEMENT CONCERNING NORMAN P. GRUBB (RUBI)

WEC's Co-ordinating Council affirms that:

1. WEC honours Rubi as the one who laid much of WEC's foundation after the period of crisis before and after the death of C.T. Studd (16 July, 1931). Here is a worthy quote:

> In the years since Studd's death, WEC witnessed steady growth, and by the 1970s it was reaching all over the globe with more than five hundred missionaries – among them the courageous Dr. Helen Roseveare, who began her service in Ibambi where Studd himself tirelessly served. In analysing the phenomenal comeback of the WEC, it would be difficult to overestimate the outstanding leadership of Norman Grubb, a man possessed of a rare honesty in admitting his own shortcomings and, though a relentless defender of his father-in-law, wise enough to recognise his flaws and learn from them. (Ruth A. Tucker, *From Jerusalem to Irian Jaya. A Biographical History of Christian Missions,* Grand Rapids, Zondervan, 1983, p.268.)

Humanly speaking, WEC owes its existence to the outstanding leadership of Rubi as its first International Secretary (1931-1965).

2. We recognise that there are statements of Rubi's in his later years that seem to be overly provocative and/or, at times, appear even unscriptural or to lack scriptural support. We recognise that such statements can have a negative impact on the public image of WEC, especially with people that do not sufficiently understand Rubi's statements in their context and intention.

Therefore the confusion and reaction of the Christian public in USA and, to a lesser extent, in Britain, made it necessary to distance WEC from these controversial statements.

3. Nevertheless, we feel that this should not cause a breakdown in personal fellowship. Where this has occurred we encourage people to clear the matter up with Rubi and to renew fellowship in the bond of love.

4. We realise that negative reactions from the public could have been one factor that stopped us emphasising Rubi's basic message of 'Christ in us' (Col. 1:27) and of the need of our union with Christ ('being in Christ' – Col. 1:28). We believe that there is a great need to return to this emphasis. It is one of the key factors that played such a vital role in WEC's growth and development in the early years. It is essentially intertwined with our emphasis on faith, holiness, multiracial fellowship, and sacrifice.

At the 1990 Intercon Dieter made the following statement:

> I believe that antagonism to some of Norman Grubb's provocative statements has held us back from fully embracing the core issue. I believe that strongly. It also overlooks the simple fact that Rubi prefers, as he often stated, to overstate a truth deliberately, rather than understate it. As an original thinker he is not afraid of going close to the border of heresy.

We come now to the closing years of Rubi's long and fruitful life.

Because Sandie was too ill to care for him he was given a home for a time by his friends, Page and Tom Prewitt of Jackson, Mississippi. Page wrote a circular in March 1990 to Norman's friends giving a full run-down on his physical condition. From this horrific report it is totally amazing that he continued to have any kind of ministry for a further three years. (He always minimised his physical limitations.)

> Norman was in the hospital (Mississippi Baptist Medical Centre) from February 4th through February 28th (24 days). He is at home with us now. He has been under the care of five different doctors: an internist, who was his general doctor; a urologist, who admitted him and checked him to determine the cause of his loss of bladder control; a pulmonologist, who took care of his lung and chest problems; a surgeon, who was called in to insert a chest tube which was necessary to drain the infection that surrounded his infected lung; and a neurologist, who checked him to be sure the bladder problem was not caused by a slight stroke. (He also ran tests to determine the degree of nerve damage in his legs.)
> In addition to the pneumonia and infected chest, it was discovered

that Norman had a stomach ulcer. The ulcer causes two problems: the loss of appetite and a reflux stomach acid which he in turn aspirates into his lungs. This was determined to be the primary cause of his lung abscess.

Norman is very weak; this weakness makes him unable to do anything for himself (he can feed himself). He has to have help with everything else – walking, getting out of bed or a chair, dressing and using the bathroom. He can walk a little but to do so has to use a walker and have someone help him. At the present time we have to have nursing help with him all day, every day and until he goes to bed at night (11 pm).

Norman has just begun to read his mail again. He stopped reading at the end of January. He now has about 150 letters that are unanswered.

Extreme anaemia is one of the causes for Norman's weakness. His lack of appetite and refusal to eat like he should doesn't help this condition. His legs are very weak also, so they easily give way when he tries to walk.

In March, 1990 Norman was moved to other friends in Hopkinsville, KY. – Billy and Mimi Anderson. They provided much the same care as he received at the Prewitts. He improved a little but still needed nursing care.

Some time after that he returned to his home in Fort Washington, PA., the journey being interrupted when he had to be hospitalised en route. Sandie wrote to a WEC worker in August, 1991:

Papa is about the same although he is either in bed or a nearby chair. His nurses care for him well and, in the process, Papa has had time to share the Lord with them.

I am taking one day at a time. Some close friends – Dee Dee Winter of Arlington, TX., and Linda Bunting and Harriet Wearren of Louisville, KY., have been here on a rotation basis for the past few weeks helping me. My cousin and his wife, Daniel and Marlene Grubb, have been visiting and helping on a regular basis. I am so thankful for them all.

Sandie, Norman's beloved grand-daughter, died in October, 1991. A WEC worker close to him at Camp Hill confided that he wept for three days and refused to eat. Some time after that he wrote to Patrick and Jill Johnstone (also suffering from cancer) at WEC's International Research Office.

How I always greatly welcome your general letter. I have been with you in spirit, Jill, in this suffering part of your life.

You will know by now how the Lord took my precious grand-daughter, Sandie, who meant so much to me here. I don't know when I have suffered so much as in this sudden loss. You will have received the copy of my general letter about the Lord giving me the last eight to ten of her years and all she meant as she drove through every state of the USA taking my Total Truth message which is now in print. I enclose a copy also of my recent one on *Intercession in Action*. I am not really expecting to write more, though still by God's enabling have clarity of mind as I come to 96 in a year's time.

It is the fact of my leg helplessness (I fall when I try to walk) that keeps me in my bedroom on a chair, lovingly supported by my Pris. No one has volunteered to type and so she has to take it down by hand. She is God's final mercy to me with Sandie now with God, and I at 96 expect to follow her to our eternal union with Jesus. Meanwhile I am lovingly cared for as necessary by nurses and Pris and with a weird instrument which carries me like a sack of potatoes from bed to chair.

I shall greatly look forward to your new children's book, *You can Change the World*.

The glory is to follow.

Norman Grubb.

In August 1993 Norman wrote to a wide circle of friends.

My loving friends of our Christ family,

This is likely to be the last letter I write as I am 98 years of age now. I believe I have said these same words a year ago; as you can see, I remain part of our Lord's plan here on earth. Thus by the grace of God, I am beginning my 99th year. It is by His grace that I can continue to keep in contact with you.

Many of us have opened our whole hearts to each other for many years and find refreshment in doing so. I have so much to be thankful for – especially your loving contact and corrrespondence all these years.

In front of me are 50-60 precious letters, many of which are quite lengthy. But no matter how short or how long, many reiterate how much the Holy Spirit has given to me to share with you. Once again, a sign of our Living Jesus expressing Himself to you.

The Lord's amazing goodness shines through over and over in our lives. Even though I am bedridden with one of my legs so out of gear that I would fall if I tried to stand, the Lord blesses us in our tight spots. He has given me wonderful family support.

In my own family circle, I am blessed with my son, Daniel, a recently retired college professor; and his loving wife, Rosemary at his side. He is also an ordained priest in the Episcopal church and ministers to a lovely countryside congregation in Western Pennsylvania. Priscilla, my daughter continues to stay on here at the house with the support of my grandson, Daniel Jr., and his wife, Marlene. My son, Paul, and his wife, Madge reside in England and are content in their own lives.

And finally, you, my extended family, continue to be at my side during my final years. The Lord's amazing goodness shines on me since Jesus revealed Himself to me as my personal Saviour in 1914. I spent my entire life getting Him known as Saviour to the world.

I was side-by-side with my father-in-law, C.T. Studd, who originally began his journey in 1912 into the Congo via the Nile. Over the years our crusade has grown vastly covering the Congo and other various areas worldwide. [Over 50 countries.] We have converts now becoming missionaries, combined with CLC which was born out of WEC – approximately 2,800 workers altogether. I hate writing just these present glorious facts, and not touching the exact needed reply to most of your letters. At 98 years, and with many limitations that come with age, this is my best. You are all ever in my thoughts and prayers to our Heavenly Father. I thank you for your gifts of love that you all continue to send my way. Your letters and visits bring much joy.

Lovingly yours,
Norman.

On Sunday, December 12th, 1993 Norman complained of nausea and the doctor prescribed medicine to settle this, but by Tuesday, December 14th he was in decline. He passed into glory on Wednesday, December 15th at 11.06 pm. He was 98 years old.

He had no pain, although his breathing was heavy. His last words were, 'Abba, Abba take me, please take me.'

His funeral was at the George Washington Memorial Park, Plymouth Meeting, PA. on December 21st, with the Rev. Daniel S. Grubb (Norman's younger son) officiating.

Memorial services were held at the National Christian Conference Centre at Valley Forge, PA., at Gold Hill Baptist Church, Chalfont St Peters, Bucks., England (close to the headquarters of WEC International) and in Louisville, Kentucky, where he had a circle of close friends whose lives had been immeasurably enriched by his ministry.

Priscilla continues to live at the Fort Washington home and Daniel S. Grubb, Jr. (Pris's nephew) and Marlene, Daniel's wife will keep Pris safe and loved along with the help, as needed, of Pris's brother and his wife, Daniel Sen. and Rosemary.

APPENDIX A

A CHRONOLOGICAL LIST OF NORMAN GRUBB'S
BOOKS AND BOOKLETS (English Titles only)

YEAR	TITLE	PUBLISHER
1925	Fenton Hall, Pioneer and Hero	WEC, London
1929*	Priscilla Livingstone Studd	WEC, London
1929*	Throne Life	WEC, London
1933	C.T.Studd, Cricketer and Pioneer	Lutterworth Press, London
1936	Modern Crusaders	WEC, London
1936*	Life out of Death	WEC and HAM, London
1937	Penetrating Faith in Spanish Guinea	WEC, London
1939	After C.T.Studd	Lutterworth Press, London
1940	Touching the Invisible	Lutterworth Press, London
1942	Mountain Movers	Evangelical Publishing House
1942	Ploughing Through	EPH, Colchester
1942	Alfred Buxton of Abyssinia & Congo	Lutterworth Press, London
1943	The Price They Paid	EPH, Colchester
1945	The Home Church and the Missionary Candidate	Christian Literature Crusade, London
1945	Christ in Congo Forests	Lutterworth Press, London
1946	Concrete Evidence of a Faith that Works	CLC, London
1947	The Law of Faith	Lutterworth Press, London
1949	Successor to C.T. Studd	Lutterworth Press, London
1950	A Mighty Work of the Spirit	Studd Press, London
1951	Mighty Through God	Lutterworth Press, London
1952	Continuous Revival	CLC, London
1952	Rees Howells, Intercessor	Lutterworth Press
1953	The Growth of WEC	WEC, London
1954	This is That	CLC, London
1955	J.D. Drysdale, Prophet of Holiness	Lutterworth Press, London
1955	The Liberating Secret	Lutterworth Press, London
1958	The Deep Things of God	Lutterworth Press, London
1961	Modern Viking	Zondervan, Grand Rapids, Mich.
1962	God Unlimited	Lutterworth Press, London
1962	Leap of Faith	CLC, Fort Washington, Pa.
1963	First the Blade	WEC, London
1963	The Four Pillars of WEC	WEC, London
1964	The Key to Everything	CLC, Fort Washington
1966	The Spontaneous You	Lutterworth Press, London

1969	Once Caught, No Escape	Lutterworth Press, London
1974	Who Am I?	Lutterworth Press, London
1974	Nothing is Impossible	CLC, Fort Washington, Pa
1982	Yes I Am	CLC, Fort Washington, Pa
1984	Are We Still On Target?	Christian Outreach Inc. Nashville, TN
1985	Summit Living (Ed. by S. Dinnen)	CLC, Fort Washington, Pa
1989	It's as Simple as This	Christ-as-us Literature Center, PO Box 43579, Louisville, Ky
1991	Intercession in Action	Zerubbabel Inc, Jackson, MS
1992*	Romans Six to Eight	Zerubbabel Book Ministry, Canton, MA
1993*	No Independent Self	Christ-as-us Literature Center, PO Box 43579, Louisville, Ky

* Indicates that no publication date appears on the book/booklet. Date is approximate.

APPENDIX B

SUMMARY OF MAIN EVENTS
IN THE LIFE OF NORMAN GRUBB

1895	Born at Oxton, Nottinghamshire, to Rev. Harry Percy and Margaret Grubb.
1909-1914	At Marborough School.
1914	Conversion.
1914-1919	Army Service, Britain and France.
1919	Discharged from Army.
	Commenced at Cambridge University.
	Instigated the commencement of Inter-Varsity Fellowship.
	Discontinued at Cambridge.
	Applied to WEC and accepted.
	Marriage to Pauline Studd.
	Sailed for Congo.
1920-1923	Missionary service in Congo.
1921	Birth of Noel.
	A 'Galatians 2:20' experience.
1922	Death of Noel at Ibambi.
1923	Returned to Britain.
1924	Birth of Paul.
1925	Returned to Congo alone.
	Birth of Priscilla.
1926	Returned to Britain.
1927	Returned to Congo.
	Birth of Daniel.
1928	Returned to Britain.
	Tour of Amazonia (five months).
1929	Tour of Canada (six months).
1930	Short visit to Congo with Pauline.
	Commissioned by C.T.Studd to return to Britain and take leadership at base.
1931	WEC and Unevangelised Fields Mission became separate missions.
	Death of C.T. Studd.
1932	Recruitment of 'The Ten'.
1933	Recruitment of 'The Fifteen'.
	Publication of *C.T. Studd, Cricketer and Pioneer*.
	The Colombian field of WEC opened.
	'Kashmir & Frontier Mission' of WEC formed.
1934	Recruitment of 'The Twenty-five'.
	Publication of *Touching the Invisible*.

1935	Work opened on Nepal border.
	Recruitment of 'The Fifty'.
1936	Recruitment of 'The Seventy-five'.
	Canadian Base established in Toronto.
	Canary Islands opened.
1937-1938	Building of the London Hostel.
1939	Tour of Canada and USA.
	Commencement of centres in Pittsburgh, Seattle and Charlotte, NC.
1939-1946	World War II.
	Portuguese Guinea, Ghana and Dominica opened.
1940	New Zealand base established in Auckland.
1941	British Staff Conference and vision for 12 regional centres in UK.
	Australian Base established in Sydney.
1942	Commencement of Christian Literature Crusade.
1946	Tour of USA and Canada.
1947	Move to USA.
	Thailand, Taiwan fields opened.
1949	Return to Britain.
	Tour of Congo and visit to CMS in Ruanda. The revival message.
	Pakistan and Indonesia commenced (Kalimantan – 1949, Sumatra – 1951, Java – 1953).
1950-1951	Temporary leadership of N. American WEC.*[1]
	Japan, Uruguay and France opened.
1951	Return to Britain.
	Writing of *Rees Howells, Intercessor*.
1952	In N. America.*
	N. American* staff proposes that Grubb be recognised as 'General Secretary of WEC'.
	(Later changed to 'International Secretary'.)
1953	Based in Britain.
	Tour of Australia and New Zealand.
1954	Tour continues in India, Indonesia and Japan.
	Returns to Britain.
	Venezuela opened.
1957	Relinquished British leadership and moved permanently to USA.
	Appointed Co-leader of N. American WEC.*
	Gambia and Brazil opened.
1958	Appointed leader of N. American WEC.*
1958	Participated in Presidential Prayer Breakfast, Washington (and also in many subsequent years).
1960	Relinquishment of leadership in N. America.*
1961	First International Leaders' Conference at Kilcreggan, Scotland.
	19-point programme for advance adopted.
	The Consultative Council established (International Secretary + 5 Sending Base leaders).

1962	Indonesian Missionary Fellowship (an outgrowth of WEC) established.
	Chad field opened.
1963	Iran field commenced.
	Celebration of WEC's Jubilee.
1964	Italy opened.
1965	Decision to retire from position of International Secretary, effective Dec 31st.
	Consultative Council (later Co-ordinating Council) requested Grubb to remain a member.
1966	Freed from WEC responsibilities, Norman's itinerant teaching ministry escalates.
1968	Wrote autobiography – *Once Caught, No Escape*.
1974	Attended WEC's Co-ordinating Council in Britain.
1974	Link established with Union Life Ministries.
1981	Death of Pauline Grubb.
1984	Addressed WEC Leaders' Conference in Britain.
1985	Criticised in *Seduction of Christianity*.
1986	Link established with Zerubbabel Inc.
1989	Opposed appointment of a 'Council of Reference' in USA.
1990	Serious illness. Cared for by Prewitts of Jackson, Miss.
1991	Returned to Fort Washington and is tended by granddaughter, Sandie.
	Death of Sandra Grubb.
1993	(Nov.) Last Activity for WEC. Wrote Foreword for *Rescue Shop Within a Yard of Hell*.
1993	Dec 15. Died at his home in Fort Washington, Pa.

[1]*USA and Canadian staffs functioned together until 1970 when each became autonomous.

INDEX